*Claiming a Tradition*

*Ad Feminam: Women and Literature*
*Edited by Sandra M. Gilbert*

*Christina Rossetti*
*The Poetry of Endurance*
*By Dolores Rosenblum*

*Lunacy of Light*
*Emily Dickinson and the Experience of Metaphor*
*By Wendy Barker*

*The Literary Existence of Germaine de Staël*
*By Charlotte Hogsett*

*Margaret Atwood*
*Vision and Forms*
*Edited by Kathryn VanSpanckeren and Jan Garden Castro*

*He Knew She Was Right*
*The Independent Woman in the Novels of Anthony Trollope*
*By Jane Nardin*

*The Woman and the Lyre*
*Women Writers in Classical Greece and Rome*
*By Jane McIntosh Snyder*

*Refiguring the Father*
*New Feminist Readings of Patriarchy*
*Edited by Patricia Yaeger and Beth Kowaleski-Wallace*

*Writing in the Feminine*
*Feminism and Experimental Writing in Quebec*
*By Karen Gould*

*Rape and Writing in the* Heptaméron *of Marguerite de Navarre*
*By Patricia Francis Cholakian*

*Writing Love*
*Letters, Women, and the Novel in France, 1605–1776*
*By Katharine Ann Jensen*

*The Body and the Song*
*Elizabeth Bishop's Poetics*
*By Marilyn May Lombardi*

*Millay at 100*
*A Critical Reappraisal*
*Edited by Diane P. Freedman*

*The House Is Made of Poetry*
*The Art of Ruth Stone*
*Edited by Wendy Barker and Sandra M. Gilbert*

*The Experimental Self*
*Dialogic Subjectivity in Woolf, Pym, and Brooke-Rose*
*By Judy Little*

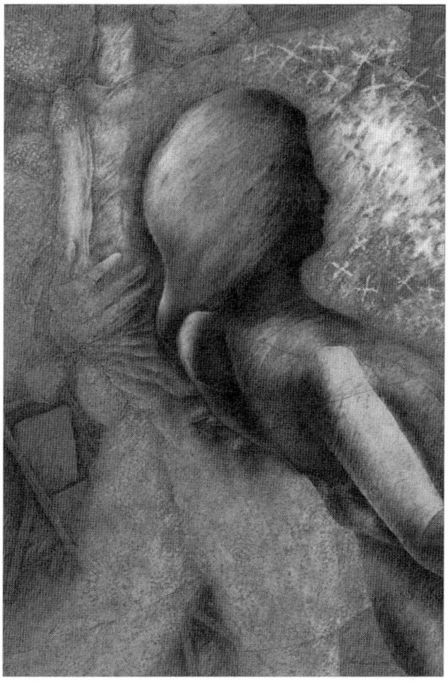

# *Claiming a Tradition*
## *Italian American Women Writers*

*Mary Jo Bona*



*Southern Illinois University Press*
*Carbondale and Edwardsville*

*Printed in the United States of America*

02 01 00 99 4 3 2 1

*Title page illustration:* Mixed media work on paper, *Turn Back,* by Christine Perri is reproduced courtesy of the collection of Florinda Bayod. Photo courtesy of Ruyell Ho, Chicago.

**Library of Congress Cataloging-in-Publication Data**

Bona, Mary Jo.
Claiming a tradition : Italian American women writers / Mary Jo Bona.
p. cm. — (Ad feminam)
Includes bibliographical references and index.
1. American literature—Italian American authors—History and criticism. 2. American literature—Women authors—History and criticism. 3. Women and literature—United States—History. 4. Italian American women—Intellectual life. 5. American literature—Italian influences. 6. Italian Americans in literature. 7. Italy—In literature. I. Title. II. Series.
PS153.I8B66 1999
810.9'9287'08951—dc21 99-21410
ISBN 0-8093-2258-7 (alk. paper) CIP

The paper used in this publication meets the minimum requirements of American National Standard for Information Sciences—Permanence of Paper for Printed Library Materials, ANSI Z39.48-1984. ♾

*To my parents, Vincent J. Bona and Florence L. Orlando*
*To my sister, Carmen Jeanne Bona*
*In memory of our beloved, Phillip J. Bona, D.D.S.,*
*July 5, 1959–July 24, 1992*

# *Contents*

# *Ad Feminam: Women and Literature*

Ad Hominem: to the man; appealing to personal interests, prejudices, or emotions rather than to reason; *an argument ad hominem.*

—*American Heritage Dictionary*

Until quite recently, much literary criticism, like most humanistic studies, has been in some sense constituted out of arguments *ad hominem.* Not only have examinations of literary history tended to address themselves "to the man"—that is, to the identity of what was presumed to be the *man* of letters who created our culture's monuments of unaging intellect—but many aesthetic analyses and evaluations have consciously or unconsciously appealed to the "personal interests, prejudices, or emotions" of male critics and readers. As the title of this series is meant to indicate, the intellectual project called "feminist criticism" has sought to counter the limitations of *ad hominem* thinking about literature by asking a series of questions addressed *ad feminam*: to the woman as both writer and reader of texts.

First, and most crucially, feminist critics ask, What is the relationship between gender and genre, between sexuality and textuality? But in meditating on these issues they raise a number of more specific questions. Does a woman of letters have a literature—a language, a history, a tradition—of her own? Have conventional methods of canon-formation tended to exclude or marginalize female achievements? More generally, do men and women have different modes of literary representation, different definitions of literary production? Do such differences mean that distinctive male- (or female-) authored images of women (or men), as well as distinctly male and female genres, are part of our intellectual heritage? Perhaps most important, are literary differences between men and women essential or accidental, biologically determined or culturally constructed?

Feminist critics have addressed themselves to these problems with increasing sophistication during the last two decades, as they sought to revise, or at times replace, *ad hominem* arguments with *ad feminam* speculations. Whether explicating individual texts, studying the oeuvre of a single author, examining the permutations of a major theme, or charting the contours of a tradition, these theorists and scholars have consistently sought to define literary manifestations of difference and to understand the dynamics that have shaped the accomplishments of literary women.

As a consequence of such work, feminist critics, often employing new modes of analysis, have begun to uncover a neglected female tradition along with a heretofore hidden history of the literary dialogue between men and women. This series is dedicated to publishing books that will use innovative as well as traditional interpretive methods in order to help readers of both sexes achieve a clearer consciousness of that neglected but powerful tradition and a better understanding of that hidden history. Reason tells us, after all, that if, transcending prejudice and special pleading, we speak to, and focus on, the woman as well as the man—if we think *ad feminam* as well as *ad hominem*—we will have a better chance of understanding what constitutes the human.

Sandra M. Gilbert

# *Acknowledgments*

My gratitude runs deep. I thank members of my writing group who patiently read early versions of this book and gave me useful advice on feminist criticism and the developmental novel: Eloise Buker, Gena DeAragon, Rose Mary Volbrecht, Joy Milos, and Julie Tammivaara. My colleagues Jane Rinehart and Beth Cooley, invaluable writing group participants, also offered insightful criticism on later chapter versions, asking hard questions that compelled me to clarify those traditions distinct to Italian American *women's* cultural background.

Scholars working in the area of Italian American literature have been my greatest champions: Fred Gardaphé, Anthony Tamburri, and Edvige Giunta have generously shared resources and insights, helping me strengthen the book's organization and focus. Without them and the venue of the American Italian Historical Association, where initial chapters of the book were read, Italian American studies would be much less vibrant and advanced.

Preliminary research for this book began under a Gonzaga University Research Council Grant, which allowed me to travel to the Immigration History Research Center at the University of Minnesota. I thank in particular Rudolph Vecoli, the center's director, for providing me with several articles on the stonecutting industry in Barre, Vermont. Gonzaga University's support of my sabbatical enabled me to complete this book. I thank interlibrary loan officer Connie Som, who never failed to locate and retrieve the many—and often rare—books I ordered, and librarian Linda Pierce, whose expertise on the computer and in the stacks expedited my own inquiries into the writers' lives. I also thank Sandra Mortola Gilbert for her enthusiastic response to the subject of this book and her good wishes for its completion. With their continued support and careful advice, my editors Carol A. Burns, Tracey Sobol, and Julie Bush helped me through the painstaking and time-consuming activity of editorial work.

My family's love during the process of writing this book was crucial for its completion, and my special thanks go to Judy, who makes all things possible. Owing them a debt is a happy obligation. Finally, to the writers themselves, whose stories run deeply along my pulse: their words, most fundamentally, gave this book its raison d'être.

# *Claiming a Tradition*

# *Introduction*

In her 1977 Douglass College Convocation speech, Adrienne Rich urged female students to think of themselves as *claiming* an education, not as passively *receiving* one. She defined "to claim" as "to assert in the face of possible contradiction" and in contrast defined "to receive" as "to act as [a] receptacle or container for." The way a female student approaches her education is vital: "The difference is that between acting and being acted-upon, and for women it can literally mean the difference between life and death" (*On Lies, Secrets, and Silence* 231).

Much of the same can be said for Italian American women writers. Their work has come to light because of the assertions of writers and scholars seeking to place them within both their Italian and American cultural and literary traditions. Even in the 1990s, however, claiming a tradition for Italian American women writers is an act of assertion in the face of possible resistance. As late as 1993, the Italian American writer Gay Talese was asking "Where are the Italian-American novelists?" and offering an essentialist argument to answer his own question: Italian Americans are harnessed by a heritage of *omertà* (silence) and cannot extricate themselves from it.[1]

As early as 1949, Olga Peragallo had produced *Italian-American Authors and Their Contribution to American Literature*, reinforcing the fact that Italian Americans did not abide by the cultural code of silence. More of a biographical listing than an examination, Peragallo's book nonetheless put Italian-descended writers on the literary map. Rose Basile Green's 1974 *The Italian-American Novel: A Document of the Interaction of Two Cultures* offered a sociological reading of primarily male Italian American writers.[2] Not until the publication of Helen Barolini's trailblazing anthology, *The Dream Book: An Anthology of Writings by Italian American Women* (1985), were Italian American women writers introduced and regarded seriously for their achievements. Why did it take so long for writers such as Mari Tomasi and Diana Cavallo to be perceived for their contribution to American literary history? Both Tomasi and Cavallo published novels; Tomasi's second novel, *Like Lesser Gods*, was published in 1949, the same year as Peragallo's book. Dissemination and republication of works by Italian American writers have only recently begun, nearly forty years after Tomasi's publication.

The publication history of an African American novel, Zora Neale Hurston's *Their Eyes Were Watching God*, offers those of us committed to teaching and writing about Italian American writers a hopeful lens through which to view our present efforts. For nearly thirty years after it was first published in 1937, *Their Eyes Were Watching God* was "largely unknown and unread" (Washington vii). Writers and academics teaching in newly emerging black studies departments recognized in Janie Crawford a black woman's version of the quest for identity. In 1971, Mary Helen Washington described *Their Eyes Were Watching God* as an "underground phenomenon," taught primarily in African American studies departments by such figures as Alice Walker, who introduced the novel at Wellesley in 1971–72. By 1975, because the novel was again out of print, a petition was circulated at the December 1975 Modern Language Association (MLA) conference to get the novel republished. At another conference on minority literature held that same year at Yale University, a few copies of *Their Eyes Were Watching God* were shared with conference participants, many of whom were reading the novel for the first time. As Washington notes, "[B]etween 1977 and 1979 the Zora Neale Hurston renaissance was in full bloom."[3] The emergence of Hurston's novel as preeminently part of *American* literary history originated from the initial efforts of African American women writers and teachers who, Henry Louis Gates explains, "generated [the rediscovery of Hurston] primarily to establish a maternal literary ancestry" (186).

Following Alice Walker's example, Helen Barolini sought to establish for Italian-descended women in the United States a literary maternal ancestry by introducing fifty-six Italian American women writers in *The Dream Book*. Such a task has proven auspicious. Noting that "Italian American women have not had the critics or literary historians who would attempt to probe their background and unlock the reasons for silence," Barolini, herself an essayist and novelist, provides the historical and social context for the perceived invisibility of this group (32).[4] Aware that most southern Italian immigrants were "not wanted or valued in their land of origin," were unlettered, and immigrated to America "without a literary tradition," Barolini explains that women were "immutably restricted to home and family" and developed in the areas of "practical arts[,] not the imaginative ones" (3, 4).

Championing many of those daughters of immigrants who, with the help of education and changing familial mores, chose the pen rather than the needle to demonstrate their creativity, Barolini suggests that these writers possess a "cohesive and . . . a specific resonance as Italian American women writers" (x). At the same time, Barolini recognizes the lack of known models from the Italian culture for Italian American women writers to emulate. Just as Alice Walker found in Zora Neale Hurston the black woman "who was to be her model," Barolini is assured that Italian American women writers will discover such models for their own development: "Models are important inasmuch as they connect the present writer to her past, provide a continuity that makes a shared culture a valuable resource; one's own culture is important to the spirit of the writer and to the writing itself" (33).

For a writer like Tina De Rosa, the Neapolitan folk culture of her paternal grandparents provided the connection to the past and the cultural ingredients for her first novel, *Paper Fish* (1980). Indeed, the figure of the grandmother becomes central to many Italian American literary texts, Barolini's multigenerational novel *Umbertina* included. Along with the southern Italian culture of her grandparents' generation, Tina De Rosa, a third-generation Italian American, was also influenced by her undergraduate and graduate education. Although she might not yet have discovered a maternal literary ancestry, in *Paper Fish* De Rosa demonstrates her virtuosity as a modernist devoted to recreating the Italian American community of her childhood.[5]

Italian American writers and scholars have been recently engaged in *claiming* Italian American literature as part of the American literary tradition. Placing Italian-descended writers into the mosaic of American literary traditions enlarges the wholeness of American literature. By emphasizing cultural and gender differences in their narratives, Italian American women writers in actuality move toward the heart of American literature. Like many quintessential "American" texts (for example, *The Adventures of Huckleberry Finn* and *To Kill a Mockingbird*), Italian American novels share a sense of otherness and alienation. At the same time, Italian American women's novels demonstrate how ethnic American women in the second half of the twentieth century claim affiliation as central to their personal development. Unable fully to acculturate to American ways or maintain old-world customs, Italian American women writers complicate the meanings of American identity by emphasizing cultural and sexual identity, influenced by regional provenance, modification of familial control, changes in generational relationships, and attainment of education.

Keeping Italian American novels available must be of central concern to those of us committed to establishing visible Italian American literary traditions. In the past several years, for example, novels by Mari Tomasi, Diana Cavallo, Tina De Rosa, and Dorothy Bryant have been republished, thereby providing teachers and scholars with books in print. *From the Margin: Writings in Italian Americana*, edited by Anthony J. Tamburri, Paolo Giordano, and Fred L. Gardaphé, anthologizes both male and female writers, further recognizing the contributions of well-known (Jay Parini, Diane di Prima, Sandra Gilbert) and lesser-known (Diane Raptosh, Phyllis Capello, Jonathan Galassi) writers of Italian origin. The collection includes both critical and creative writings, providing an analytical apparatus with which to read the fiction and poetry.[6] Two journals, *Italian Americana* and *Voices in Italian Americana* (*VIA*), include critical and creative writings by Italian and Italian American writers, providing a forum for critical debate about Italian American ethnicity in the 1990s. Rose Romano's journal devoted to Italian American women, *la bella figura*, ran from 1988 to 1992, culminating in her anthology, *la bella figura: a choice*, published in 1993.

My own commitment to offering a critical reading of Italian American women writers stems from my interest in the ways in which previously underemphasized cultural traditions enrich the corpus of American literature (see Bona, *The Voices We Carry: Recent Italian/American Women's Fiction*).[7] Those scholars dedicated to disseminating the contributions of ethnic writers, particularly Werner Sollors and William Boelhower, have been instrumental in conceptualizing the idea of ethnicity itself as a category worthy of investigation. Sollors warns against viewing ethnicity as an ahistorical and "quasi-eternal essence" ("Ethnicity" 290) and ethnic groups as natural and real ("Introduction" xiii, xiv). Recognizing that ethnicity is based on a contrast, Sollors explains that, like the idea of nationalism, ethnicity is a modern phenomenon, coming into existence as a result of the American and French Revolutions, remaining "a powerful force in political history ever since" ("Ethnicity" 288, 289).[8] In his introduction to *Through a Glass Darkly: Ethnic Semiosis in American Literature*, Boelhower also issues a warning: "[E]thnic literature should not be ghettoized by separating it either from so-called American mainstream literature or from national cultural issues in general" (9). Italian American literature is neither mainstream nor ghettoized; its narratives offer another discourse about American identity, often using the Italian family as its central focus.

For Italian American women writers, the task of recovery and establishment has just begun.[9] Such work necessarily requires an analysis of the interpenetration of their novels with the literary and cultural American context and an awareness of their position as *Italian* American *women*. W. E. B. Du Bois's well-known meditation on "double consciousness" offers a reading on the position of people who try to negotiate between two cultures: "One ever feels his twoness,—an American, a Negro; two souls, two thoughts, two unreconciled strivings" (3).

In a similar way, immigrants from the booted country came to feel their "twoness" in American culture. For Italian American women who write, the category of gender functions as an equally necessary lens through which to interpret their negotiation between the Italian familial culture and the American milieu. The issue of gender modifies Italian American women's treatment of Italian ethnicity in illuminating ways. For example, in southern Italian culture, the father was said to function as *capofamiglia* (head of the family), supervising the behaviors "of the members of the total family" to ensure stability and respect in the community (Covello 157). Because loyalty to the family supersedes all other alliances in southern Italian communities, any deviation from proper behavior was met with an immediate response from the father, the central authority in the family.

In *The Right Thing to Do* (1988), Josephine Gattuso Hendin explores the ramifications of such conduct on an Italian American woman. The daughter's rebellion against the outmoded beliefs of her father causes harm and grief to both of them. Because he holds fiercely the Italian familial belief of controlling and monitoring the conduct of his daughter, the father refuses to adjust to the imminent independence of his American-born child. In nineteenth-century southern Italy, a girl would have been chaperoned and separated from the opposite sex until her marriage. As Phyllis H. Williams notes, "[A] girl had her career pretty well mapped out for her," and such a career insisted upon careful selection of a husband, marriage, and children (83).

The father in *The Right Thing to Do* attempts unsuccessfully to chaperone his college-aged daughter, following her on the streets of New York's boroughs. Although he wants to live out his responsibility as head of the family, the father in Hendin's novel suffers in ways unique to his position as an aging Italian American father. The daughter does not exhibit proper female behavior, according to old-world southern Italian standards. Thus, she is thought by the father to bring shame on the family, the loss of honor considered a tragedy for *la famiglia*. For the daughters depicted in several Italian American women's novels, the "unreconciled strivings" to which Du Bois refers have to do with their positions as "ethnic" Americans and as women from a patriarchal cultural tradition whose code of *onore* (honor) was entwined with their virginity (Alba 33).

Italian American writers often reveal what is called an *italianità* in their narratives, that is, a flavor of things Italian. Despite differences in regional settlement and distance from the immigrant past, Italian American women incorporate into their novels basic features of Italian culture. The editors of *From the Margin* agree that *italianità* evades a uniform definition and instead comprises several meanings, such as "real and mythical images of the [home]land, the way of life, the values, and the cultural trappings of [the writers'] ancestors." The concept of *italianità* also includes "language, food, a way of determining life values, a familial structure, a sense of religion." The writers whom I am analyzing share with many of the others anthologized in *The Dream Book*, *From the Margin*, and *The Voices We Carry* the impetus of recovery of *italianità*. Recognizing that "*italianità* is an inheritance," Italian American women are critiquing and recreating their relationship to the Italian culture in their novels (Tamburri, Giordano, and Gardaphé 6, 9).

Before introducing specific qualities of *italianità* that Italian American writers incorporate in their narratives, it is essential to give historical background on the Italian experience of immigration to the United States in the latter part of the nineteenth century and early part of the twentieth century. In doing so, I hope to show why the southern Italian cultural experience is paradigmatic in the novels under consideration, despite that some of the writers' ancestors originate from northern villages in Italy. Northern Italians were among the first to emigrate from Italy to America. Of the 47,000 Italians who arrived on American shores in 1861, most were from the north.[10]

After 1880, primarily southern Italian peasants (*contadini*) and unskilled laborers immigrated to the United States. Of the 2,300,000 immigrants who arrived from Italy between the years 1899 and 1910, only 400,000 were from the northern provinces. At least 85 percent of all Italians who emigrated from Italy were from the *Mezzogiorno*, areas south and east of Rome.[11] During the years of peak migration—1890 to 1910—approximately 80 percent of the emigrants were male.[12] Those women who did emigrate rarely traveled alone but thought of themselves as "part of the family economy, and left [Italy] to help their families" (Ewen 51). As Barolini explains, "[A]n uneducated Italian woman could not exist, economically or socially, outside the family institution which defined her life and gave it its whole meaning. She came, almost an indentured servant, bonded to her traditional role" (*The Dream Book* 7).

As Leonard Covello notes, distinctions formulated between northern and southern Italians were always made "to the detriment of southern Italians" (16–17). The northern Italians' assumed position of superiority was shaped by their closer contact with other industrialized European countries such as Switzerland and France (Rolle 64). Immediately after the country was unified and the north "had taken power in the Mezzogiorno," the north "began to foster the slander of the 'innate inferiority of the Mezzogiorno and its people,' first insidiously, then quite openly" (Gambino, *Blood of My Blood* 65). The United States immigration authorities ignorantly reinforced the distinction between northern and southern Italy, though very little was known about southern Italy by either northern Italians or Americans.[13] When immigrating to the United States, those from the northern regions of Italy upon reaching America "repudiated kinship with Italians from the South," the negative attitudes having successfully survived the transatlantic crossing (Covello 16–17, 30). By the late nineteenth century, Italian immigrants were primarily emigrating from the *Mezzogiorno* and were subjected to hostility in America, culminating in discrimination and violence against those "low" Italians from *Italia bassa* (lower Italy).[14]

According to historians of southern Italian culture, the family in the *Mezzogiorno* was the only institution that afforded comfort and could be trusted. The family was considered *soprattutto* (above all) because of the social and historical conditions in southern Italy and Sicily that compelled families to trust no one but themselves for survival.[15] The reasons for such an attitude stem from the geography of southern Italy and the historical pattern of constant invasion of foreigners. Superadded to their lack of power was a pernicious combination of natural disasters (floods, volcanic eruptions, famines, earthquakes), an insalubrious and scarce water supply, and widespread malaria and outbreaks of cholera. The most pressing motivation to leave their regions was extreme poverty, abetted by exorbitant taxing by the northern Italian government. Despite the tendency of northerners to assume a changeless and timeless world south of Rome, in actuality a dying economy in the *Mezzogiorno* soon impelled a mass exodus. If their conditions proved insufferable enough, southern Italians did and could change (Mangione and Morreale 54–85).

While it is true that the conflict between northern and southern Italians remained at times fiercely evident in the United States, the prose works under consideration tend to diminish the antagonism for two interrelated reasons. First, Italian American women write novels about Italian familial culture from the perspective of the disenfranchised—as women and as immigrants. Impoverished and, for the most part, uneducated, Italian immigrants from both the north and south sought a better life in America. Second, despite slanderous epithets hurled at each other from both sides, southern and northern Italians were often categorized by the host citizenry as inferior, whether their original region was from the north or from the south. Thus, the southern Italian paradigm functions to highlight the position of the marginalized immigrant family in the fiction under consideration.

Nonetheless, such a position in time changed. Second- and third-generation Italian Americans often identify themselves according to their ancestors' original region in Italy. Because less stigma is attached to those children whose relatives emigrated from southern Italy and Sicily, the writers of the third generation are less interested in representing themselves as good Americans and more engaged in revitalizing regional customs by incorporating them into their novels. The phenomenon of *campanilismo* (village spirit), in which "not only each region, but each town considers itself a self-contained, unique culture" (Gambino, *Blood of My Blood* 65), survived the transatlantic crossing in the emergence of Little

Italies.[16] Several of the novels are set in Italian American neighborhoods, in which distinct regional customs form part of the daily life of the community.

Nevertheless, Americans, as Phyllis Williams explains, had their own tendency of "lumping together . . . all Italians," regardless of the distinct traditions of single villages or communes. Americans were "oblivious to these differences," characterizing the Italian as "'a dirty, undersized individual, who engages in degrading labor shunned by Americans'" (13, 14).[17] Especially in the first decades of their new life in America, Italians from both northern and southern Italy were denigrated by non-Italians; the derogatory nomenclatures dago, wop, and black guinea were attached to Italian immigrants in America en masse, regardless of their regional origin.

The *italianità* revealed in the novels by Italian American women writers is no mere defense against being perceived narrowly and injudiciously by the American culture. Rather, it is a strategy of commemoration, recovery, and re-creation of their Italian familial cultures. The stories they give us comprise several features of *italianità*: the portrayal of what Gambino calls *l'ordine della famiglia* refers to the unwritten but uncompromising code of duties and responsibilities to the family (*Blood of My Blood* 3). As Leonard Covello writes, in southern Italy

> family solidarity was the basic code of such family life and defiance of it was something akin to a cardinal sin. . . . The family solidarity was manifested by uniformity of behavior, adherence to family tradition and, also, a community of economic interests. (150–51)

Because of the migration experience, the historically necessary solidity of *la famiglia* diminished, and so did the woman's role within the family. In the critical literature about the Italian family, however, a typical description of the mother goes like this:

> She is the family's emotional sustenance. While yielding authority to the father, she traditionally assumes total control of the emotional realm of the family. Her life centers around domestic activities, and she is expected to receive her primary pleasure from nurturing and servicing her family.

Her personal needs take second place to those of her husband, and in exchange she is offered protection and security from all outside pressures or threats. (Rotunno and McGoldrick 347)

The saying *una madre, molti padri* reinforces what Colleen L. Johnson cites as the two predominating themes in the writings of southern Italian culture: "the centrality of the family and the elevation of the maternal role" ("The Maternal Role" 235).

Closely tied to the centrality of the Italian mother's role is the "strong cult of the Madonna—the Holy Mother who prefigured all other mothers and symbolized them" (Barolini, *The Dream Book* 9). Describing peasant women in southern Italy (Lucania/Basilicata), Ann Cornelisen recognized the Marian cult as part of "the core of local belief" and peasant women's role in the family as parallel to the Madonna's of the Catholic church: "all-forgiving, all-protecting" (27). In his analysis of Italian women, Gambino describes the ideal of womanliness as she who possesses *serietà*, "seriousness," crucial for maintaining the strength, honor, and cohesiveness of the family in southern Italy. That the most common invocations in southern Italy in times of trouble are "*mamma mia*" or "*Madonna mia*" reinforce for Gambino the elevated status of the mother (*Blood of My Blood* 150).

Both features of *italianità—l'ordine della famiglia* and the elevation of Italian mothers—are modified by the experience of migration and resettlement patterns in the United States. Although her stature may have been inviolate, Cornelisen admits that few Italian peasant women could achieve the ideal behaviors of the all-forgiving and all-protecting Madonna: "[T]his is the aim of most mothers, but they seldom carry the weight of total responsibility" (27). Italian American women writers portray the mother's role in the family in complicated and varying ways. An analysis of the mother figure in Italian American women's novels reveals a differentiated identity: she is both strong and weak; articulate and silent; traditional and rebellious; assertive and ineffective. She is not categorically depicted as trapped by her "timeless" peasant mentality, accepting with resignation her heritage of fatalism.[18] That is not to say that the incorporation of another feature of *italianità*, a belief in *destino* (destiny), is fully overridden by American optimism in these texts. Similarly, the mentality of *miseria* (desperate poverty), reinforced by the impoverished conditions in America for those immigrants from the *Mezzogiorno*, is not an immutable feature in the prose works of Italian American women.

Perhaps the conflict most insistently dramatized in these novels has to do with a struggle in the family between the Italian belief in *la via vecchia*, "the old way," and the American emphasis on innovation and liberation from old beliefs. The following well-known Italian proverb encapsulates the Italian family's investment in *la via vecchia: Chi lascia la via vecchia per la nuova, sa quel che perde e non sa quel che trova* (Whoever forsakes the old way for the new knows what he is losing but not what he will find) (Gambino, *Blood of My Blood* 2). Traditionally subordinate to the men in her life—father, brothers, husband—the Italian woman's stake in the old ways perpetuates her inferior status. In certain instances, the female characters interpret the belief in *la via vecchia* through the lens of their status as mothers: responsible for transmitting to their children the moral heritage (for which they were highly valued in Italy), Italian immigrant mothers felt particularly threatened by the public schools of America, which they feared underrated their roles as educators of their children.

Defined through family affiliation, the Italian immigrant mother's role was potentially attenuated in America, especially when she was required by economic or legal necessity to send her children into a strange public world outside the confines of *la casa*: the factory and the classroom. Social historian Elizabeth Ewen believes that maternal authority over children was not weakened in America. Rather, mother and children were intensely involved in adjusting to a new land. Like other first-generation immigrant women, the Italian American mother "had very little formal contact with the dominant value system of American life; her immediate context determined her energy, organization skills, and familial responsibilities" (96). The novels in the Italian American tradition at times portray mothers as defensive and resentful toward their children's American ways, but in other cases, mothers in fact succeed in maintaining the cultural authority and economic stability of the family.

Novels focusing on second- and third-generation Italian American women tell another story. The inherent struggle resulting from a devotion to *la via vecchia* and an allegiance to the new world is often meliorated by the Italian American writers' inclusion of another feature of *italianità: comparaggio* or *comparatico* (godparenthood). In Italy, this term refers to "a system of relationships whereby men or women were included as members of a family upon their assuming the role of godfathers or godmothers to a child of whom they were sponsors at baptism or confirmation" (Covello, appendix A).

Although godparenting in the religious sense is not emphasized in the novels, the creation of what Micaela di Leonardo calls "nonreligious fictive kin" offers a writer like Mari Tomasi the means by which to depict the struggle between immigrant parents and their increasingly Americanized children (119). The godparent in *Like Lesser Gods* mediates between old and new worlds, aiding in the young Italian American's formulation of an identity that is neither Italian nor American but a combination of both. The Italian family insisted on the privileged status of elders, in accordance with *la via vecchia*: "The elders are prudent and experienced; do as they do and you will learn and prosper" (Mangione and Morreale 233). That Italian American women writers employ such a figure as a mediator between two contrasting cultures attests to the resiliency of the role itself and the innovative aspect of ethnicity, which is open to "modernizing feature[s]," not to one, set definition (Sollors, "Introduction" xiv).

The code of *omertà*, the cultural injunction to be silent, may very well have originated in the Sicilian countryside where bands of brigands fought against governmental authorities. Such conditions "gave rise to a morality in which justice was regarded as a private matter, not a public one. This . . . is the real meaning of the code of *omertà*, the so-called code of silence" (Alba 37). This feature of *italianità—omertà*—has peculiar resonance for women of Italian origins and for women who want to write. Perhaps the codes informing the southern Italian family were considered inviolate in Italy, but they were subject to an authority closer to home in America: the wife, the mother, the sister, the daughter. That Italian American writers have chosen to use the family as the focus of their novels, to write of the family and tell its secrets, is a profoundly courageous act of autonomy.

The proverbs and expressions relating to words themselves attest to a tradition of wariness about their function and efficacy. Consider the following proverbs: *La migliore parola è quelle che non si dice* (The best word is that which is not spoken); *A chi dici il tuo secreto, doni la tua liberta* (To whom you tell a secret, you give your freedom). For Italians, "words are not meant literally. They give expression to the moment; their purpose is not logical or measured" (Rotunno and McGoldrick 353). The gender of the speaker also affects the putative value of the word. Thus, we have the proverb *Le parole son femmine, e i fatti son maschi* (Words are female; actions are male). When males use words, they are given fuller legitimacy. Italian men are said to use words more sparingly than females, and the words they use are connected with loyalty and *onore*. Hence, we have the expressions *Ti do la mia parola* (I give you my word) and *parola d'onore* (word of honor).

Women's words, on the contrary, are supposedly used for hurtful and useless gossip, revealing their lack of loyalty and inability to form "superior" relationships (that is, male friendships). In *Women of the Shadows*, Cornelisen suggests that women's language is used as a source of protection and information: "They meet, as all cliques do, to exchange useful gossip, to laugh at the expense of others and to avoid the danger of being themselves the victims. They know that somewhere else in town they *are* the victims" (7).[19]

Coupled with this attitude toward words is the code of *omertà*. Although the imposition of silence may very well have pervaded the psyches of Italian immigrants, it did not necessarily prevent them or their children from using the family as the focus of their writings. One method women use of overcoming inhibitions placed on them implicitly or explicitly by the family is to write through the silence. Italian American writers, like their Asian

American and African American sisters, start out from what they know—the family—and tell the secrets in order to (as King-Kok Cheung explains) "defend themselves with words; . . . discover their potential—sound themselves out—through articulation" (162).[20]

Italian Americans from southern Italy and Sicily may very well have come from a nonreading, premodern culture in which nearly 62 percent of the men and 74 percent of the women who came to the shores of Ellis Island were illiterate (Gambino, *Blood of My Blood* 78–79). They may very well have come to America deeply distrusting education "because it is an attribute of the very classes who have exploited you and your kind for as long as memory carries" (Barolini, *The Dream Book* 4). Nonetheless, as second-generation writer Pietro Di Donato, author of the critically acclaimed novel *Christ in Concrete* (1939), predicted in 1978, a "renaissance" of Italian American writers was inevitable: "Our time is now. I see it because you are no longer *figli di muratori* (children of construction workers); you go to school and you are children with brains" (qtd. in Mangione and Morreale 427). Even though he might not have been considering women as part of this rebirth, Di Donato's prediction has come to fruition in the past twenty years.

As if in anticipation of Gay Talese's discussion of the Italian's inherent reticence, Jerre Mangione and Ben Morreale, authors of *La Storia: Five Centuries of the Italian American Experience*, explain that Italian American novelists write "with the distinctive advantage of listening to tall stories. . . . The least educated immigrant was often naturally endowed with a strong gift of narrative that planted the seeds for [his or her] offspring's form of storytelling." Mangione and Morreale suggest that Italian Americans possess a natural capacity to create stories and explain that, even though the immigrants were illiterate, "they did bring with them a form of literature in their proverbs, their legends, and in the oral tradition of their *cantastorie* (the village storyteller)" (365, 353).

We hear the voices of those immigrant storytellers in the novels of nearly all the Italian American writers analyzed in this book, though Barolini, Hendin, and De Rosa most directly incorporate oral traditions into their fiction. When the speaker in Maria Mazziotti Gillan's poem announces to her Anglo-Saxon teachers that she has found her voice, she simultaneously embraces the legitimacy of exploring ethnic identity:

> Remember me, Ladies,
> the silent one?
> I have found my voice
> and my rage will blow
> your house down. (13)

Like Gillan, the Italian American writers examined in this book have found their voices and can no longer be perceived as silent.[21]

Locating the origins of Italian American women's traditions is subject to different interpretations, depending on whether a critic is analyzing multiple genres (for example, autobiography, poetry, memoir, nonfiction) or writers who possess an Italian surname, even if their focus is not necessarily on Italian American cultural experience.[22] My analysis of Italian American women writers begins with Mari Tomasi's second novel, *Like Lesser Gods*. I do this for several reasons. First, it is the earliest novel in the women's tradition concerning the development of the Italian family in America. The novels in the Italian American literary tradition focus primarily but not solely on the familial experience and are often set in an ethnic neighborhood, which undergoes dismantling, rebuilding, and sometimes wholesale obliteration of the community itself.

Second, even though Tomasi might have been writing without the benefit of a literary ancestry, she seems to have conceived of herself as a writer, whether or not she gained critical acclaim or visibility for her work. In fact, Tomasi became an expert on the quarrying industry in Barre, Vermont, where her northern Italian ancestors settled. She worked on the Vermont Writer's project and served as city editor of the *Montpelier Evening Argus*. In 1941, Tomasi won a Breadloaf Writer's Conference Fellowship (Rosa, Afterword 292). On her dedication page to *Like Lesser Gods*, Tomasi thanks her sister, "Marguerite, who kept the study quiet," recognizing the detachment necessary while she honored her family in writing.

Third, Tomasi employs narrative structures and themes that subsequent writers utilize in their novels to varying degrees. Tomasi conveyed a fidelity to the story of immigration and resettlement that shapes the constructions of so many of the later novels. Perhaps the narrative strategy most creatively employed by Tomasi can be seen in her renovation of the bildungsroman to meet the needs of ethnic groups in America, including Italian Americans. Understanding development as relational and family oriented, Tomasi compels a rethinking of separation and autonomy, the traditional markers of maturity. In subsequent novels analyzed in this study, the bildungsroman is refigured in other innovative ways, adding texture and depth both to the novel of development and to the Italian American text. Tomasi's use of a godparent figure who mediates between Italian and American cultural heritages is also adopted by several other writers, some of whom inherently doubt the efficacy of such a figure (Waldo) while others subsume the role of godparenthood under the domain of grandparenthood (Barolini, De Rosa, Cavallo).

Certainly, Tomasi did not initiate the tradition of equating America with illness and Italy with health, but her insistent emphasis on the diseases from which immigrant workers suffered underscored the negative consequences of coming to America. Tomasi's depiction of America as unhealthy reverses the trend quite popular in nineteenth-century novels in which Italy was depicted as malevolent and insalubrious, stripping Americans of their innocence and health. Despite its optimism, *Like Lesser Gods* does not overlook the fact that immigrants suffered in the new world and did not always overcome their illnesses. Tomasi explores the fatal illnesses resulting from Vermont stoneworkers inhaling the noxious dust in closed sheds. Dying prematurely at the height of their artisanal careers, these men—often quite young—left families to cope with a new world on their own. Tomasi offers her readers historically accurate information about the fate of stonecutters before proper dust-removing equipment was installed. Tomasi's suggestion that illness itself represents the immigrant experience in America is thematized more insistently in the later novels.

Several ideas shape the novels under consideration: the depiction of immigration and resettlement in America; the tension resulting from immigrant parents' devotion to *la via vecchia* and the second-generation children's adoption of American values; the family as the shaper of identity, claiming affiliation as essential to development; the presence of a godparent figure who aids in the young person's development of an Italian American identity; and finally, the persistence of illness, both physical and mental, from which characters suffer. It is the aim of this study to examine how Italian American women writers incorporate and challenge such ideas in their creative imaginings.

Chapters are organized roughly chronologically and along thematic lines. In chapters 1 through 4, I examine paired texts, focusing on shared features of *italianità* and on innovative structural techniques. I begin chapter 1 with Mari Tomasi's *Like Lesser Gods*, the earliest in the novelistic tradition written by a woman, but I pair it with Marion Benasutti's *No SteadyJob for Papa*, published in 1966, nearly twenty years later. (Both Diana Cavallo's *A Bridge of Leaves* and Octavia Waldo's *A Cup of the Sun* were published in 1961 but share thematic and structural features better analyzed in separate chapters.) Benasutti's novel depicts the early years of the immigrant experience, as Tomasi's novel does, inviting a comparative analysis of their narratives.

Chapter 1 analyzes the early years in Italian immigrant history, in which gaining employment and sustaining the family in the United States were of paramount concern. Tomasi and Benasutti write developmental novels that depict the coming-of-age within the Italian family in America. The immigrant saga begins with the journey from the homeland to the adopted country; attendant upon such a transition are the difficulties of adjusting to a foreign culture, not only physically (that is, finding work, providing food and shelter) but also psychologically—adjusting to being perceived as different from the American culture.

Both Tomasi and Benasutti produce immigrant narratives that reconcile the conflict of cultures through their adherence to a communal definition of prosperity. Upward mobility and separation from the family are deemphasized in these novels while an emphasis on seeking work within the community and maintaining family relations is essential to each author's definition of success. Chapter 1 seeks to demonstrate how the traditional bildungsroman is reshaped by Italian American core values: group affiliation, family cohesion and relatedness, identity derived from ongoing communication with the family. Thus, what is produced structurally in these novels might be called a communal or ethnic bildungsroman, tracing the development of family and community as they mature and recognize more completely their role(s) in America.

In chapter 2, I analyze how *l'ordine della famiglia* becomes the subject of contention between parents and children. This chapter focuses on the conflict between masculine core values—authority, discipline—and the child's desire to liberate herself from a world she finds both alluring and demeaning. No longer benevolent or ineffectual, some of the fathers in Waldo's and Hendin's texts subscribe to the code of *onore* with a ferocity bordering on the maniacal: their behavior has the potential to destroy their relationships with their children. At the same time, however, when the increasingly Americanized child challenges the father's parental authority, she is met not merely with resistance but with stories that offer her the cultural reasons undergirding the father's distrust of American emblems of personal success. Pervading both novels with disturbing frequency is the manifestation of illness—both physical and psychological—which informs and modifies the characters' development.

Chapter 3 presents two novels that most resemble the traditional bildungsroman in their emphasis on an individual whose autonomy permits reflection and development. In this chapter, I offer a brief overview of the critical literature on the bildungsroman in order to reveal its resiliency of form, stretching both thematic and structural boundaries. Modified by the categories of ethnicity and gender, the characters' developments in Diana Cavallo's and Dorothy Bryant's novels are crucially influenced by their positions in the Italian American family. As the characters struggle to negotiate an identity that can accommodate their dual heritage—Italian and

American—they inscribe illnesses specific to their personalities. In order to become well, the characters in these texts must recapture and accept their losses. To forget the cultural past, Cavallo and Bryant suggest, is to suffer a spiritual death that cannot be remedied by material prosperity or higher education.

Commemorating and renegotiating the past is the subject of chapter 4. In their devotion to Italian cultural heritage, Helen Barolini and Tina De Rosa ostensibly produce family bildungsromane reminiscent of Tomasi's and Benasutti's. Nonetheless, Barolini's deliberate incorporation of feminism and De Rosa's experimentalism function innovatively in these novels. While they remain keenly interested in the Italian American family, each writer's specific emphasis transforms her novel, highlighting the relationship between ethnicity (origins, ancestors, "the old country") and innovation (feminism, modernism).

Barolini's and De Rosa's primary concern is to reinvent the lives of their grandmothers, who inspire their stories, reinforcing the centrality of the grandparent figure in the Italian American tradition. Barolini modernizes her multigenerational saga by focusing on the changing roles of women from one generation to the next. De Rosa employs modernist narrative strategies, especially in her nonlinear plot, to probe the secrets and silences of an Italian American family. In both novels, the grandmother functions as wise seer, giving advice, anticipating problems in the future, and telling stories to ease the family's suffering. Without recovery of the grandmother, Barolini and De Rosa believe, the foundations of *italianità* will crumble.

These women writers have been overseeing the reconstruction of Italian American households. Because of increasing awareness of and critical literature written about Italian American women writers, recent writers of the 1990s may turn to their foremothers to discover their future models. Italian American women continue to write about the family and Italian American identity. Some of the writers continue in the literary traditions of realism, depicting family life in social settings and communities. Others move away from a strict emphasis on realism, employing instead modernist literary strategies to delve into the thought processes of characters with Italian American backgrounds. Still others move completely away from any overt depictions of Italian American ethnicity and yet continue to show interest in exploring the ways in which identities take shape.

Chapter 5 offers an overview of the various styles of fiction employed in recent years. Three areas in particular have produced writings that complicate an analysis of Italian American ethnicity: the portrayal of lesbianism and its effect on family relations; novels that incorporate Italian American ethnicity as a thread in their narratives but not as the sole focus of their texts; and the short-story collections in which Italian American ethnicity seems submerged, though a probing of the stories reveals dualities that bring the concept of ethnicity to light. The final chapter functions also as a beginning of future studies of Italian American writing. Italian American women's voices are clear and inescapably present. Claiming and clarifying these traditions are the tasks of this study.

# 1 *Family Novels of Development*

## *Mari Tomasi's* Like Lesser Gods *and Marion Benasutti's* No SteadyJob for Papa

For Mari Tomasi and Marion Benasutti, gracefully negotiating American customs is central to attaining happiness and accruing material prosperity for their Italian American families. Both northern Italians, Mari Tomasi and Marion Benasutti depict the gradual and sometimes painful assimilation of Italian families who immigrated to the United States in the early decades of the twentieth century. *Like Lesser Gods* (1949) and *No SteadyJob for Papa* (1966) refashion in specific ways the generic program of what has been called the immigrant saga. The way in which the immigrant saga has been defined by William Boelhower tends to overlook the female experience of emigration: "[A]n immigrant protagonist(s), representing an ethnic world view, comes to America with great expectations, and through a series of trials is led to reconsider them in terms of his final status" ("The Immigrant Novel" 5).

While the above paradigm works well for Italian male immigrants, many of whom provided the United States with an unskilled labor force, it does not fit the Italian immigrant woman's experience, which centered around the family. What Boelhower proposes here is a cultural script that excludes a communal focus—individual men leave their homelands to achieve prosperity (in most cases, to contribute to the family's economy). The cardinal values of Americanism are emphasized: individualism, material success, and personal achievement. What is omitted from the script is the Italian immigrant woman who invariably came with her father, brother, or husband and was defined within the context of her immediate family. Though circumscribed by a patriarchal family structure, Italian women perceived family life as their province and were valued for their roles as caretakers and teachers of their children. Moreover, family life has been perceived by historians of Italian culture as the focal point of a woman's abiding concern, a perception shared by several of the novelists in the Italian American tradition (Winsey; Rotunno and McGoldrick).

Both Tomasi and Benasutti expand Boelhower's definition of the immigrant text to include the Italian *family* who came to America to escape poverty and attain a sense of comfort in the new land. The journey to another world lends itself to writing the traditional form of the bildungsroman, the novel of quest leading to self-realization and spiritual maturation. Berndt Ostendorf, a critic of ethnic literature, suggests that behind the journey from one land to another looms that old sense of "travel as travail; [the bildungsroman] is a literature of the adventure of Americanization, and adventure also has that old meaning of arriving." The phrases that highlight the journey motif recognize the male experience: "rise," "odyssey," "out of . . . ," "from . . . to," "journey to," "the education of" (159).

The traditional novel of quest in the American literary tradition is primarily utilized by male writers, from Mark Twain's *The Adventures of Huckleberry Finn* to Abraham Cahan's *The Rise of David Levinsky* and John Fante's "Odyssey of a Wop," but it fits neither the structural nor thematic purposes of the Italian American women's narrative. Just the titles of Tomasi's *Like Lesser Gods* and Benasutti's *No SteadyJob for Papa* reveal a concern for the family's economic survival in the new world. Both titles refer to the father's employment (or lack thereof) in America, but Tomasi and Benasutti do not focus solely on one character's rise or fall, odyssey or misadventure. Rather, these authors are dedicated to tracing the *family's* intellectual and spiritual development in the new world.

Feminist critics have been instrumental in analyzing the way women writers have reformulated the bildungsroman, aware of the impact of gender in qualifying literary representations of development. The traditional novel of formation traces the development of a male protagonist's mind and character. The novel begins in childhood and ends with the character resolving his conflict and coming to maturity and recognition of his role in the world.[1] In fictionalizing women's formation, women writers do not necessarily value separation and autonomy as measures of development. As Elizabeth Abel explains in her introduction to *The Voyage In: Fictions of Female Development* (Abel, Hirsch, and Langland), women do not sever family ties as easily as men, nor have they been socialized to do so. If boys have been encouraged to separate themselves from the family to achieve autonomy at a young age, girls, in contrast, have been compelled to reproduce their mother's life as wives and mothers themselves, often achieving self-authentication much later in life and for different reasons.

When a bildungsroman is written to meet the needs of the Italian American family in the United States, the structure and thematic content of the genre are transformed. Tomasi and Benasutti are dedicated to exploring the primary assumption underlying the novel of formation: the evolution of a coherent self.[2] At the same time, the authors reformulate that assumption to include the development of the Italian American family in the United States. To preface the Italian family with the word "stable" or "coherent" would be to suggest that they arrive in the United States unstable or incoherent, which can be construed as an ethnocentric notion; nonetheless, I agree with Ostendorf in his assertion that the "very act of emigration forces a disintegration of self, culture and society. . . . The self is pushed into marginality" (149). In their attempt to portray examples of successful adjustment to American society, Tomasi and Benasutti deemphasize the Italian family's struggle to find acceptance, which often required them to deny their heritage. What the authors emphasize instead is the fact that gaining American stature is a process, often painstaking and relentless, occurring neither quickly nor accidentally.

Rather, like the female characters depicted in Anglo-American women's novels of development, immigrants often develop later in life, having had to overcome an inimical milieu that excoriates difference and reduces a cultural group to two or three pernicious stereotypes. Tomasi and Benasutti explore the topics of ethnicity and gender by reevaluating what being identified as Italian and a woman means in a country—America—that has often valued neither. In doing so, the authors present a view of the Italian American family that is highly influenced by women and by behavioral patterns traditionally associated with women, for example, interdependence and cooperation.

Women who write out of an English and Anglo-American tradition have demonstrated in their fiction that the impact of gender has traditionally limited a woman's development, forcing her to abide by cultural standards that limit her creativity.[3] Tomasi and Benasutti do not overtly subscribe to the ideas that marriage and family necessitate self-effacement and stifle expression. Both authors firmly believed that it was the family itself that loosened their tongues and gave them the materials out of which to create their family narratives. Perhaps, also, Tomasi's and Benasutti's fierce loyalty to *la famiglia* prevented them from negatively criticizing the Italian family's attitudes about gender, for example, fearing reprisals from the family to which they were beholden. More insistently, I believe that both authors recognized the ease with which ethnic groups in America were misunderstood and diminished. Their novels attempt to portray Italian American families who are loyal *Americans*, working steadily toward achieving the dream of owning a home and educating their children.

Werner Sollors explains that the concept of ethnicity is based on a distinction between "individuals (of the nonethnically conceived in-group) and ethnic collectivities (the out-groups)" ("Ethnicity" 288).[4] However much Tomasi and Benasutti recognize the contrasts between cultures, their novels attempt to explore the relationships between Italian and American values, rituals, and beliefs. As a result, both *Like Lesser Gods* and *No SteadyJob for Papa* are filled with proverbs, recipes, and rituals distinct to each author's Italian homeland villages. Tomasi and Benasutti introduce features of *italianità* to non-Italians in an attempt to construct a bridge between both worlds. In their optimism, Tomasi and Benasutti create novels that offer models of successful negotiating between the nonethnically conceived in-group (the "Americans") and the ethnic collectivity of Italian immigrants.

Both categories—gender and ethnicity—help formulate a sense of identity for the Italian American characters fictionalized by Tomasi and Benasutti. *Like Lesser Gods* and *No SteadyJob for Papa* offer affirmative depictions of the Italian family in America. The authors define *la famiglia* in neither static nor stereotypical terms. In this way, both Tomasi and Benasutti controvert narrow definitions of the Italian family provided by scholars in sociology and history who have in the past interpreted the Italian American family as immutable.[5] Tomasi and Benasutti do not grossly exaggerate the benefits of their own culture; they do propose a belief in what Gambino has called "creative ethnicity," that is, building upon "inherited ethnic characteristics [the author] judges to be valuable." Drawing upon two cultures—Italian and American—allows these writers to "shape the emerging synthesis of contributions," without favoring either culture (*Blood of My Blood* 329).[6]

Mari Tomasi ably combines the strengths of both cultures in her second novel, *Like Lesser Gods.* Born in Montpelier, Vermont, Tomasi eventually chose writing to memorialize her love of Barre, Vermont, and the history of quarrying in that area. Her depiction of granite workers in *Like Lesser Gods* reveals her expertise concerning the quarrying industry. Tomasi's 1960 article "The Italian Story in Vermont" further informs us that pioneer emigrants from Carrara arrived in Sutherland Falls, Vermont, in 1882. Displaying her fervent love for both Italy and America, Tomasi writes:

> It was the highly prized marble of the hills of Carrara, Italy, that provided the world with masterpieces of art created by the sculptors and carvers of antiquity; and it was the equally prized marble and granite of Vermont hills that centuries later attracted the descendants of these artists and craftsmen to Vermont.

Italian cutters and carvers from the Como area, Carrara, and other stone-working districts of Italy began to immigrate to Vermont in the 1880s. The city of Barre, "the world's greatest granite center, . . . proved to be Vermont's magnet for Italians emigrating from the north of Italy" (73, 75).[7]

Tomasi's earlier story "Stone" anticipates *Like Lesser Gods* and has been anthologized with other Vermont regionalist writing. Tomasi's novel traces the growth of an ethnically diverse community of Irish, Welsh, French, Scottish, Spanish, and Italians, showing how the residents of a small quarry town gradually adjust to American ways within the span of a generation. Tomasi explores the difficulties of living in the United States as an immigrant person who is cognizant of her difference from American culture but who feels compelled to acquire the mainstream's value system without completely relinquishing her culture of heritage. Tomasi makes clear in *Like Lesser Gods* that one of the most significant ways in which the Italian American person retains her ethnic heritage is through her unwavering allegiance to *la famiglia*, the institution understood by Tomasi to provide an identity and continuity in one's life. *Like Lesser Gods* suggests that in America, the Italian's dependence on the family increasingly is less a result of economic constraints and more a desire to retain family heritage. At the same time, dependence on the family, especially for women, is often the result of lack of freedom. For the Italian mother, the family may have been the sole source of her power and status. As a result, the family was less a space of freedom than a place of safety: shelter from a foreign culture and language.

Tomasi's highly affirmative depiction of the Italian American family deserves fuller commentary. It is not the family represented by media in magazine advertisements and film characterizations, limiting Italian Americans to big appetites or violent natures. Rather, Tomasi values the Italians' ability to assimilate into American culture without jettisoning Italian values, especially *l'onore della famiglia*, reverence for family solidarity and maintenance of family tradition. Nor does formal schooling diminish the influence of the Italian family. Rather, Tomasi insists on the possibility of being educated without familial resistance, a belief she might very well attribute to her northern Italian background, as evidenced by her own need to distinguish herself from her southern neighbors:

"The northern Italian differed in temperament, and usually in education as well as in physical appearance, from the southern Italian" ("The Italian Story" 75). Despite Tomasi's own predilection about southern Italians, her novel and several others written by southern-descended Italian Americans controvert the oft-repeated southern saying, *Fesso chi fa i figli meglio di lui* (It is a fool who makes his children better than himself). In America, this belief placed in the context of formal education reinforces the image of the Italian family as narrow-minded, inward-looking, and preventing the mobility of its children. Tomasi insists in *Like Lesser Gods* that the values of being both *ben educato* (well mannered) and *ben istruito* (well instructed) are tacitly shared and enforced by family members.

In conjunction with the centrality of the family to the Italian American novel, *Like Lesser Gods* reinforces three themes often highlighted in Italian American writing: the immigrant's desire to maintain Italian customs and yet adopt some of the dominant culture's values; the emotional and intellectual development of second-generation children, who feel increasingly alienated from their immigrant parents' culture; and the godparent figures, who not only serve as guides for the young person reaching maturity but often serve as mediators between inherited and adopted cultures. The anthropologist Michael M. J. Fischer notes that one of the tendencies of a narrative work that takes ethnicity as its focus is its discovery that there is no role model for being ethnic American. Assuming an ethnic identity, Fischer argues, "is a matter of finding a voice or a style that does not violate one's several components of identity" (196). Tomasi takes the traditional Italian emphasis on *comparaggio* and invents a new role for selected outsiders who traditionally functioned as sponsors at baptism or confirmation. Tomasi suggests that the godparent in America might function as a role model for a young person and help her become something new: neither an Italian in America nor an American, she is encouraged to choose a multifaceted concept of self in becoming an Italian American.

In keeping with the primary assumptions undergirding the bildungsroman—a belief in a coherent self and faith in the possibility of developing that self—*Like Lesser Gods* expands literary representations of development by including the coming-of-age not only of a young person seeking an education but of the Italian family itself. The novel depicts the lives of working-class Italians and other ethnic groups in Granitetown, a fictionalized Barre, Vermont. Divided into two periods of social history, 1924 and 1941, *Like Lesser Gods* traces the community's development from first- to second-generation Italian Americans.

The novel opens with the fifty-five-year-old, unmarried Piedmontese schoolteacher *Maestro* Michele Pio Vittorio Giuseppe Tiffone taking his first boat trip to America to visit his nephew. After the untimely death of his relative, Tiffone is invited to live with his former student, Pietro Dalli, and his family. Tomasi introduces the schoolteacher immediately in *Like Lesser Gods* to reinforce her belief in the sustaining nature of the Italian culture as it is represented in this educated, wise, and practical man. That he possesses the names of the sacred and secular heroes of his land—Saint Michele, Pope Pio, King Vittorio, and his father—parallels his function as a storyteller and a mentor, embodying the country of his heritage in his name and in his role as a teacher.

That Michele Tiffone also possesses the same first initials and the same syllabication as his creator is no coincidence. As a child, Mari Tomasi sat behind her parents' grocery store counter and listened to the "chatter of the Montpelier stonecutters." Inspired by their stories, Tomasi suggests that from her early memories "grew the seed for the novel *Like Lesser Gods*" ("The Italian Story" 78–79).[8] Returning to the family home after two years of college (at Trinity) to work as a journalist and writer, Mari Tomasi remained the unmarried teller of tales like her most essential character, Michele Tiffone.

Refiguring herself in her character, Mari Tomasi gave Michele Tiffone the expert voice on quarrying in Carrara and Barre. Tomasi's meticulous scholarship and careful research are embodied in the maestro, who roams about the town, sharing his ideas with the residents. Perhaps Tomasi could not imagine or dared not imagine creating a woman for such a role, though by remaining single Tomasi chose a path different from her mother's path of marriage and motherhood. Tomasi also chose not to recreate the heated conflicts between strikers and strikebreakers in the stonecutting industry, between Scotch and Italian settlers, and between anarchists and socialists.[9]

In keeping with Tomasi's dedication to depicting the growth of family and community, *Like Lesser Gods* focuses exclusively on the immigrant enclave in Vermont. Granitetown is both unified and divided by the work of the granite industry, thus complicating the immigrants' ability to develop personally and communally. The stone industry provides the "little city of imported bloods" with a necessary pay envelope to ensure the maintenance of family needs (42). At the same time, the industry ceaselessly threatens death to the men who inhale dust particles from the granite they work. Tomasi's reverence for stone does not prevent her from discussing the deleterious effects of quarrying.

As Alfred Rosa states in his afterword to the republication of *Like Lesser Gods*, Tomasi was no stranger to the irony inherent in the quarriers' vocation: "The more the workers dedicated themselves to the stone, the more they created their own figurative and literal tombstones" (297).[10] Unlike Pietro Di Donato, whose novel *Christ in Concrete* parallels *Like Lesser Gods* in its devotion to the concept of work, Mari Tomasi's vision of America working is ultimately affirmative, one quality overwhelmingly denied the Italian Americans in Di Donato's proletariat novel.[11] Tomasi's novel traces the growth of several immigrant groups from Granitetown and in doing so redefines the novel of formation to include a vision of *cooperative* development, one that depends upon the members of the family and community to ensure successful adjustment into American society.

The relationship between Maria and Pietro Dalli demonstrates on a small scale the way the granite industry both unites and divides its people. This Italian couple reinforces Tomasi's belief in the qualities of endurance and resignation that allow both Maria and Pietro to survive as immigrants in America. The novel begins in 1924 with Maria and Pietro at odds about Pietro's work in the granite houses. Aware of the health hazards of working in closed sheds, Maria ceaselessly urges Pietro to quit stonecutting and open up a family grocery store.[12] Pietro's own persistence at working the stone equals Maria's, though his reasoning stems from a religious and artistic devotion to the work.

Maria's "female realism" prohibits her from perceiving stonecutting aesthetically like her husband does.[13] Rather, Maria's practicality compels her to be solicitous for her children's welfare, and receiving a regular paycheck is integral to this concern. Maria, like most immigrant women, is defined by her role in the family. Her position as a mother might be depicted as prohibitive from the perspective of an Anglo-American woman's bildungsroman. In contrast, Tomasi traces Maria's growth as a woman within the family and thus challenges the understandable belief that marriage and community often mean sacrificing personal integrity and work (outside the confines of the family home).

Like many of the Italian American mothers fictionalized in this tradition, Maria embodies the characteristics described in Gambino's model of *serietà*: pragmatism, shrewdness, and assertiveness (*Blood of My Blood* 146). Maria's solicitude for her family's well-being does not preclude her from acting in a rash, passionate, highly individualistic way. Analyzing Maria's thoughts leading to her midnight vigil to the quarries reveals the extent to which she will go in order to ward off eventual illness for Pietro.

Maria's regard for her husband's health indeed stems from the unconditional love she holds for him. She admits temporarily to losing individuation in his arms: "'Yet the moment Pietro touches me, I am no longer Maria—I am Pietro, thinking and feeling as Pietro'" (15). Despite the fact that Maria is solely defined by her role within the family structure, she is neither denied sexual fulfillment nor individual determination. In this way, Tomasi overturns the Italian stereotype of the *mamma mia*, a position that reduces the importance of sexuality in favor of the perpetually dolorous, Madonna-like role.[14] Maria's function as a mother never prevents her from experiencing sexual delight in her husband. Although her sensual life is privatized and relegated to the nighttime, Maria Dalli realizes a completeness to her womanhood that includes sexual fulfillment. Yet, Maria's love for Pietro is ultimately modified by her anger at his insistence on working the stone.

Maria Dalli's strong-willed nature manifests itself most prominently in her determination to prevent her husband from working in closed quarrying sheds. The same qualities Maria displays in Tomasi's text were ingrained in nineteenth-century southern Italian girls, qualities, we are reminded, that are "indistinguishable from the expectations for all *male* Americans" (Barolini, *The Dream Book* 13). Throughout American history, white men have been encouraged to be independent and self-assertive; from the industrial revolution on, they derived much of their identity from the work they did outside the home. Although Maria Dalli's self-assertion and practicality are not given expression outside the province of home, they are not to be interpreted as possessing lesser value. Rather, such qualities as commitment to work and activism are honored in Tomasi's text *within* the context of a family. There is no doubt that once women enter the work force themselves, their exclusive focus on family necessarily diminishes. Not until Dorothy Bryant's novel *Miss Giardino* do we see these values transferred to the outside world in the central character's capacity as a teacher and single woman responsible for her own livelihood and emotional fulfillment.

Tomasi's account of Maria Dalli's midnight trek occurs toward the end of book 1, emphasizing the extreme to which Maria will go in order to prevent her husband from ever entering the quarries again. At the same time, Tomasi's narrative functions structurally as the climactic ending of one phase of this community's history. The climax anticipates necessary changes in Maria's attitude if she is ever going to reconcile herself to her husband's artistic commitment to carving stone.[15] At this point in the narrative, Maria's anger prevents her from forming any resolution about her husband's vocation.

As I discussed in the introduction, proverbial Italian culture has traditionally understood deeds to be the province of masculine behavior. In *Like Lesser Gods*, Tomasi overturns this assumption by having Maria take action against the granite industry. While it is true that pitting herself against stone is safer than directly abusing her family, Maria Dalli's behavior ultimately reveals her lack of power to effect change in her family. When Pietro stumbles to bed (after the rituals of grappa making and drinking), Maria plunges into the night air, determined to actualize the words Pietro had spoken fervidly before: "If by accident my hand should sometime err, just let my boss give me hell. I would throw the job in his face, and quit" (142). By putting these words into the mouth of her male character, Tomasi reverses the traditional Italian attitude that distinguishes between words and deeds according to gender; that is, words are associated with women's behavior and therefore inferior to male action.

Undoubtedly, Maria inchoately realizes that her husband's words are not to be taken literally, since words quite often in Italian perception merely give expression to the moment (Rotunno and McGoldrick 353). Nonetheless, Maria's activism is motivated by her immediate concern for *la famiglia*. Maria attempts to control her husband's destiny by stealing into the stonecutters' shed at night and destroying Pietro's masterpiece: a nearly-finished carving of a cross. Maria's vandalism of the memorial undermines her hope of making her husband's employer think that it was a careless slip from Pietro's hand. Though her deed is never discovered by Pietro, Maria's self-imposed penance thereafter silences her on the subject of her husband's work. Engaging in action that is concrete but destructive, Maria Dalli eventually learns that her resignation is not synonymous with passivity. Maria's quiet endurance may very well be a sacrifice of her will to act, but it keeps her family together. Tomasi's concluding description of Maria's trip to the quarries is appropriately filled with images of death, readily anticipating Maria's failed plans: "[I]n the harsh moonlight the Vitleau sanatorium site was a grotesquerie of exhumed maple roots, standing watch over their open graves" (143).

After maliciously destroying Pietro's cross, Maria shakes an angry fist at the other memorials as though they were witnessing her act of violence. Maria's action in this episode suggests more than just deep-seated willfulness. Even if she is strong and assertive, Maria's anger and bitterness reflect her lack of power as an immigrant mother. Rather than vent her anger on those whom she loves, Maria takes arms against the unreasoning stone. To Maria, the stone symbolizes the senseless oppression granite workers (the majority of whom are immigrants) confront on a daily basis. In this regard, Maria is disempowered just as much by her ethnicity as by her gender. Tomasi clearly suggests in this scene the mother's potential for violence against the family, even though Maria justifies her action by blaming the larger industry that employs her husband.

In contrast to Pietro, who has the luxury of regarding stonecutting as sacred artistry—stonecutters memorialize life like lesser gods—Maria does not have the freedom of viewing it from an artist's perspective.[16] Instead, Maria must perceive the job from the standpoint of her role as wife and mother, that is, in the context of a relationship. By equally including Pietro's and Maria's perspectives, Tomasi gives neither special advantage; rather, she suggests that different experiences result in different priorities, though the issue of gender influences what those priorities will be. Obviously, Pietro's work is hazardous and will inevitably lead to his death, thus leaving Maria a widow with four children. In book 1, Tomasi characterizes Maria as challenging the larger force that threatens the small but vital community of her family.

As if to solidify the connection between the impregnable stone and Maria's endurance, in book 2 Tomasi includes Pietro's final thoughts before succumbing to occupational disease. Though Pietro eventually contracts tuberculo-silicosis, he lives to see each of his children grown, his youngest son, Americo, preparing to leave for college. On his deathbed, Pietro sees only one face in the group not "grief-ravaged," and that face is Maria's: "[H]e was proud of her. As strong, as unflinching as granite she was" (256). Pietro never learns that it was Maria who had vandalized his work, so his perception of her is limited by his failure to account for Maria's needs as a mother. Nonetheless, Pietro compares Maria's strength and determination to the permanence of stone. Maria's choice of design for her husband's memorial is fittingly taken from a sketch of the rococo cross that Pietro had nearly completed but never resumed after its destruction. Having come to appreciate the beauty of Pietro's artistry and the spiritual nature of the stonecutter's job, an older Maria has long been reconciled to her husband's work well before she honors his life in stone.

Tomasi legitimizes Maria's position as wife and mother throughout *Like Lesser Gods* by exploring the depths of her emotion and intelligence. As Maria wrestles with a force beyond her capacity to control, she gains an endurance that strengthens over time. Unlike victims of novels written in the vein of naturalism who are inexorably crushed by unrelenting forces, Maria gains the power of endurance in Tomasi's realist text. What occurs in this novel is the evolution of a coherent self, one of the assumptions implicit in the bildungsroman. Neither the ties of marriage nor community prevents Maria from developing into a model of strength for her family, especially for her daughters. Maria's eldest daughter, Petra, may be named after her father, but the meaning of the name—rock—also symbolizes the impressive, but very human, strength with which Tomasi endows Maria. It is no irony that when Tiffone discusses da Vinci's role at the Carrara quarries, he refers to the artist's painting called *Madonna of the Rocks*, connecting stone with the strength of woman.[17] Surely Maria's strength reflects her namesake, the Madonna. Human reconciliation, which necessitates both compromise and courage, is Maria's greatest strength, one that she increasingly gains throughout the novel.

Despite their earlier conflict, Maria and Pietro's marital relationship is emotionally satisfying to them. Pietro is neither weak-minded nor irresponsible, qualities attributed by writers such as Benasutti and Bryant to their fictionalized Italian men who come to America.[18] Because Tomasi's novel overwhelmingly affirms the strength of the Italian family in America, she demonstrates her equanimity by fleshing out the lives of her male characters. Constructing a bildungsroman to accord with the values of Italian Americans (for example, interdependence, family cohesion), Tomasi furthers this focus by exploring the relationships between members of the Dalli family rather than by limiting her exploration to the development of one character.[19]

Pietro's decision to cut stone assuredly leads to his death, but not to his morbid deterioration of spirit. In book 2, when Pietro learns of his illness, he disconsolately leaves the doctor's office and walks down to the riverbank. Throughout this section, we hear the thoughts of a man tormented by the realization of his imminent death and his need to tell Maria. Though he refused to heed his wife's warnings throughout his younger adulthood, Pietro understands his personal situation in the context of a relationship and deems it his responsibility to share this with his spouse. At the riverbank, Pietro briefly considers immersing himself in the cold water, a perverse baptism that would quicken his death. Rejecting this option, Pietro's final months are spent accepting the hazards of his life's work. In other words, Pietro's adulthood represents what Carol Gilligan describes as "the interdependence of self and other, both in love and in work" (170).

Finally, Pietro "plods to his Calvary," walking with Maria and Petra up the hill to the neighborhood sanatorium (220). Tomasi uses religious imagery much like her contemporary Pietro Di Donato does in *Christ in Concrete*, depicting immigrants as suffering Christ figures. Pietro's final vision before dying includes Italian and American images, reinforcing Tomasi's belief in a consciousness of identity that is neither all Italian nor American but a combination of both. Pietro's boyhood on the hills of northern Italy is superimposed on a scene of granite workers stopping work at the sound of the whistle screeching. The deathbed plea of the old-world *paesani*—"*Gesù, Giuseppe e Maria!*"—are Pietro's final words. The last word simultaneously recalls his wife, Maria, and the blessed Mother. Invoked in times of great pain, the Madonna was considered neither remote nor otherworldly to the Italian. Rather, the Holy Mother possessed an immediate power directly accessible to the believer. The old-world plea reinforces Pietro's acceptance of the interdependent nature of his life. He develops into the gentle, generous man that he is because he possesses equal dedication to his family and to his work.

Tomasi uses the relationship between Maria and Pietro as a commentary on the homeland culture's strength in the face of adversity. As immigrants, Maria and Pietro provide their children with impressive examples of endurance and resiliency. While Tomasi proposes that the same qualities the couple demonstrated in their marriage be cultivated in the community for the successful adaptation of American mores, she does not promote obsequious acceptance of mainstream culture. Instead, she mediates the two cultures in *Like Lesser Gods* through her creative use of the schoolteacher, Michele Tiffone.

One of the ways that mentoring takes place in Italian American women's novels is for the godparent to mediate between seemingly contradictory values systems. The godparent teaches the confused heirs of two cultures how to embrace both of them without slavishly adhering to one or the other. Tomasi's use of a godparent figure enlarges our understanding of the way writers have employed the mentor figure in American literature. For example, the guide depicted in an early-nineteenth-century story about America, Hawthorne's "My Kinsman, Major Molineux," functions to help the protagonist to adjust to a new society. In effect, Robin is encouraged to forget his past in order to survive in a world that is indifferent to a commitment and a desire to remain with the family. His failure to adjust to the demands of a new culture may result in pain, violence, or even death. In contrast, a text like Tomasi's insists on the strength of the original culture to provide succor from the difficulty of adjusting to a foreign environment. In this way, Italian American women's novels can be usefully compared to other novels that emphasize the power of familial heritage such as Leslie Marmon Silko's *Ceremony* and Toni Morrison's *Song of Solomon*. Each of these novels aligns itself with the power of the home culture to give meaning to their characters' painful lives in America.

The fact that Tiffone decides to come to America at age fifty-five attests to his resiliency of character, despite his rheumatic legs. His immediate adoption of Petra's nickname—Mister Tiff—presages his ready adjustment to changes within the American milieu.[20] Because he remains unmarried, Mister Tiff is liberated from the demands of rearing a family, allowing him the time to ramble about the community freely and to place himself in the thick of emotions felt by others. His marginality (as an Italian, as a scholar, as an elder, as a man distanced from his biological family) gives him insight into the problems facing other characters, old and young. Mister Tiff's role as mediator places him somewhere between a saint and a *furbo* (shrewd person); he is neither wholly self-effacing nor deceptively conniving for his own aggrandizement. As a result,

Tiff helps others adjust to the social demands of American culture and by his own example shows them the possibility of maintaining homeland values as well.[21]

The Americanization of the immigrant enclave in Granitetown called Pastinetti Place is ostensibly shown in its nomenclatural shift to the anglicized "Pleasant Street." The immigrants' gradual adjustment into American culture is not as insipid as the new street name suggests. Mister Tiff returns to his former job as maestro because of a need stemming from the second and third generations' ignorance of the Italian language. Once a week, he teaches Italian to six of the immigrants' grandchildren. In contrast to writers like Pietro Di Donato and Julia Savarese (*The Weak and the Strong*) whose works are primarily directed to exposing the hostility of the dominant culture, Tomasi dedicates the second half of her book to exploring the ways in which characters have adjusted to the gradual immersion of American values. As a result, Tomasi investigates the idea of marginality with regard to the always difficult but achievable interplay between two cultures.

Tomasi's creation of Petra, the eldest daughter, remains the most provocative example of the process of assimilation in *Like Lesser Gods*. Petra enters one of the few professions open to white women—she becomes a nurse.[22] This vocation extends her mother's role as caretaker into the larger world, but it also prepares Petra to aid in the treatment of her father's illness and anticipates her equally vital role as nurturer to her future husband, Denny Douglas. Undoubtedly, Petra's role is defined by her relation to men, a situation that obviously perplexes her creator, who waits until the penultimate scene to resolve Petra's story.

Quite late in the narrative, Petra thinks that she, like the maestro, needs no partner in this world. Petra sees in Mister Tiff a viable model of being in the world, one that agrees with her own personal development. Yet, Tomasi gives only her most unconventional female character, La Tonietta, the option of singlehood in *Deep Grow the Roots*, her first novel (1940). Midwife and mother, the unmarried La Tonietta can say unflinchingly to her accusers, "'I do not consider myself a sinner—I never have. . . . I did not want a husband—I *did* want children'" (140).[23] In her imaginative recreation of her parents' northern Italian homeland, Tomasi produced a daringly unconventional woman who was dependent on no one but herself for her welfare. Perhaps because moving to an alien land is often fraught with painful changes, Tomasi chose a traditional route for Petra—marriage and family. It's almost as though Tomasi lost her nerve once she was writing about life close to home.

Tomasi complicates the conventional situation of marriage by having Petra decide to marry not another person from an immigrant background, as her brother Vetch does, but an Anglo-American. Before Tomasi unifies Italian and Anglo-American cultures through the ceremony of marriage, she equalizes relations between these two groups early in Granitetown history. Tomasi places Mister Tiff in a position of teaching the neighborhood children Bible stories and stories of the saints. Included in the privileged trio who take part in field trips to St. Michael's church is Denny Douglas, the son of Scotch quarry owners. Tomasi describes the children as "grimy pilgrims" who are transfixed by Tiff's Bible stories of St. Michael as they stand under the sculptured wings of the archangel. That Denny is indelibly moved by Petra's religious background is reflected in the fact that, as an adult, he uses his skills as a carver of miniatures to reproduce a faithful replica of the wooden archangel, beside which stand Mister Tiff and three smaller figures huddled under the angel's wings. When Petra sees Denny's figurine, she is filled with awe. The fact that Denny preserves that union in stone validates Petra's heritage.

Tomasi's perplexity regarding intermarriage is resolved in a violent way: Denny's hand is mutilated during a quarrel he breaks up at his father's quarry, compelling him to relinquish his avocation of carving. Yet his penchant for capturing moments of life affects him artistically. After the accident, Denny sketches the half-dreaming expression on Petra's face when she had first seen the figurine. By having Denny sketch a picture of a woman looking at a carving, remembering her cultural past, Tomasi integrates Catholic, Italian values with Anglo-American interest in those values. Tomasi's creative ethnicity reveals her own desire to capture both cultures, though she repeatedly suggests that the Douglas family denigrates the efficacy of art. Denny's parents frown upon his artistic aspirations, and they actively try to frustrate his ambitions. Symbolically and literally, they reduce their son to an artist of miniatures.

Denny's later mutilation reveals Tomasi's own concern about the element of power in relationships. To strip Denny of his power of expression parallels the immigrant experience of being disempowered in America. Denied the option of expressing themselves solely in their original language, Italians, like other ethnic groups, had to invent ways to express themselves. They weren't simply allowed to be who they were, as in Italy, so the immigrants had to find new avenues of expression—through the English language, through the work force, and through education. Tomasi's debilitation of an Anglo-American character suggests her awareness of both the issues of ethnicity and gender in Petra's decision to break away from family to marry outside the Italian culture. Anglo women writers have physically handicapped their male characters in order to equalize relations between the heroine and her mate. In the case of Elizabeth Barrett Browning's *Aurora Leigh* and Charlotte Brontë's *Jane Eyre*, for example, both male characters are maimed before they can become appropriate helpmates for their spouses. Mari Tomasi follows in the same tradition of diminishing male power so that the male character learns to empathize with his wife's position as a woman. In the situation of *Like Lesser Gods*, the Anglo-American male must learn to embrace his future wife's cultural heritage, realizing that Petra's homeland values will continue to enrich her relationship to his cultural background.

The relations between Anglo-American and Italian American traditions are often characterized by contention, especially in the novels depicting immigrant life in the early decades of the twentieth century. When the writers begin to voice the sentiments of the Italian American characters without self-consciously pitting their group against mainstream culture, they begin to explore more exclusively the psychology behind Italian American behavior. For writers such as Tomasi and Benasutti, their parents' trip to the new world and the subsequent adjustment in America remain preeminent in their memories. Both were born in the first decade of the twentieth century to parents who courageously left Italy to make a better life in America. The writers focus on the success and bravery of their parents, despite overwhelming odds.

Such courage is demonstrated in detail in Marion Benasutti's *No SteadyJob for Papa*. Benasutti claims to have limited her novel to writing about the family, but in actuality she acutely explores American society through the eyes of the adolescent narrator, Rosemary. Rosemary's position as a first-generation Italian American often compels her to regard Anglo-American culture warily, if not negatively. Nonetheless, like Tomasi's novel, *No SteadyJob for Papa* is insistently concerned with the family. Devoted to writing from childhood on, Benasutti was inspired by her writing classes at Temple University to create fictions out of what she knew most—the family.[24]

Using her mother as her central source of inspiration, Benasutti produced a novel that revolves around the lives of an Italian American family in Philadelphia during World War I. The narrative event that maintains its immensity of purpose in many immigrant sagas is the transatlantic crossing; Benasutti's novel follows in this tradition as she describes her parents' journey to America and their subsequent move to Goat Hill in South Philadelphia, an insulated and impoverished ghetto. The sense of travel as travail informs Benasutti's description of the mother's difficulties after she immigrates to the new world. At first, the mother remains in her northern Italian village, fruitlessly awaiting word from her husband in America. Though he is literate, the father never writes to tell his wife that he hasn't yet accumulated enough money for her passage. Ignoring the irresponsibility of her spouse and the protestations of a recalcitrant mother-in-law, the mother arrives at Ellis Island literally in bare feet, her *pianelle* (slippers) stolen from her in steerage. Benasutti's reference to the immigrant woman's arriving without shoes also comes to symbolize the mother's willingness to start anew in order to survive in America.

That the mother's travel is filled with hardship anticipates further struggles living in the new world—her move from one land to another is less a fact of the adventure of Americanization, as Ostendorf contends, than it is a struggle that requires resiliency

(159). Benasutti's reenactment of the mother's journey commemorates an unlettered woman's assertiveness and her devotion to work, qualities closely akin to Maria Dalli in *Like Lesser Gods*. These behaviors are intimately connected with each woman's commitment to *la famiglia*, influenced by her role as a mother. While her husband unsuccessfully attempts to make a living, the mother in *No SteadyJob for Papa* successfully raises a family and brings to America her ability to do hard work and to sacrifice to meet the family's needs. Both mothers exhibit what Gambino rather chauvinistically calls "the ideal of womanliness," *la serietà*—serious awareness of the crucial role they play in sustaining the family economically and socially (*Blood of My Blood* 146).

The original jacket cover of *No SteadyJob for Papa* belies Benasutti's focus by emphasizing the fact that the father is temperamentally unequipped for all forms of work: "[H]is natural ebullience rebels at routine, yearns for the singing breeze of spring."[25] Such a description merely reinforces the stereotype of the guileless, unchanging peasant, an image often associated with Italian immigrants in America. In her article "The Making of an Italian American Writer," Benasutti explains that her novel is really about the activities of her mother, "the ambitious one," the one who is the guiding force for the family as they gradually adjust to American ways (31). Ultimately, then, the novel is another example of an ethnic bildungsroman as it charts the maturation of the Italian family in America.

Just as Tomasi redefines the novel of formation according to the needs of the whole community, Benasutti traces a young girl's growth into adulthood as she becomes educated within and outside the perimeters of the family. The young narrator's sense of identity is determined by the perception her family shares of themselves as immigrants in America. The most telling difference between Tomasi and Benasutti is the fact that Tomasi had a clear sense of place in her work and thus can be compared to other regional writers like Sarah Orne Jewett and Sherwood Anderson. Like them, Tomasi writes a narrative that revolves around the lives of people who are either sustained emotionally or virtually destroyed by their region. In contrast, Benasutti's narrative revolves around the mother's scrimping and saving in order to move into a neighborhood that will allow her family to live decently.

Benasutti's novel is neither as thematically sophisticated nor as structurally complex as *Like Lesser Gods.* Yet its depiction of the mother-daughter bond provides an overview of the contrasting needs of different generations and a reinforcement of the necessity of family cohesion for determining the success or failure of the girl-narrator's psychological development. Like the narrator in Tomasi's text, Rosemary records with understanding and animation the historical period in which her mother experienced her early adulthood—during and after World War I. Endowing her mother with grandiosity, Rosemary lends credence to Mamma's actual name, Europa, which refers both to a Phoenician princess and the country she leaves behind. The Greek myth portrays Zeus taking the form of a white bull and carrying Europa off to Crete. While Papa neither raped his spouse nor provided her transportation to the new world, he permanently took her away from her northern Italian provenance and was thereafter unable to support the family financially without her and the children's assistance.

According to one anthropological study of Italian behavior, the attitude toward being victimized is assumed by the culture. The statement *La vita è una fregatura*, "Life is brutally unfair," unfortunately accords well with the situation of the immigrant woman who comes to America—she is forced to come to the new world because of a marital arrangement in which she is defined by the man who chooses her.[26] While Europa in *No SteadyJob for Papa* arrives on Ellis Island without her husband's summons, she comes as a married woman with an infant in her arms. In other words, her choosing to leave Italy is modified by her service to *l'ordine della famiglia* and to her perception of herself as a woman of *serietà*.

The family, not the individual, was the social unit of necessity honored by Italians. As the mother knows, her relationship to *la famiglia* gives her special status and accords her a measure of security. Understandably, many immigrant Italian women have responded negatively to their early years in the United States with searing comments such as, "I was only thirteen when I came. After three months I got married. . . . I got white hair when I was twenty-six. My life was finished," and, "I would never have come here. I would never have made this life" (Winsey 203–4, 206). These declarations reveal that utter lack of choice deprived immigrant women from determining their lives, having had their careers as wives and mothers rigidly arranged for them at an early age.

In *No SteadyJob for Papa*, Europa's persistence in believing in her strength as a wife and mother liberates her from the obvious constraints associated with her position. Her arrival in America requires resiliency and aggressiveness, qualities that she possesses as a young girl of *serietà*. The Italian maxim *Non ti far vedere senza far niente* (Don't be caught doing nothing) applied most rigorously to girls being trained in household duties (Gambino, *Blood of My Blood* 151). The mother's determination to achieve all the comforts of the new world precludes her from lamenting her disenfranchisement in America. In contrast to her mother-in-law, who relentlessly contends that America is a sick place, the young mother is determined to consent to the ways of a foreign culture even while she maintains her descent from and love for her Italian village.[27]

Benasutti quite deliberately contrasts the older woman from the younger to suggest the danger involved in harboring a resentment toward a world where one intends to stay a lifetime. For the mother-in-law, America is *maledetta*, an accursed land that has no room for old people. She has spent the better part of her life in Italy and has no desire to incorporate American ways. Despite her negative attitude toward the new land, the grandmother in *No SteadyJob for Papa* at times functions to mediate between old and new ways. In fact, Benasutti suggests that she functions much like Michele Tiffone in her ability to establish peaceable relations between various ethnic groups, including the owners of the homes and apartments in the neighborhood:

> It was Gran'ma who established international relations in the Back street. She spoke to everyone in her native tongue. . . . Gran'ma had even succeeded in cracking the rigid façade of the building inspector's aunt by using the oldest trick known to man—or woman: artful, significant flattery of the most insidious sort. (79)

In this way, the grandmother eases relations between immigrants and owners, unknowingly functioning to allay her daughter-in-law's anger over living in such impoverished surroundings. Because she remains certain in her conviction that America, despite its allure, is a sick place, the grandmother's mediation is ultimately less efficacious than Tiffone's in *Like Lesser Gods.*

Like Tomasi's book, Benasutti's is a novel of development that overwhelmingly affirms the ability to assimilate successfully in the United States. Nonetheless, her choice to have an older woman define the new world as ill reveals Benasutti's cognizance of the potentially harmful effects of living in America as an ethnic person. The concern with illness is integral to these Italian American novels and dramatically differs from the way Anglo-American writers have traditionally interpreted America and Italy. Often, in nineteenth-century American literary depictions of Italy, the booted country is treated as symbolic of the decadence of the European world. A writer like Henry James places his ingenue Daisy Miller on Italian soil, and she literally dies from inhaling the noxious Colosseum air. In obvious contrast, the immigrants literally die from inhaling the dust fumes of granite quarries in Tomasi's *Like Lesser Gods.* Daisy Miller in the novella of that title and Isabel Archer in *The Portrait of a Lady* are deprived of their American innocence and health. Experienced and manipulative characters (often American expatriates) cruelly treat the female protagonists, who become ill and/or psychologically wounded as a result of such treatment.

In contrast, Italian American women writers, especially those writing about the early decades of the twentieth century, regard Italy as the place of health. Receiving an unmediated vision of Italy from their parents, Tomasi and Benasutti never modified the original place: it remained an Edenic world, much like America has been at times perceived by the early writers of the republic.[28] For Italian Americans, illness and suffering are equated with America, not Italy. Their perception of the original culture is often tied to a childhood memory of beauty, a memory that is unchanging and ahistorical. Recently, however, Italian American writers depict characters who travel abroad to Italy in order to regain a part of their identity that has been muted and denied in America.[29] To go to Italy is to return to America healthy, a contrast to nineteenth-century American writers whose characters abroad are often hurt by their experience. For immigrants, the brutal conditions exist in America. But while a writer like Benasutti critically evaluates the new world, she does so without depriving herself of her belief in the generosity of America.

The mother in *No SteadyJob for Papa* possesses an undaunted belief in one of the myths of America: hard work brings about success. If hard work means that she must pave the streets with her own two hands, then so be it. When the mother moves to an indigent neighborhood in South Philadelphia, she is deeply troubled but never relinquishes her commitment to purchase a house. Her struggle continues for years; perhaps in spite of the dream of American success, the mother maintains her desire to protect the family. Central to achieving this dream is the desire for permanence: buying a space she can control not only stems from her belief in the dream of owning property but also results from the marginalization she experiences as an Italian immigrant. Buying a home is not merely a sign of American success; it is a way to preserve her dream of America as a right choice and a way to purchase a protective space for her family. While Benasutti exposes the vulnerability the mother feels living in poverty, the author also pointedly and repeatedly comments on the Anglo-American women who step "daintily over the dust of the Back street" to retrieve the velvet dresses Mamma sews them (32). Rosemary becomes the voice of her mother's suppressed rage, articulating her immigrant mother's lack of power: "I think she hated the *feeling* of being poor that the street gave her. It seemed to rob her of her innate dignity" (33). Pride of place affects the immigrant in America, and Benasutti controverts the notion that too readily presumes a connection between the intimate villages immigrants left and the ethnic enclaves they filled.

Because of the overwhelming shame she experiences when living in the ghetto, the mother becomes a frustrated, angry woman who expends an exorbitant amount of energy cleaning and working for her family and for the wealthy. That she bangs pots and pans about in a "fine fury" and uninterruptedly works in the house attests to Mamma's essential lack of control over her world. For the immigrant women depicted in Italian American novels, motherhood meant interdependence, never autonomy. One of the common ways of expressing utter loss of control, Adrienne Rich points out, is by "furiously and incessantly cleaning house" (*Of Woman Born* 264). The narrator repeatedly refers to her mother's anger by describing her ceaselessly working, thereby reinforcing the relentless drudgery of her mother's life.[30]

It is no coincidence that Benasutti equates the mother's situation with the war itself. A bloody fight breaks out in Mamma's kitchen when she runs a boarding house in a western Pennsylvania coal-mining town where the family first settles. Images of strife and suppressed anger characterize the mother's behavior when she vents her spleen on cooking vessels. World War I finally provides the father with temporary work, but after the war he loses his job, subjecting the family to yet another financial setback. What saves the mother from inflicting violence on herself or on her children is her unremitting belief in the American dream, however tarnished it becomes through long waiting and financial hardships.

The saying *Con un pezzo di terra mai si dispera* (With a piece of land, one never despairs) applies well to Rosemary's mother, for she refuses to relinquish her dream of owning land. For the Italian American, the desire to purchase a house is tantamount to achieving the dream. Although from northern Italy, Mamma's determination to own her home parallels southern Italian immigrants' desire to purchase a house. Such a need stems from the values of the *Mezzogiorno*. For southern peasants, land meant power and was the key to all economic security. According to Gambino, a legacy of this belief is the Italian American's obsession with owning his own home, however humble it may be (*Blood of My Blood* 128). With unfailing perseverance, the mother continues to save for the house she sees materializing in the distant future.

Unlike Maria Dalli of *Like Lesser Gods*, Europa's anger in *No SteadyJob for Papa* is efficacious—she converts it into concrete action to reach her dream. Like Tomasi's mother, the immigrant mother in Benasutti's text is the doer, the achiever, and more readily submits to the American value of upward social mobility than the immigrant father. When she finally purchases her house, the mother's anger is replaced by a sound foreign to Rosemary's ears: laughter. Late in the narrative, Rosemary celebrates her mother's coming-of-age in America by describing her as a "new, exciting stranger" (241). Strategically placing this chapter at the very end allows Rosemary to remember her formative years as leading up to something positive in the future. Her ethnic memory is thus grounded in the future, not the past, suggesting that ethnicity itself is to be reinvented by each generation (Fischer 195).

Benasutti's treatment of the immigrant mother's development is closely integrated with the narrator's maturation. It will be recalled that one of the primary elements of the ethnic bildungsroman is its emphasis on the interdependence of family members. Because identity is derived from affiliation with the family, Benasutti structures her novel of development around the bond between mother and daughter. Rosemary interprets her personal experiences by relating them to her mother's. Although she is dependent on her mother for guidance, Rosemary's life is equally influenced by her love of writing, encouraged by her father, who "believed passionately in *La Educazione*" (36). *No SteadyJob for Papa* emphasizes Rosemary's creativity, but not to the exclusion of her responsibility to the family. If Benasutti writes a *kunstlerroman*, it is dramatically modified by the imperatives of actual life for a poor, immigrant family in America. Devoted to the Latin prayers that she recites every morning and evening, Rosemary exclaims that she is "in love . . . with all words" (60). While Rosemary indeed recognizes her artistic tendency, she does not "master" it by the novel's end, an assumption implicit in the genre. When she enters a writing contest, Rosemary's hope of winning is intimately connected to the financial reward her family will receive during a time of impoverishment for them.

In one scene in the narrative, Rosemary begins equating the hardships of immigrant life with her specific vision of apocalypse: "[T]he end of the world came in small bits and pieces. When Mamma left the Old Country, and Gran'ma gave up her beloved land; . . . when you lost your job—the world ended like that, a little bit at a time" (130–31). Benasutti's belief in the power of the written word is demonstrated in Rosemary's second-place win in the contest; thus she becomes a veritable Jo March of *Little Women*.[31] The fact that Rosemary writes in hopes of winning a financial reward places her alongside the nineteenth-century women writers of "popular" fiction who wrote because they needed money (Baym 30).

Mamma's skepticism regarding Rosemary's prize reveals her basic indifference to the power of words—*parole femmine*, words are feminine and therefore unimportant. While the mother expresses pleasure that Rosemary was financially rewarded, her reaction is grounded in disbelief over the fact that her daughter received money *per niente*, "for nothing," for mere words. Although she fails to value the usefulness of the written word, the mother in Benasutti's novel is neither jealous nor resentful of her daughter's success, because it is assumed that such a monetary reward will contribute to the family's well-being. Benasutti ultimately opposes the narrow belief that Italians prevent their children from advancing educationally by having the mother consider Rosemary a potential candidate for college.

Benasutti's portrayal of Rosemary's growth as a woman and a writer includes the family that instructs her in practical matters of living. Rosemary's concern for her family's survival increases her desire to work and to write well, two areas of activity not necessarily in conflict. Offering an alternative for a young woman who aspires to be a writer, Benasutti suggests that she need not remain unmarried, celibate, and alone in her creativity. Marriage and sex do not of necessity preclude women from being accomplished writers or artists. Rather, intimacy and involvement with the family sustain the woman in her writing. As hopeful as this scenario may sound, Benasutti herself produced only one novel in her lifetime, perhaps mute testimony to a life in which family matters took priority over artistic invention.[32]

Rosemary's initiation into adulthood is punctuated by three events: she is the victim of an ethnic slur; she has her first menstrual cycle; and she takes part-time work as the paid companion to the housebound Mrs. Pierce. In each of these experiences,

Rosemary comes closer to accepting her identity as an Italian American woman. While Benasutti is sometimes critical of the dominant culture, she incorporates values of American identity that will be useful to Rosemary's emotional development, thus demonstrating her allegiance to creative ethnicity.

At the age of twelve, Rosemary begins preferring solitude to the companionship of her Irish friend, Helen Lacey. The prerogative of being alone is unusual for an Italian, especially for a woman, because she is exclusively defined by her service to the family. Radical individuality may exist in one's personality, but it is consciously repressed. For Rosemary, however, becoming an American encourages autonomy, a position reinforced by her literary aspirations. In chapter 9 of the novel, Rosemary has two experiences that disturb her sense of identity as an Italian American and as a woman. In the first, Rosemary enters an empty tennis court house (located on "Front street" as opposed to where she lives, "Back street"), a symbol of Anglo-American leisure. In the corner of the room, she sees a picture of a naked woman symbolizing Spring. Having never seen nakedness before, Rosemary is intrigued, but her sensual experience prematurely ends when the tennis court attendant and tennis players enter the room and hurl a derogatory word at her: "'It's one of those wops from Goat Hill,'" one of the boys says, propelling a shocked Rosemary out of the setting (84).

Emotionally wounded by the incident, Rosemary internalizes the stinging epithet. At the same time, she compares her feelings to those of her mother's, forcing her to feel the "bitter stifling shame" of living in a poor neighborhood.[33] Having been defined as other, Rosemary's first response is to perceive her living conditions through Anglo eyes: she's a wop kid from Goat Hill. It is understandable, then, for Rosemary to feel hate for "my mother and father, [and] the place I lived in." She powerlessly accepts the status of inferiority placed on her by the dominant culture that uses "a single cruel word" to diminish her (85). Confronting her cultural background for the first time helps Rosemary learn to recognize her difference because of the way she has been identified by the American culture. Such an awareness compels her to see the squalid living conditions in which she and her family live but at the same time forces her to find another context in which to make sense of her experience.

Benasutti explicitly compares Rosemary's negative experience to the black experience in America, both groups having been victims of racism in the early decades of the twentieth century. In an attempt to overcome self-loathing, Rosemary recalls her first encounter with an African American man in Philadelphia, where she acknowledges his contrast to her own skin color without equating difference with inferiority. In saying hello to the man, Rosemary diminishes their difference by using a shared term of greeting. Thereafter, the narrator perceives blackness to be a particular pigmentation, not a radical departure from human nature. Rosemary's experience with the black man is romanticized and singular; it does not prevent her from feeling superior toward southern Italians, her own racism evidenced by the way she earlier described her southern neighbors: "their faces darker, their features thicker, their voices not melodious as the ones I was used to" (4).

Recalling her encounter with the black man is useful instruction for Rosemary, but it does not necessarily teach her about the origins of racism in the United States and the qualitatively harsher effects of racism on blacks. Her mother's response to the tennis court episode reinforces the Italians' refusal to place value on words: "'What is real? Sticks and stones, these are real! I have known them. But names! *Mamma mia*, names are for fools who, rather than remain silent and be thought fools, speak out and remove all doubt!'" (89). Despite the fact that the mother disparages words in this response, she continues to instruct her daughter by encouraging her to employ the weapon of language rather than fists in order to teach ignorant "name-callers" the Italian descent of renowned figures such as Columbus and the pope.

However much Rosemary is satisfied with her mother's verbal response, she perpetually yearns for her physical affection. The narrator's second initiation—this time into womanhood—is signaled by the beginning of her menses. During this time, Rosemary vainly tries to win the affection of her mother: "I used to throw myself onto her knees and hug and kiss her for no reason at all except that I was frantic with love for her" (94). Unable to be intimate, the mother cannot reciprocate her daughter's pleas for physical love. Embarrassed by matters of the body, Mamma consigns them to closed doors and dark rooms. Her mother's clandestine activity of hanging out the white squares of menstrual cloth during the night hours further reinforces the privatized nature of this woman's sexuality.

Coming to the aid of her sick daughter, Mamma recognizes Rosemary's pain as part of her entrance into womanhood. Her explanation is both instructive and misleading: "'You have become a woman, that is all. It is nothing to be frightened'" (95). To be a woman is not perceived to be a positive rite of passage into adulthood for Rosemary. Because of her position as a poor, disenfranchised immigrant, the mother in *No Steady Job for Papa* has reconciled herself to a life of birth-giving and motherhood (eight children), perhaps even denying to herself the dire consequences of menstruation when placed in the context of marriage and sex.[34] That Rosemary at this juncture begins secretly desiring to be a nun can be viewed in two ways. First, it suggests Rosemary's inchoate understanding of her lack of control over her own womanhood. Second, it reveals Rosemary's intuitive realization that in choosing to be a nun, she may be choosing to be autonomous.[35] It is only when Rosemary is provided a cherished room of her own that she comes to understand and empathize with the restrictive nature of her mother's life.

It is not surprising to know that Benasutti chooses an Anglo-American household as the site for Rosemary's initiation into adulthood. Separation from her familial household during the week does not prevent Rosemary from identifying closely with their needs. After the wartime prosperity ends, Rosemary is compelled to seek regular work outside of the house. She is thirteen years old at this time and is *ben educato*, which makes her a fitting candidate to become the paid companion of old Mrs. Pierce, an invalid woman whose daughter must work during the day. Benasutti suggests by her choice to situate her protagonist in an Anglo-American environment the necessity of silence and autonomy for reflection and integration of the self. Rosemary's life during the week exposes her to another mother-daughter relationship, one that helps Rosemary realize that her mother's inability to express affection reveals that part of her that is *invalid*, like Mrs. Pierce, a part of her emotional makeup she has been unable to develop.

Alone for the first time in her life, Rosemary views herself naked in the mirror. Introduced to the physical part of herself that she, like her mother, has kept hidden, Rosemary initially does not recognize herself: "This was the first time we'd met, she and I, face to face. Naked, I did not know myself" (115). In her analysis of looking-glass literature, Jenijoy La Belle explains that a woman's "mirror consciousness" is a fundamental paradigm of female self-definition in Western culture (26). If the mirror is one of the major avenues toward self-creation, then Rosemary's response to herself suggests a duality in her identity that is reinforced by the doubleness of her pronouns "she and I." While it is true that the image in the mirror is always, as La Belle explains, "at once the self (at least in the visual sense) and not the self" (42), Rosemary is in the process of defining herself in a complex way, not merely seeing in the mirror an object of derision and hatred as occurred in the tennis court episode. Women have traditionally perceived the mirror as male, that is, as representing the patriarchal values that threaten to transform the female self into an object perceived by the male culture. For an ethnic woman, the objectifying is also enacted by the dominant society, threatening to estrange a person from her culture of heritage through enforced assimilation and ethnocentrism.

Benasutti incorporates the mirror scene to suggest its potential to help Rosemary achieve self-possession and a viable identity. Rosemary's initial nonrecognition is less an indication that she is psychically divided than it is a realization that her familial home provides no access to introspection and self-analysis. Like Tomasi, Benasutti asserts her ethnicity creatively by integrating useful facets of both Italian and Anglo cultures. In this initiation scene, Benasutti establishes the importance of individuality to form a coherent self-image without diminishing the essential fact that Rosemary needs her family's culture to achieve a healthy identity. While Rosemary gazes at her naked body, she intimately connects herself to her mother, who has always privatized her sexuality: "And suddenly I thought of Mamma who . . . must have had, too, a flawlessly beautiful body, though nobody could attest to this for Mamma always undressed in the dark. . . . So much beauty, I thought now, lost to the world" (115). Allowed time for introspection, Rosemary is able to realize her burgeoning adulthood in the context of her mother's life, and what she learns is that she and her mother share beauty, not merely the ugliness of their neighborhood. Instead of rejecting her mother, she recognizes that her mother's incapacity to love herself stems from cultural mores to which Rosemary, as an Italian American, will not subscribe.

Rosemary interprets her ability to achieve adulthood in the context of her relationship to her family, especially to her mother. Rosemary interprets the words "be true to yourself" according to her family's needs. She sees no conflict in becoming an adult *and* maintaining strong ties to the family. To reinforce the interdependent nature of the Italian American family, Benasutti has Rosemary appropriate her mother's dream, using the language of consent (Sollors's term) to affirm her belief in the family's future in America: "'We'll go forward, Mamma, we will. . . . We'll be true to ourselves, Mamma, and God will let us have a nice house'" (120–21). Rosemary's vision of the future is communal; its potential depends on its shared nature. Benasutti, like Tomasi, values the compelling force of her ethnicity and defines the struggle to achieve an identity as a creative ethnicist would do—by adopting useful aspects of several cultures, including Anglo-American.

Tomasi and Benasutti share an optimistic, though not naive, vision of Italians in America. They depict the family coming-of-age as the central concern of their novels. The fact that the family is successful depends upon the cooperation of each family member but also on their acceptance of American beliefs in upward mobility, education, and personal achievement. These works are distinctly Italian American in their unabated belief in the family's ability to nurture its members without depriving them of incorporating personal desires. But in fact, the personal desires of the mothers in these texts are often repressed in order to achieve a modicum of comfort for their families. Their struggle is to make the best of limited opportunities; they need to believe in the American dream despite experiences to the contrary. Without hope, they lose their justification for emigrating from Italy to America. If these novels are optimistic, they also show signs of struggle to maintain that optimism.

# 2 *"Growing Down"*

## *Arrested Development in the Family Narratives of Octavia Waldo's* A Cup of the Sun *and Josephine Gattuso Hendin's* The Right Thing to Do

Mari Tomasi and Marion Benasutti provide the Italian American women's tradition with developmental narratives that depict successful economic and emotional negotiation with the American milieu in the early decades of the twentieth century. In contrast, Octavia Waldo and Josephine Gattuso Hendin provide no such reassurances. Rather, they critique the same core values that Tomasi and Benasutti honor in their novels.

Waldo and Hendin examine the conflict between generations, especially between fathers and children. *A Cup of the Sun* (1961) and *The Right Thing to Do* (1988) thematize a narrative strand that focuses on the changing role of the father as head of the household. Both Waldo and Hendin highlight the father's anguished relations with his children, whether that father lives in an Italian American community in 1940s Philadelphia (*A Cup of the Sun*) or a late 1970s Queens, New York (*The Right Thing to Do*). In addition, both authors examine how the concepts of honor and shame dictate the father's behavior toward his children.[1]

Gambino explains that in southern Italian culture, the father functions as the "ultimate retainer of *la via vecchia*" and as such "made all important decisions concerning the family" (*Blood of My*

*Blood* 6). Since the family was the basic social unit for the southern Italian, supreme emphasis was placed on its honor or dignity. Any deviation from the family's rules made family members subject to attack. The immigrant father's authority was perhaps attenuated even more dramatically than the mother's after the migration to America. One study suggests that in the transition between the first to the second generation, "Italian fathers may lose their high status and their power in decision making" (Rotunno and McGoldrick 350).

Unable to command the proper respect, the fathers in Waldo's and Hendin's novels react defensively toward their families, especially their children. Immigrant parents in general tend to exaggerate the traditional core values of the family in reaction to the experience of living in an alien culture.[2] In attempting to compensate for what they perceive as a loss of control, the fathers in these novels unceasingly coerce their children to behave in ways that the children have trouble understanding. Because mediator figures—*compare*, *comare*—are either less effective or absent in these books,[3] the children struggle without guidance in their parents' world, a place they find alarmingly strange and confusing.

In describing the most conservative branch of the female bildungsroman, Annis Pratt notes that the genre utilized by certain women writers pursues the opposite of its original intent—"it provides models for 'growing down' rather than for 'growing up'" (14).[4] In a similar way, Waldo and Hendin structure their novels around the development of young Italian Americans but forcefully suggest that the model of behavior that overwhelms the children and stymies their progress is that imposed on them by Italian fathers, who require submission to the old ways. Both standards—in the conservative women's novels and in Hendin's and Waldo's texts—require suppression of desire and reinforcement of a standard ultimately harmful to those on whom it is successfully imposed.

For example, by leaving home, the female protagonist in *The Right Thing to Do* falsely assumes that she is successfully rebelling against her father's rules, but she has already suffered the consequences of his surveillance of her activities. She is hounded, spied on, followed, and trapped by a father who refuses to accept the American independence of his daughter. In this way, Hendin's novel also parallels later nineteenth- and early-twentieth-century women's texts that represent "the suppression and defeat of female autonomy, creativity, and maturity by patriarchal gender norms" (Lazzaro-Weis 17). Though the father's behavior can be perceived as tyrannical and unjust, Hendin complicates this by refusing to portray him one-dimensionally. The fathers in both novels offer their daughters an alternative way of understanding a world that the fathers perceive as dominated and controlled by the American dream of acquiring material wealth, achieving personal autonomy, and countenancing alienation.

Both *A Cup of the Sun* and *The Right Thing to Do* explore the development of second-generation children who are at odds with their dual identities as Italians and Americans. Unlike their immigrant parents, the children are not always confused by or critical of the expectations of American culture: that they be educated, that they seek the adventure of independence, that they perceive themselves as independent from the family. Rather, what confuses these characters is Italian culture and their parents' belief in such cultural concepts as *onore*, *destino*, and *mal'occhio* (evil eye). Incorporated into both novels in varying degrees, these beliefs form part of the externally imposed norms reinforced by the family and the Italian American community. Waldo and Hendin examine such beliefs from the perspective of both parents and children, thereby exploring their function and efficacy in America.

Unlike Tomasi and Benasutti, Waldo and Hendin explore southern Italian and Sicilian practices and beliefs. The characters about which they write originate from the *Mezzogiorno*. As discussed in the introduction, southern Italian peasants relied on the strength of the family to guard against unforeseen natural disasters and the constant condition of *miseria*.[5] The immigrants who came from southern Italy and Sicily, most of whom were *contadini* and *artigiani* (artisans), carried with them a strain of fatalism. The term *destino* reinforces the belief that one's life is predetermined. Such an attitude is not categorically held in either novel, but evidences of its existence continue to hold sway over the mentality and behaviors of many of the characters.[6] Historian Rudolph Bell makes an important distinction with regard to the Italian peasants' acceptance of destiny: for them, the attitude of *destino* or fatalism was less about "cosmic determination" and more about a "generalized sense of powerlessness" to effect change for the better in their lives (1).

Coupled to the belief in *destino*, moreover, is the inclusion of the concept of *mal'occhio*. The evil eye belief holds that a person can project harm or illness on another simply by looking at him or her. The evil eye is also called by other names: *fascino* or "fascination" refers to the fact that some unknown and destructive power has fascinated or ensnared its victim. As anthropologist Willa Appel clarifies, when the fascination takes a human form, it is called *mal'occhio*, "evil eye," or *invidia*, "envy" (17).[7] According to Phyllis Williams, the evil eye is the consequence of envy; thus, people who are particularly vulnerable to *invidia*, such as pregnant women and children, are encouraged to remain inside, out of the gaze of strangers (143).[8]

One of the manifestations of the evil eye is embodied in the *jettatore*, who involuntarily attacks everyone, regardless of wealth, beauty, or status (Di Stasi 35). Centrally important to the myth of the *jettatore* is the fact that he acts *without* volition, involuntarily bringing harm to the victim.[9] In their analysis of the introduction of Enlightenment ideas into eighteenth-century Naples, both Appel and Di Stasi attribute the involuntary destruction of the *jettatore* to his inability to put into action new ideas, making him feel like an outsider in his own culture (Di Stasi 35). Frustrated by his inability to act positively in the world, the *jettatore* is incapable of not acting harmfully toward others.[10]

Once the evil eye is cast, varying forms of illnesses occur: headache, exhaustion, depression, fever, and the like. The curers are usually women who pass down the ritual cure matrilineally. Cures differ from region to region, but most often they include determining whether the illness is organically based or caused by the evil eye; blessing the afflicted person; and repeating the ritual cure while dropping olive oil in water.[11] Like the belief in *destino*, the evil eye cannot be ultimately obliterated; as Appel explains, "[I]t is a latent and inevitable part of life" (19).

Waldo and Hendin dramatize the interconnection between *destino* and *mal'occhio* through the father-child relationship. In extreme cases, children are psychologically and literally paralyzed by the father's vigilant surveillance of their activities. As much as they try to rebel, the fact that they have been scrupulously watched by their fathers produces in them an internalized surveillance, depriving them of the ability of acting in accordance with their own desires. The child's destiny is in the hands of her family; to insist on self-determination (which is impossible for the most repressed children) directly challenges the family's belief in its interdependence and honor. Compelled to uphold *l'ordine della famiglia*, the fathers in these novels refuse to surrender power. Because the second-generation children are also obliged by the culture of the classroom to conform to American standards, they do try to rebel against family patterns, some more successfully than others. For the fathers in *A Cup of the Sun* and *The Right Thing to Do*, their children's success has little to do with becoming autonomous and challenging the old ways. Rather, maintaining *onore* guaranteed the family's strength and unity.

To old-world parents, childhood and early adulthood were a time of work, responsibility, and cooperation, not education and leisure. The concept of adolescence simply did not exist as a developmental stage in the "old" country (Ewen 99). When it seems to the immigrant parents that their Americanizing children are defying their responsibilities to the family, the father traditionally intervenes to ensure that his children continue to serve *l'onore della famiglia*.[12] There is a saying attributed to the ideal man of *pazienza* (patience) that reflects his ability to maintain family harmony: *Uomo che sa pensare alla sua casa* (A man who knows how to think after his home) successfully protects his family and advances their security and power (Gambino, *Blood of My Blood* 118, 122). The basis for the southern Italian father's parental role stems from the social need to cooperate within and outside the family in order to survive economically.[13] As one proverb explains, honor is worth more than money.

*A Cup of the Sun* bears comparison to the communal bildungsroman of *Like Lesser Gods* in its portrayal of the children of immigrants who grow up surrounded by things Italian: beliefs, rituals, and behaviors. The neighborhood children in Waldo's novel are highly influenced by their parents' beliefs and often develop identities according to the reputed honor or dishonor of their families. Not every child in the community of Waldo's text "grows down," but two of the children remain incapable of forming sexually and emotionally satisfying relationships, and one dies tragically young.

In 1946, Octavio Waldo received a Board of Education scholarship for four years to Temple University and the Tyler School of Fine Arts, graduating with honors from Temple in 1952. Her work both as an artist and as a writer is reflected in the imagery that she incorporates into *A Cup of the Sun*.[14] Waldo's subsequent short stories recall the themes basic to her novel: using a national crisis (such as war) as a backdrop for examining the conflicted emotions displayed by characters; emphasizing the powerful nature of *la famiglia*; and suggesting the necessity and humanizing capacity of memory.[15]

*A Cup of the Sun* revolves around the lives of Italian American families in a small town on the outskirts of Philadelphia during the years 1941 through 1945. The children in the community experience the onset of World War II, and several of the older boys enlist in the armed forces. The organization of the novel departs from the traditional linear narratives that inform the novels of Tomasi and Benasutti. Though it does follow a particular chronology, *A Cup of the Sun* is more impressionistic than realistic; that is, Waldo is more interested in capturing the emotional moods of the characters than in objectively depicting character, setting, and action.

Part 1 (summer 1941 through summer 1942) introduces the three families who comprise the major focus of the novel, each of them suffering from a mental lethargy that they find difficult to overcome. The Rossi family consists of the silent *Signore*, Filippo

Rossi (or the Old Man, as he is called), and his spinster sister, Rose, who cares for his two children, Laura and Pompeii. This household has been damaged by the father's "forgotten past": when he was in the priesthood, he personally buried hundreds of corpses during World War I. As a result of seeing such carnage, the Old Man loses his faith in what he considers a merciless God and leaves the church. He later marries a woman of questionable reputation who bears him two children. Of the two, only Pompeii is his. "Silent and empty without even the will to die," the Old Man gives his children a legacy of confusion and pain (113).

Both children are destined to repeat in different ways the dramas of their parents' pasts. Without a mother, Laura and Pompeii are victimized by the neighborhood because the family has lost honor. As discussed in chapter 1, the mother in the Italian American family is embraced as its center, a woman of seriousness who responsibly serves *l'ordine della famiglia*. Her reputation already in question, the mother in the Rossi household deserts her demanding husband, a gesture that was not approved of in American society at this time and was considered unforgivable in an Italian American family. Being without a mother is like experiencing a spiritual death, which the children intuit but do not acknowledge. Of the three families, the Rossi family's destiny most closely parallels the plot of exhaustion in Waldo's depiction of Laura's tragic death.[16]

Part 1 also introduces the quintessential family of *onore*, the Bartolis. A restorer of antiques, Mr. Bartoli's status as an artisan gives the family economic security and ensures their stature as a family of good means. Aldo Bartoli's artisanal status, however, does not preclude him from referring to himself as a peasant, recalling the unjust treatment of the church and nobility toward poor people in southern Italy.[17] Of the three families under discussion, the Bartoli family overtly appears the most stable: it consists of a living mother and father and two children, Andrea and Niobe. A product of peasant mentality, Mr. Bartoli has been taught to rule his family through force and anger. Waldo captures the family's anxiety when the father enters the room: "*He* was the head of the house in whom love and hate boiled in restless confusion. *He* was Mr. Bartoli, and every inch of his towering robust structure said so. . . . They did not look at him, were afraid of him, of his strength, his rule, and, most of all, his anger" (26). To emphasize the effect of this patriarch, Waldo deliberately leaves indeterminate the voice of the internal narrator; it could be any one of the characters—Mrs. Bartoli, Andrea, or Niobe.

Sexual relations between the Bartoli parents are mutually satisfying, though their sexual natures strangely impinge on the oldest boy, Andrea, who intensely hates his father. Waldo, like Tomasi and Barolini, offers an example of a loving sexual relationship between parents, thereby overturning the image of women as only suffering Madonna figures. In an extreme reaction to his feelings of powerlessness, Andrea commits incest with his younger sister, who suffers profoundly as a result. Father and son are mutually jealous of one another, a trait Mrs. Bartoli attributes to southern Italian culture. The saying *Fesso chi fa i figli meglio di lui* is a transported *contadino* fear (Covello 257).

Despite his artisanal skills, Mr. Bartoli identifies himself as a peasant and fears any change or departure from his control as head of the family. Yet the father comes to learn that such dominance has only incurred the wrath of his children, not guaranteed their obedience or love. Andrea Bartoli was born in America, and his schooling prevents him from being apprenticed under his father's tutelage.[18] Possessing little practical experience regarding his father's work, Andrea is nonetheless educated and talented. Like Laura Rossi, Andrea Bartoli feels suffocated by the family name and the neighborhood that identifies him solely by his relation to them.

Although less fully developed, the third family consists of Concetta and her severely retarded brother, Romeo. Like the good child of an immigrant mother, Concetta has assumed the responsibility of caring for her brother, despite her anger and impatience: "She pointed to Romeo. . . . 'I never get any peace. Wherever I go, I have to drag him along'" (17). As Elizabeth Ewen says of the female child in Italian and Jewish immigrant households, "child or no," the daughter sees the "situation with her mother's eyes; she assume[s] the maternal burden, and put[s] aside her own needs to meet the needs of others" (100). Concetta is fatherless and troubled by the constant necessity of watching a young retarded child, who emblematizes the confusion and pain of the community at large. In fact, each of the children—Laura, Pompeii, Andrea, and Niobe—identifies with Romeo, seeing herself or himself as confused and sick as he is.

Part 2 of the novel (September 1942 through November 1944) explores more fully the conflicts that result from the tension of World War II and the possibility of Italian American soldiers committing fratricide. Many Italian American men returned to their homeland to fight against Fascist Italy, which often translated to killing their own kin.[19] Andrea and Pompeii enlist for reasons that have little to do with their loyalty to the American government. Each of the young men is trying to escape his family but fails. In the classical sense, each young man tries to escape his destiny but runs headlong into it.

For Andrea and Pompeii, *destino* has as much to do with cosmic determination as it has to do with lack of individual power. Suffering from shell shock, Andrea is hospitalized. His story left unresolved, Andrea will eventually return to the family that he so desperately tried to escape. Pompeii's enlistment likewise brings him closer to the unstated demands of his perversely silent father. While away, Pompeii learns what he has always known, that his father hasn't given him "the desire to live like other people" (228). Like the buried city for which he was named, Pompeii's personal desires remain untapped in this novel. His fate, like Andrea's, is determined by parental control. Like his father before marriage, Pompeii becomes a priest.

Ostensibly celebratory, part 3 (New Year's through summer 1945) begins with feasting. The war has ended, Concetta marries, and Niobe will leave for college. Because of its communal emphasis, *A Cup of the Sun* is a novel about the emotional development of a neighborhood, especially its second-generation children, who have felt most intensely the demands of the Italian culture and the temptations of American independence. The children not only are victims of what they perceive is an untranslatable family system, but also they feel misplaced in the larger American society. Without proper guidance from godparents, they struggle individually to negotiate both worlds. For some children, the struggle ends in psychological illness or death.

In her study *Madness in Literature*, Lilian Feder distinguishes between actual forms of madness in the culture and "literary" madness, in which a character makes an exploration into the mind. As a social representation, illness, like madness, can be interpreted as a necessary movement away from a repressive society.[20] An alternative and equally plausible view is that mental illness can ensure survival in a world where the imposition of rigid regulations makes living in it untenable and leaving it impossible.

Waldo's dedication to exploring occurrences of physical and mental illness parallels other writers of Italian American traditions. Illness is revelatory: disabling diseases (for example, lung cancer, diabetes, heart failure) have often been the result of impoverishment or dangerous working conditions. The obsolete definition of disease also pervades *A Cup of the Sun*. Characters are uneasy about their confusion and often do not know how to act in ways to diminish it. The meaning of "disease" as a transitive verb complements the work of the evil eye: to cause illness or sickness in; infect. Those accused or deemed suspicious as casters of *mal'occhio* infect the victim with an illness that needs healing. Unfortunately, in Waldo's text, the curers of *mal'occhio* are suffering from the inception of World War II and the fear of losing their sons in America and their kin in Italy. They cannot fully act as healers of the sick because they are suffering too much themselves.

*A Cup of the Sun* suggests that illness in Italian American characters stems from several sources: from the expectation placed by the dominant culture on the Italian American to be mobile and independent; from the pressure of the Italian culture to maintain an identity based on an idealized image of the family; and from the inability of the young person fully to understand or contextualize the demands of either culture or either identity. At times, characters of the first and second generation suffer from disorientation, as though in the wink of an eye they have been relocated to another place and can neither adjust to the new place nor forget the confusions of the old.

The Rossi children's stories are located in the painful dramas of their parents. Because he perceives himself to have failed in roles of traditional power—priest and husband—the Old Man deliberately wills silence upon himself, a behavior that becomes pathological. As a priest, he was unable to control the carnage he saw in World War I. As a husband, his need to dominate and consume his wife made him incapable of loving. This knowledge causes the Rossi father to dehumanize himself through silence. Concerning the capacity of growth, Mrs. Bartoli comments, "'Only things that are alive can feel pain,'" but the Old Man has lost the capacity to feel (231). Detached from his past and his present, the Old Man silently sits in his chair, never once speaking to his children.

Although Mr. Rossi has lost his capacity to feel, he has not lost his will to power located in the vigilance of his gaze. In "Foucault, Femininity, and the Modernization of Patriarchal Power," philosopher Sandra Lee Bartky explains that in contemporary patriarchal culture, a "panoptical male connoisseur resides within the consciousness of most women: they stand perpetually before his gaze and under his judgment" (72). Though Bartky limits her discussion to examining the ways in which the idea of femininity is impressed upon women, of importance here is the gaze of the male judge, who expects to *see* the mirror image of his creation. Like the patriarchal male judge, the Old Man in *A Cup of the Sun* resides within the consciousness of his son, Pompeii, who is hypnotized into accepting his future role as a priest.

Waldo suggests the imposing nature of the father's behavior in an early description of Pompeii, who lies on the ground suckling a goat: "Above him slid the evasive shadow of a storm cloud. Its form was a heavy figure in a fluttering soutane. But the boy could see only the goat's belly. . . . The Old Man near the corner let the shadow pass over him, sensing something portentous in it" (13). The image of a priest in the sky is reinforced by the constant watching of the father, who waits for his son to fulfill his tacit expectation that Pompeii enter the priesthood.

Enlisting in the army allows Pompeii temporarily to forget his confused sexual feelings for Concetta and his father's unstated demands. When he returns on furlough, Pompeii remembers the fate that has been assigned to him by his father. Returning home one night drunk, he calls himself the son of "'a priest and a whore!'" The neighborhood itself impresses this identification upon the Rossi child. Acting like chorus figures, the women in "black sackcloth" chant the traditional sayings the neighborhood possesses about a family of lost honor (149). Pompeii mimics their words in his inebriation, having heard them all of his life. As a young man of Italian heritage, Pompeii is defined by the culturally sanctioned gossip used against him.

Ultimately, Pompeii realizes that his future has been "preordained and ill-omened" and his dual identity as an Italian American has been buried (151). The connection between *destino* and the workings of the evil eye is epitomized by the Old Man's constant gaze, whose "single eye opened in the night and pierced the boy with its firing indignation" (152). The father himself casts the diseased eye upon his son, making Pompeii incapable of fulfilling his sexual urges and developing emotionally. The caster of the evil eye traditionally acts involuntarily, but Waldo suggests that the Rossi father consciously controls his son.

Projecting his failed past upon Pompeii, the Old Man perversely attempts to make reparation for the wrong in his life:

> Yet this was the Old Man's son, flesh of his flesh, named Pompeii not so much out of love for the Old Man's heritage, as out of symbolism for the resurrection of the past. The resurrection to come, not to the boy, but to the Old Man who had wanted it, who would live to *see* it happen. The resurrection would come beneath the smoldering intensity of that *single shining eye*. (italics mine, 152)

The legacy given Pompeii by his father is tragic from the perspective of the son's position as a second-generation Italian *American*: he is deprived from choosing a role that is different from his father's. Mr. Rossi hypnotizes his son into dramatizing and reenacting the tragedy of his life, his "single-purposed determination" as monomaniacal and destructive as Ahab's (246).

Waldo suggests the potentially malevolent nature of the Old Man's purpose in the concluding pages of *A Cup of the Sun*. For the first time, the Old Man speaks out loud, and he appears to be concluding his bargain with the Devil himself, assuring Pompeii's safe return from the war: "'Enough! My son is home. Alive and home. I have saved him.' 'Yes, you have.' 'He will take my place and be priest?' 'It is what you have bargained for'" (247). Before dying, the Old Man realizes that he cannot remember what his son looked like, ironically having committed his life to gazing upon him.

Truly, Laura Rossi's fate is the most tragic of any of the children. Laura's pain results from the way she has been defined by the community because of her mother's flawed past. Pompeii may be called the son of a priest and a whore—which will enforce his future celibacy—but he is not the illegitimate daughter of a *puttana* (whore). Although Laura's mother was married to the Old Man when she bore her daughter, Laura is not his child. After her mother abandons the family, Laura remains with the Old Man, his sister, Rose, and Pompeii, but Laura is anathematized by her community.

Unlike the other mothers in this novel, Laura's mother deviated from her prescribed role within the family. The rigid standards of Italian American motherhood assume the mother's centrality to the family, her demonstrated power and resilience within the family, and her capacity to sustain the family emotionally and financially. Because Laura's mother refused to abide by such cultural standards, she was marginalized by the community, considered *malafemmina* (woman of ill repute) and a caster of *il mal'occhio.*

Suffering from the whispered accusations of her community, Laura learns of her illegitimacy and her mother's past in her youth. Young men in the neighborhood feed on past stories of the "unspoken truth of her birth, on the tantalizing memory of a blond woman they had never known. . . . The Old Man's woman. The whore" (19). Defined by her mother's reputation, Laura is unable to secure the love of Andrea Bartoli, a young man whose family honor would be sullied if he were to court Laura Rossi. Laura's fate is more tragic than her brother's: her reputation as the daughter of a *puttana* deprives her from securing respect and love from the Old Man and the community at large.

Quitting high school and becoming sexually involved with a noncommittal neighborhood boy, Laura moves closer to reenacting the scenario of her mother's past—a woman defined by her body, by her lack of chastity, and by her lack of adherence to family regulations. Laura, too, is defined in sexual terms, and she seeks to be nurtured outside herself in the advances of men. Waldo nonetheless clarifies that Laura's search has nothing to do "with man but with woman" (148). The absence of a preceding article in front of the word "woman" suggests that the daughter is seeking a maternal figure in her life. Without other viable models—the Madonna, the saints, a *comare*—Laura cannot dilute her need for a maternal presence. Seeking her mother, Laura seeks an image of nurturance and stability denied her by the transported Italian American culture. In America, Laura has neither the protection of the extended family (which she might have experienced in Italy) nor the advice of a godparent figure who might have protected her. In his persistent silence, the Old Man deliberately ignores Laura, whose mere presence vividly recalls the absent wife and mother. Refusing to acknowledge her existence, the father emotionally annihilates Laura.

Laura tells her family's story to Niobe Bartoli, her childhood friend and a central character in the novel. In what she subsequently realizes is their final conversation, Niobe receives from Laura the cultural script of Laura's life. Laura eagerly encourages her younger friend to rewrite it. Their discussion takes place in a drugstore, anticipating Laura's inability to be healed by family or community. Recalling her past as a young girl, the eighteen-year-old Laura reminds Niobe that even though youth unified them, Laura was marginalized by the very neighborhood she sought to claim as hers:

> "People whispered, and their tongues never touched me then. They put compassionate fingers on my head and said, 'Poor child of God—ah! pity! A victim of circumstance, but she doesn't look like *Her*!' *Her* was my mother! My mother . . . I didn't know that then; they never let me know." (173)

The neighborhood women guard the sanctuary of motherhood, protecting what was in Italy the life force of the family in an often ruthlessly unstable environment. In doing so, they define Laura negatively, imprisoning her in a role from which only death will liberate her.

Laura continues to describe the neighborhood mothers who "'followed me with their rosaries and crossed themselves when I passed, as if I were the evil eye walking in the street'" (173). Laura's outsider status threatens the putative stability of the community. The ritual of blessing oneself wards off *mal'occhio* but also tacitly tells Laura that she is cursed, diseased—a threat to *la famiglia*. The evil eye is thought directly to threaten the regenerative process, and those outside the regenerative cycle are likely to cast the evil eye (widows, childless women, priests and monks). Laura's parents strayed from conservative familial models and are thus targeted as casters of the *mal'occhio*.

As if intuiting the inexorable connection between her cultural background and her identity, Laura explains to Niobe: "'People don't have to look long to know who I am. I am *Her* daughter! The whore's kid! And where's that poor child of God? Dissolved in tits and ass—that's where!'" (173). In this scene, Laura is already dying from infection brought on by a self-induced abortion. After Laura dies, the women gossip and repeat stories about the abortive procedure: "'Imagine doing that with a shoehorn [and a mirror]—imagine seeing it while doing it!'" (183). Laura is literally killed by her body, but she is symbolically killed by her community. Their final description of the abortion reinforces Laura's monolithic identity as a diseased body.

Throughout the drugstore scene, the girls hear the noise of ringing apothecary bottles, reinforcing the connection between illness and the Italian American community. Laura's legacy to Niobe not only includes death and punishment but also hope and determination; she encourages her girlhood friend to revise her script: "'Go as far away as you can and grow; . . . because you're the only one of us who can do it'" (176). At the same time, Laura's tale is cautionary; she warns Niobe of the error of forgetting her Italian identity: "'What are you replacing us with? Have you forgotten you're a Wop too?'" (175). Niobe's self-hatred is not only connected to her identity as a woman but also as an Italian American who seeks to conceal the evidence of her birth by refusing to confront feelings of shame she has at school for her cultural heritage. Like her brother, Andrea, Niobe feels embarrassed of things Italian and is critical of her neighborhood—the "fig trees—and superstitions—and ancient rights and wrongs" (91). Laura pleads with her friend to accept the possibility of developing an identity that neither relinquishes the past nor excludes new growth. Niobe's choice to leave her neighborhood to attend college expresses what Rachel Blau DuPlessis calls a "critical dissent" from the narratives of punishment and death that have dominated twentieth-century women's writing.[21]

Throughout *A Cup of the Sun*, Waldo exposes the illusion in too rapidly making an assumption about stability based on an outward reputation of honor. Like many families of the *Mezzogiorno*, the Bartoli family is governed by the idea that, as Lola Romanucci-Ross says of the people in Ascoli Piceno, "most of you is outside of you," that is, families are coerced by public opinion; "they are thus shame-sanctioned, not guilt-sanctioned" (213, 215). The Bartoli family epitomizes the need to guard against opprobrium, but the children's stories reveal the consequences of intergenerational conflict and the difficulties of living as second-generation Italian Americans during the war years. Unlike Laura's, Niobe's development is not irreparably arrested; she is able to grow up. Niobe Bartoli's growth into womanhood is underscored by her incestuous experience with her brother, Andrea; by her relationship with two other guides besides Laura, Mrs. Bartoli and the local artist, Giambelli; by her break with the Catholic church; and by her decision to leave the community at the end of the novel, attesting to the fact that the concepts of *destino*, *onore*, and *campanilismo* have not wholly circumscribed Niobe's life.[22]

Anticipating Niobe's experience of incest when she is fourteen years old, Waldo utilizes the imagery of the evil eye. Andrea lasciviously watches his younger sister from the courtyard "in the shadow of a marble Leda who never altered her stone embrace around a stone swan" (30). Raped and impregnated by Zeus, Leda is primarily depicted in art and poetry as overpowered and helpless. Unlike Leda, Niobe becomes aware of her brother's fascination. Spying on her while she gazes at her naked body in a mirror,

Andrea interrupts Niobe's privacy by whistling. Feeling powerless himself, Andrea seeks to control his sister's body and her self-image. He is literally fascinated by her body. Di Stasi explains that Fascinus was a phallic Roman god and the word "fascination" is itself another name for the evil eye; "thus, in Latin, the word *fascinum* may mean 'fascination by evil eye' as well as 'phallus'" (43).

Alerted to her brother's behavior, Niobe asks her mother's permission to move to another bedroom, one that is out of Andrea's eyeshot. Mrs. Bartoli denies her daughter's request, unknowingly promoting Andrea's desire for his sister. Andrea is both fascinated by his sister's beauty and by the way he fascinates her, that is, bewitches her with his eyes. Andrea's gaze negatively influences Niobe's image of herself, compelling her to see herself through the eyes of her brother, whose unresolved internal rage against the father endangers the life of his sister.

After the incident of incest, Andrea enforces silence upon his sister, threatening self-emasculation should she confess to the family. Unable to confess within the family, what remains imperative for Niobe is religious confession, an obligation to tell the truth about illicit sex. Niobe attends weekly mass and observes the Catholic rituals of penance and communion. Unable to take the sacrament of communion without confession—and thereby call attention to herself at mass—Niobe eventually tells her secret after weeks of confessing nothing to the priest. Withholding sins in the confessional, the priest warns Niobe, will send her directly to Hell and ceaseless torment. Realizing inside the confessional box that the church offers confession for comfort "and nothing to grasp hold of afterwards except fear" (69), Niobe continues her confession, answering the detailed questions of the priest, who warns her not to "so much as meditate upon what has happened" (71). Already condemning herself for what occurred, Niobe realizes that the church is not strong or understanding enough to assist in her development.

The confessional discourse between Niobe and the priest is less an indictment of the individual priest than it is an exploration of the limitations of religious confession. As Foucault explains, the ritual of confession "unfolds within a power relationship" (61). As such, the priest traditionally follows the meticulous rules governing the "confession of the flesh," including "insinuations of the flesh: thoughts, desires, . . . combined movements of the body and the soul" (19). At the same time, the priest, according to precept, involves the fourteen-year-old Niobe in a question-and-answer format about the details of her sexual encounter, in effect intensifying Niobe's memories about her act with Andrea. The confession of Catholicism parallels what Foucault describes as an "institutional incitement to speak about [sex] . . . a determination on the part of the agencies of power to hear it spoken about" (18), which occasions the priest's subsequent oratory of condemnation.

The priest's words, however, are overshadowed by Niobe's internal thoughts that dramatize her personal struggle:

> She wanted to tell [the priest] it hadn't been her fault; yet she was not certain that she hadn't wanted Andrea. What was it, she asked herself, that made them need love so suddenly and completely? Was it the war? She was certain she had needed love then. Always at the back of her thinking she knew that if she had cried out Mr. Bartoli would have come and killed them both. (71)

Both agents of control, the priest and the father require the obligatory measure of obedience; they threaten punishment but do little to help Niobe heal.

Recalling her experience of incest, Niobe thinks "she had felt herself divide: what was inside her thinking was one person; her body was someone else" (70). When she observes her body in a mirror, Niobe can no more negotiate an identity with herself than can any woman whose body has been prematurely taken away from her. In her failed attempts to become whole again, Niobe realizes the limitation of both Italian and American cultures. Though it offers her expiation, the Catholic church is unable to aid in her reintegration as dramatized by the confessional scene. The American classroom offers her a route to autonomy as a means of protection from getting hurt again, but it does not guarantee emotional sustenance. Internalizing a hatred of her body, Niobe initially thinks that she will escape the reminder of her emotional pain by entering a world of alienation, which she equates with the culture of the classroom: "'I will belong then. I will be consumed within a world of divided, detached people who peer at each other from behind books'" (134). Aware of the Anglo-American prerogative of an independence reinforced by schooling, Niobe briefly thinks that she can find a sanctuary in college education. Although she might find temporary safety, Niobe comes to realize that the American behavioral model of distance and detachment will not help her achieve wholeness.

Despite the fact that her family and neighborhood limit autonomy in their desire to define and restrict the self to place, Niobe finds her voice within her community before she enters mainstream culture. She does this through the help of Mrs. Bartoli and Giambelli. Lacking the serendipitous nature of Mister Tiff in *Like Lesser Gods*, the characters who aid Niobe Bartoli's development are also suffering from the tension of war and the threat of loss to the community and the homeland. Because Andrea has gone off to war, Niobe is able through privacy and reflection to wrestle with her identity as a victim of incest and as an Italian American woman.

Mrs. Bartoli perceives her daughter's distance from the family as a kind of sickness, magnified by the American milieu. Although she never learns of her daughter's sexual liaison with Andrea, Mrs. Bartoli intuits her pain and longs to embrace her daughter. Unable to respond to her mother's physical overtures, Niobe distances herself by reading a novel, an act of autonomy often treated with suspicion by Italian American families. Mrs. Bartoli encourages conversation about the novel Niobe reads, *Death in Venice*. Claiming that Mann's novel is a love story, Mrs. Bartoli offers an unsolicited interpretation of the text, which accepts and honors the existence of homosocial love: "'[I]t happens. Right around us; if we could look into all these houses whenever we wanted to, we'd probably see stranger things than that'" (122). Later on, Niobe comes to the "appalling reality" that Mrs. Bartoli would have done nothing had she known of Niobe's illicit sexual encounter (197). Niobe slowly learns to listen to her mother's parabolic way of expressing truths. Recalling the words her mother said to Andrea, Niobe interprets them as a glossary of ethnic survival: "'You live in a world that would deny you differences. Yet that is all your Mamma can give you'" (140). From her mother, Niobe learns that it is possible to be different without denying or repressing the self.

From her father, Niobe learns that it is possible to be domineering and loving. In a heated argument, Niobe finally breaks the imposition of *omertà* that has been enforced upon her by her father. During this second confessional scene (one that might never have happened in Italy), Niobe speaks forthrightly about the possessive nature of her father's rearing practices, which enforce silence and obedience with no regard for the child's personal needs. For the first time in the Bartoli family, Niobe says out loud that her brother is sick, that her father is domineering, and that her familial life has prohibited her and her brother from being able to love. Challenging her father's rigid control of the family, Niobe questions his own ability to love: "'What could you possibly know about being a woman? You, with your desire to rule over everything. You, who talk about freedom and free choice, who would allow none of it for Andrea or for me'" (212).[23]

Mr. Bartoli neither denies the conflict between father and son nor his own capacity to bully a family into submission. At the same time, the father admits to loving his wife profoundly; his hope for Niobe is that she will experience such deep love. Unlike the Old Man of the Rossi family, Mr. Bartoli is not incapable of loving, nor is he unchanged by the American independence of his children. Shortly after the father-daughter exchange, Mrs. Bartoli reminds Niobe of their ongoing connection to one another, despite the daughter's inability to express emotion: "'I can see the tears. You will wait until you are alone to know them, but they are not unfamiliar to me. I have felt them from the beginning of your time'" (216). Both parents reinforce the interdependent nature of Italian family life, but neither parent ultimately forces Niobe to remain at home.

Mrs. Bartoli's intuitive understanding of her daughter's pain aids in Niobe's healing process. Though she is not depicted as a literal curer of *mal'occhio*, Mrs. Bartoli cures through language. In her discussion of the connection between storytelling and curing, Trinh T. Minh-ha explains that "the principle of healing rests on *reconciliation*, hence the necessity for the family and/or community to cooperate, partake in, and witness the recovery, depossession, regeneration of the sick" (140). For Italian Americans, a child who distances herself from the family is thought to be sick or in pain. Sensing her daughter's conflict, Mrs. Bartoli tells her a story about her own girlhood in Italy, where she learned from her mother not to be embarrassed over female sexuality. Although Niobe does not understand the story's meaning then, her mother passes it along, aware of its ability to soothe her suffering daughter. In this way, the mother partakes in Niobe's recovery, aware of her unhappiness.

As part of the community's "regeneration of the sick," the town's artist, Giambelli, shares the responsibility of healing one of its daughters. Niobe asks Giambelli about the causes of shell shock, the illness from which her brother suffers. Privately, Niobe attributes Andrea's illness to their illicit union before he left for the war. Refusing to tell Giambelli the secret of her past, Niobe's sadness nonetheless compels the artist to recognize her suffering. Aware that art grows from pain and never denies its existence, Giambelli accepts Niobe's pain and in his own way absolves her from the grievous experience haunting her past: "'It doesn't matter—not to anyone—not to anyone who loves you'" (203). Though he cannot identify what "it" is that hurts Niobe, Giambelli nonetheless offers hope for her healing.

Shortly thereafter, Niobe visits her brother at the hospital, liberated from feelings of confusion and guilt: "[H]e could hold her forever and never excite her or frighten her" (207). Perhaps Waldo uses Andrea's illness as one way to free Niobe from his emotional clutches. Like Tomasi's choice to disable the Anglo-American Denny Douglas before he marries Petra, Waldo's choice to have Andrea Bartoli suffer from shell shock undercuts the brother's control over his sister. It also suggests how deeply troubled Andrea is because he can only focus on hating his father (209). That Waldo's description of the hospital is reminiscent of a prison suggests Andrea's severe incapacity to change and to reconcile himself to his position as a second-generation Italian American who has been wounded by the war at home and abroad. The fact that Waldo's text does not participate in the successful formation of Andrea's character may very well suggest Waldo's concern for Niobe's emotional development. Andrea's absence from the text allows Niobe to heal and make serious decisions about her life.[24]

Waldo's portrayal of Niobe's growth into womanhood occurs within the context of a community threatened by the destruction of war and by individual suffering. Niobe's adult life will never be entirely free from her childhood, nor does Waldo suggest that complete separation from the past and from family is necessary, possible, or healthy. Niobe's journey into adulthood differs from the earlier voyages of her ancestors: she does not cross an ocean, suffer great physical hardship, or learn a new language. Instead, Niobe embraces features of both Italian and American cultures.

Before leaving for college, Niobe's final thoughts reveal her acceptance of pain as part of her experience as a woman, as an Italian American, and as a community member:

> The smell of wine, the fig trees, the broken bell in the church tower . . . [t]his Niobe would never leave behind. She could travel the world over and around and never see this place again, but it would be as present as her heart beating in her chest. . . . Woman's touch would risk comparison with the dead touch of Laura. Man's embrace would call up Andrea to her. This was more than a place. This was a way of life—the index she would carry with her. (243)

That the bell in the church tower is broken not only suggests the community's loss of *campanilismo* but also forecasts the extension of the second-generation's social and cultural boundaries. The children of immigrants will travel away from the sound of the belfry, allowing them to experience other avenues of expression.

*A Cup of the Sun* explores the emotional confusion of a community in pain. Niobe Bartoli leaves the neighborhood, but she knows that she "would see and know the future through it" (243). The same can be said for Gina Giardello of Josephine Gattuso Hendin's *The Right Thing to Do*. Hendin's novel can be seen as a minimalist treatment of the father-child conflict in its depiction of one Nino Giardello from a Little Italy in Queens and his college-aged daughter who struggles against the harsh expectations of the Italian culture represented by her father. Such a skeletal version of the Italian American family is one of Hendin's strategies for reinforcing the inevitable changes that take place as first-generation parents age and can no longer protect or control their children's lives. Another of Hendin's strategies for suggesting the increasingly attenuated strength of the Italian American family is to represent the *capofamiglia* as ill and dying. The novel sounds an elegiac note in its depiction of the father's death and the burdensome, but not necessarily negative, legacy he gives his daughter.

Hendin won the Before Columbus Foundation 1989 American Book Award for *The Right Thing to Do*, her first novel. A full professor of American literature at New York University, Hendin, like her female protagonist, was raised by a Sicilian immigrant father and a Neapolitan mother in one of New York's Little Italies.[25] Although there are parallels between the novel and Hendin's upbringing, she explains that "the parents in the novel are really a composite of many other people, of many other parents." Early intuiting the difficulty of achieving a life different from the family's, Hendin left her home, explaining that she wanted "more identification with the people in the literature I was saturated with" ("Interview" 55, 53–54). Although she did not strongly identify with her Italian background during her college years, Hendin discovered that one of the strengths of being Italian American lies in its positive difference from the pervasive self-examination seen in the Anglo-American culture:

> I don't see a very high value placed on self-examination and introspection. I think Italians can be very thoughtful, but they are not always thinking about their own feelings. Our cultural focus is very much oriented towards behavior, from whence comes the title of the novel. (54)[26]

The emphasis on proper behavior—doing the right thing—is immediately evident in the first chapter of the novel. Aunt Maria, Nino's sister, has died without receiving last rites, a situation that threatens Nino's reputation, although he is the only male of his generation still living. Hendin dramatizes the clash between Irish and Italian Catholics in her presentation of Aunt Maria and the Irish priest, who refuses to give last rites because the dying woman remarked that all religions were alike. The conflict between American Catholicism—which was dominated by the Irish during the period of Italian immigration—and Italian anticlericalism made for uneasy relations between the two cultural groups, though it did not prevent intermarriage between children of the second generation.[27]

The awkward, confused, and darkly comical way in which the family secures Aunt Maria's burial alarmingly indicates Nino's diminished capacity to maintain *onore della famiglia*. The next six chapters examine in detail the conflict between father and daughter, although what is at stake between the generations is symptomatic of the larger failure of the family. As Hendin explains, at issue here is not only the relation between father and daughter but also "a vision of the fate of the family" ("Interview" 60). Hendin chooses to concentrate on one relationship in crisis, for the Italian American community is attenuated in several ways: by marriage outside the cultural group, by relocation away from the Italian enclave, and by the death of first-generation immigrants.

Nino's suspicion that Gina is not escaping to the library on weeknights but into the arms of a boyfriend compels him to reinforce his position as a man of honor. In chapter 2, Gina's mother upholds the father's status as head of the family by showing him a photograph of her daughter with a blonde-haired man; this picture convinces Nino that his daughter is having sexual relations. Vigilantly, the father watches and follows Gina on the elevated train and on the streets of New York City, even though he struggles to keep up with her because he is ill: a stroke, "climax of his diabetes," has left him limping (*The Right Thing to Do* 13). Gina's boyfriend, Alex, works at the bursar's office at Columbia where Gina is also working in the summer to earn tuition money for Hunter College.

Alex's Anglo-American background deserves commentary, not only because it represents a stark contrast to Gina's but also because it offers another model of behavior for Gina to interpret and critique, allowing her to understand more appreciatively her own culture. At twenty-six, Alex has yet to complete an undergraduate degree; his stasis indicates an untapped rebellion against his wealthy and successful parents. Moreover, Alex's vain attempts to complete his short stories for Gina ultimately indicate that he will be unsuitable as Gina's long-term partner.

Gina later articulates the cultural expectations of her Anglo-American boyfriend, which serve as a contrast to her own. What you *become* is what matters, not what you *were*: "[Y]ou had to be a star at something to retain your position in the family" (147). In contrast to Gina's family, which emphasizes loyalty to one's relations above all else, Alex's family dramatizes the classic American belief in what Sollors calls the "culture of consent," that is, "a denial of legitimacy and privilege based exclusively on descent," and a celebration of the self-made individual, who consents to make himself anew, identifying himself through his outward achievements (*Beyond Ethnicity* 4). Having failed to achieve outwardly, Alex is unacceptable to his family; nor is he accepted by Gina's, because he neither understands nor (when he does) abides by the rules governing the southern Italian family: responsibility to and protection of the family; sexual relations within the context of marriage only; and respect towards one's elders.

Chapter 3 in particular offers a dramatic rendition of the Italian culture's need to protect its family. For Gina's father, protecting is synonymous with following his daughter in an urban milieu that makes chaperonage nearly impossible. Although Gina can easily escape her father's clutches, she deliberately allows the hunt to continue on the streets of New York City, slowing down her pace "or he would lose her" (80). Hendin reverses the hunter/prey scenario to suggest two ideas: first, Nino is losing the battle against his daughter and he knows it; and second, Gina wants her father to know that she knows he's losing. At the same time, Gina respects Nino's perseverance, though she does not accept his need to dominate her.

Exhausted and dizzy from the effort of following Gina, Nino leans against the window of a *pasticceria* (pastry shop) to rest. Gina comes out of a cafe, reaches for Nino's arm, and invites her father inside for iced coffee, effectually denying him the upper hand in the scene. What prevents Nino from striking his daughter in public is his perception of reputation, the maintenance of *bella figura*, a code of good behavior so as to prevent showing weaknesses to outsiders. Had he cracked her across the face with his cane, Nino thinks that the public (which is an Italian neighborhood) would know that it meant his daughter was a *puttana* (86). Gina refuses to allow her father to dictate her freedom. As such, she is defined by her father as a whore, a woman who refuses to be controlled by a man.

Gina's freedom implies Nino's loss of honor. The father's ideas about protection and honor spring out of a "dim Sicilian past" (96), in which a woman's chastity defines the status of the man. Protecting her sexual virtue is part of the father's responsibility toward the daughter; for Nino, losing that role makes him feel outmoded, a laughable figure from the past. Nino is doubly displaced from the American society of the late twentieth century: he is distanced from his Sicilian village of Ventimiglia and no longer recognizes his old Italian neighborhood in Queens. Profoundly depressed, Nino realizes that the indifference of the American culture toward "home values," that is, cooperation, interdependence, and fierce loyalty toward family, makes him feel abandoned and insignificant.[28]

Unfortunate as the father's subsequent illnesses are, they symbolize his loss of control as head of the family. Since his stroke, Nino has increasing circulatory problems that exacerbate his diabetes. As in *A Cup of the Sun*, *The Right Thing to Do* explores the consequences of illness on those ailing and those well. Later in the narrative, both of Nino's legs are amputated, and he loses control of his kidneys before he dies of heart failure. Hendin uses images of illness to mourn the death of first-generation Italian Americans and to emphasize the inevitable changes taking place within the family. *The Right Thing to Do* reads in part like a cautionary tale, examining the consequences of the second-generation's adoption of American values.

Nino believes that change is always bad, a belief reinforced by his proverbial culture and his literary understanding of Dante. From his father, Nino passes along the Sicilian proverb that says "When you leave the old ways, you know what you will lose, but not what you will find" (*Chi lascia la via vecchia per la nuova, sa quel che perde e non sa quel che trova*). Inherently conservative, proverbs explore the values of a culture. Sicilian proverbs about close blood ties—"those between parents and children and among siblings—form the most detailed and voluminous category in Pitre's collection" (the Sicilian folklorist who gathered a large group of proverbs in the nineteenth century) (Gabaccia, *From Sicily to Elizabeth Street* 3).

For the Italian family in America, change has sometimes been perceived as diluting the respect and honor accorded the family. Criticizing the changes he sees taking place in his neighborhood, the church, and the larger culture, Nino uses his literary ancestor Dante as proof against the positive aspects of change: "'You know one of the worst punishments in Dante's hell was to doom a soul to change forever from one thing to another. If Dante were alive today, he would say, "That soul is a spoiled kid"'" (20). His own child rebels against living with the family because she is also part of an American culture that sanctions independence and mobility. Gina's conflict with her father is not only about generational differences and sexual identity but also about her father's fear of being replaced by less protective forms of authority embodied in the classroom and the workplace. What Nino considers his parental responsibility to protect his child, Gina considers suffocating and destructive.

One of Gina's recurring dreams reflects the vital nature of the father-daughter conflict: Gina eludes six men running after her with a coffin by fleeing from one scene to another and by being transformed into a half-fish (43–44). Gina's dream suggests that change is necessary to avoid the threat of death, but she realizes the incompatibility between her need for freedom and her desire to do the right thing by her family. Hendin calls into question the influence of parental authority and the extent of filial responsibility to that authority. Both father and daughter must learn to accept the other: Nino must recognize the persistent double standard he possesses about women before he can accept the inevitable independence of his daughter; Gina must realize that her father's understanding of love includes controlling in order to protect his daughter.

Hendin utilizes images of opera heroines to emphasize Gina's gendered position in the family. As much as Nino wants Gina to be educated and rewarded for her intelligence, he has never treated women as equals to men and has blamed women for their subservience at the same time that he exacts such behavior from them. Hendin's repeated references to *Madame Butterfly*, *Turnadot*, *La Bohème*, and *Rigoletto* all engage plots that detail what Catherine Clément calls "the undoing of women." The great lament of operatic divas is appropriately uttered in Italian: *Lasciatemi morir*, "Let me die." As Clément explains, "It is the abandoned nymph's lament, the lament of every Dido and every Ariadne, the lament of woman. The only course open is death. . . . There is always a man at the conclusion" (22, 47). Refusing to be confined by an undifferentiated image of *italianità*, Gina wants to escape what she perceives to be the threat of her ancestors, who accept only submission as proper female behavior.

The fact that Nino prefers Verdi's *Nabucco* to Puccini's *La Bohème* reveals that his concern with homeland values has more to do with feelings of loss than with the desire to control the destiny of his daughter. An opera about enslaved Jews searching for their lost fatherland, *Nabucco* parallels Nino's own feelings of loss and alienation in America.[29] Although Nino is the man at the conclusion of Gina's story, she is not undone, suggesting that this Italian American narrative will not require filial sacrifice. Nino's death at the end of the story indeed liberates Gina from her father's pervasive influence, as much as Andrea's illness liberates Niobe in *A Cup of the Sun*. Nevertheless, Nino's death also compels Gina to reconsider her allegiance to the family.

The relationship between change and illness in *The Right Thing to Do* oddly unites father and daughter in their struggle. Nino makes a connection between Gina's rebellion and his own illness: "'First you get one sore, then another, then you're covered with them. . . . Like the stroke, it comes, takes a little of your sight, leaves you a little crippled, and goes'" (72–73). Although she is physically healthy, Gina comes to realize that she may be infected by another disease—the moving disease: "Once you move out, she had realized, you keep moving out. It's not something you want to stop" (201). As much as she wants to escape her father's control, Gina regularly encounters a healthy and strong Nino in her dreams, whose grip makes her feel like "an immobilized child" (182). Both father and daughter suffer from paralysis, emotional and physical. Nino understands that his illness and Gina's rebellion are parallel phenomena: diseases for which he thinks there are no cures.

As much as Gina's mother submits to the will of a tyrannical husband—Laura calls Nino a dictator—she wants a different future for her daughter. Despite her suppressed anger, Laura provides Gina with an example of a woman of *serietà* who finds pleasure "in daily things, that gave her a steady joyousness" (47). Laura's repeated attempts to help her husband regain health undercuts Nino's resignation. Refusing to succumb to the pressure of Nino's fatalism, Laura embodies characteristics of *furberia* (shrewdness), extracting the best from what might seem to be the worst of situations.

In his final years, Nino's attempts to secure his hold on the family backfire when they concern his daughter. For example, he humiliates Gina at high school by bringing her a letter of rejection from an Eastern women's college, hoping from that rejection that his daughter will learn that women cannot get what they want. Instead, Gina internalizes her anger and learns to disguise her feelings in order not to be hurt. Ironically, Gina's lack of emotion will make her a better candidate for American society. Perceiving American and Italian cultures as mutually incompatible and irreconcilable, Nino's inflexibility reveals his fear of losing his daughter to values different from his own. The father's cognizance of Gina's desire to "be one of them" makes him all the more adamant in his endeavor to prove that "she can't be" (24). In his final attempt to control his daughter's behavior, Nino barges into Alex's apartment to find Gina partially dressed. Hitting her across the shoulders with his cane and, later at home, locking her in her bedroom, Nino resorts to his ancestors' behaviors, following the restrictive rules that he deplored in his youth.

The second half of the novel (chapters 4–7) explores the ramifications of Gina's leaving the Italian American family. Three events in particular aid in and complicate Gina's emotional development.

First, by moving out, Gina enters more fully an Anglo-American life style, trading in one set of rules and problems for another. Hendin earlier has Nino disparage the rules central to the dominant culture: "'Premarital sex with contraceptives? Marriage vows you can change your mind about three weeks later? Contracts for everything that show you mistrust everyone you deal with?'" (19–20). Although at first she doesn't recognize the extent to which she has relinquished one form of captivity for another, Gina learns, in the process, that she is being controlled just as much by Alex as she was by her father.

Second, Gina speaks with Alex's father, a history professor, who specializes in Puritan and Native American relations. As a result of their conversation about the contentious struggles between the two cultural groups, Gina is able to articulate her irresistible connection to her Italian background.

Finally, after her father becomes permanently disabled, Gina, bound by filial responsibility and respect, regularly visits him at home. Shortly before his death, Nino tells her a story from the oral traditions of his Sicilian village. Nino's story to his daughter is edifying to both of them. The conclusion of the tale and Nino's interpretation of it offer, as stories from oral cultures often do, "a 'message' or a point, a truth, to remember as one confronts life's problems" (Roger Abrahams qtd. in Mathias and Raspa 10). From this story, both Nino and Gina are released from crippling ties that made them adversaries. In contrast to Gina's boyfriend, Nino completes his story, presenting his daughter with both a cautionary tale *and* a message about autonomy.

Alex, like Nino, wants to control Gina. However, their reasons for trying to dominate her differ. Nino wants his daughter to behave according to the dictates of *l'ordine della famiglia*, which requires obedience and filial obligation. Because he understands his position in the family in terms of relationships, Nino expects the family members to behave according to group standards. For the first-generation Italian immigrant in the early to mid-twentieth century, the American dream meant family solidarity and steady work, not, as sociologists John Papajohn and John Spiegel explain, "the values of individual achievement, planning for the future, and striving to improve his status in the American social system" (105). However much he fails to live up to his parents' American dream, Alex perceives himself to be autonomous and in control of his future. In actuality, Alex seeks to control Gina by changing her, as Gina thinks, playing "'Svengali to my Trilby, Pygmalion to my Galatea. He wants to free me from the burden of my working-class practicality'" (93). Alex's attempt to free Gina is a veiled disguise for controlling her. In fact, Alex regularly imagines his ideal woman as virginal, submissive, and defined by his needs (122, 124, 158).

Having carelessly risked pregnancy, Gina realizes that she must procure contraceptives. When she tries to use a diaphragm during sex with Alex, he reacts angrily by pulling it out, throwing it in the garbage can, and telling her to clean herself. Explaining to Gina that he should have been part of the decision to use contraceptives, Alex tells her that what occurred between them had to do with trust. Nonetheless, what follows this scene is a description of sexual activity that leaves Gina with welts all over her body. Alex punishes Gina for trying to assert control over her body without his permission. Gina ends up playing "Trilby for Svengali" as Alex "hypnotizes" her with his lovemaking. The script that Gina follows depends upon her vulnerability for its success. In a very real sense, Alex wants the opportunity to rape a virgin over and over again. His unfinished short story, "Princess Persephone," promises what its title delivers: to trap the heroine in a narrative for which only the hero has the key. Gina thereafter realizes that in order to guard herself against pregnancy, she will have to secretly take the pill. The female characters in *A Cup of the Sun* did not have the option of using birth control. Because she is afforded this prerogative from American culture, Gina protects herself from playing the role of the sacrificial victim in an ancient ritual, a vision of disempowerment that Gina often imagines (56, 77, 100).

Gina's moral and emotional confusion regarding Alex makes her susceptible to his need to dominate her. Regarding Alex's treatment of her family, however, Gina demonstrates close affinities to her responsibilities as a family member. She will not allow Alex to trivialize or diminish her parents, whom she protects intuitively from Alex's judgmental eye. When he visits Gina's parents, Alex offers to marry her, but Gina realizes that marriage means nothing to Alex and that he would use marriage to hurt her family: "[H]e would turn Nino into the stuff of anecdotes" (103). Here Gina is operating out of a belief in protecting the family's honor and reputation. She may have thoughtlessly accepted her boyfriend's refusal to take her seriously, but she will not countenance uninformed stereotyping of her culture.[30]

After being locked in her bedroom, Gina decides to leave the parental home, hoping to escape "the place of old humiliations and failures" (106). Even though Gina leaves the family, she remains intellectually and emotionally tied to their beliefs. Gina's affinities are best demonstrated when she is placed in a cultural context strikingly different from her own. In chapter 4, Gina and Alex travel to Philadelphia for a weekend to visit Alex's parents. For Gina, the most telling clue of having entered a culture antithetical to her own is the fact that when they arrive, the parents are not there: "The idea that parents could invite you for the weekend—their own son!—and be too busy to be home when he arrived was so alien, she took it personally" (134). The conversation Gina later has with Victor, Alex's father, reveals the incontrovertible influence Nino and the Italian American culture have had upon her. That influence, Gina begins to realize, offers her a way to contextualize the experience of emigration from another culture and transplantation in a new world. Instead of perceiving Anglo and Italian cultures as mutually opposed to each other, Gina begins to connect two ostensibly disparate groups by examining the acts of uprooting and resettling in a new world.

Nineteenth-century immigration to the new world, like the Puritans' transatlantic crossing, was often interpreted typologically as a kind of fulfillment. Relating their "errand into the wilderness" to the Old Testament exodus of the Israelites, the Puritans were motivated by religious fervor. However intensely distrustful Italian Americans were of the Catholic church, like other immigrants, they often interpreted their migration as an escape from the bondage of the peasantry and a deliverance to the promised land.[31] During her conversation with Victor, Gina empathizes deeply with the drama of cultural conflict between the two groups. Ultimately, Gina's interpretation of the Puritans' errand is influenced by her father's negative migration experience: his conception of identity was wrenched loose, and he felt as though such changes destroyed all he knew to be right and good.

In responding to the Puritans' cruel treatment of the Native Americans, Gina acknowledges that the Anglo-Americans lost their "moral bearings" in the wilderness, changing for the worse. Victor counters Gina's interpretation with a positive gloss on change. The dismantling of Puritan religious beliefs was "'maybe the ultimate triumph of the wilderness,'" leaving them with "'just a belief in the power of individuals to transform themselves'" (143). While Gina is attracted to the Emersonian belief in self-reliance and infinite possibility, she is at the same time influenced by her father's interpretation of change: "'But change is a kind of doom, too. You know the character in Dante's *Inferno* whose punishment is to keep changing from one thing to another . . . '" (144). By saying this, Gina reinforces her intellectual and emotional connection to her Italian American ethnicity as it is voiced by her father.

Gina's identification with the past and her obeisance to her Italian American family undergo change but are neither denied nor cast off. Her future legacy is presented to her by her dying father, whose illnesses are a visible testimonial of the impossibility of Nino's transcendence and positive self-transformation in America. Gina's belief in individualism ultimately coincides with her own father's, not Alex's. Both Gina and Nino reinterpret the staple American belief in individualism through the lens of *italianità*: "that is individualism like Seneca praised—personal responsibility for the good of others" (20). Gina accepts her role in the family by the end of the narrative, though her position has been modified by her father's death and her second-generation status as an Italian American.

Nino suffers tremendously in *The Right Thing to Do*. His successive illnesses immobilize him and eventually kill him at age sixty. That Hendin incorporates a sustained depiction of illness and death in her novel might very well provide a commentary on the negative effects of migration, especially for first-generation immigrants. What was the hope of a promised land in fact became a place of relentless suffering for many of the immigrants. The grandmother in Benasutti's *No SteadyJob for Papa*, for example, called America *maledetta*, an accursed land. In both Waldo's and Hendin's novels, America is often perceived by first-generation Italians to cause illness and to infect Italian Americans with disease, the only cure of which is found in the original culture. Gina may very well look at her father and think, as the daughter does in Diane di Prima's poem, "You were dying of grief from the moment I saw you" (149).[32]

Empathizing with her father's grief, however, does not prevent Gina from being wary of the possibility of Nino's illness affecting her: "It was never possible to be with him without getting hurt. He never meant ill, but he always did harm" (52). Tyrannical in his illness, Nino momentarily thinks as he lies bedridden that he is *il mal'occhio*, but his sickness necessarily diminishes the vigilance of his "watchful eye," and the severity of his diabetes causes him to go blind (178). Unlike the silent Old Man in *A Cup of the Sun*, however, Nino speaks to his daughter and gives her a legacy of words in his attempt to protect and transmit his cultural heritage. Nino functions much like the *cantastorie* or history singers of southern Italy, the preservers of local traditions whose stories entertain and edify.

Gina receives a story about her cultural heritage that will paradoxically liberate her from her father and ensure her loyalty to the family. On his deathbed, Nino tells Gina a tale from his boyhood in Ventimiglia. A young girl who was dying requested that she be buried with her father, who had died the year before. When the father's coffin was exhumed, the corpse was not decayed. Before the villagers' eyes, however, the body decays as soon as they have crossed themselves the third time in ritualistic thanksgiving for what they had assumed was a miracle. Thereafter, the people discuss what would be the best thing to do: bury Lucia with her father or alone. Having earlier sanctioned Lucia's request, the village priest regrets the error of his ways, realizing his mistake in allowing his feelings rather than his duty to dictate his behavior: "'"Our duty is to follow what has been ordained for us. The right thing is to do what has always been done. *All change is for the worse!*"'" (187–88).

Feeling cheated by the deliberate ending of her father's story, Gina accuses him of having made it up, to which Nino replies, "'No, . . . it was all the truth. Especially the end'" (188). Having engaged her in the story, Nino guarantees his daughter's emotional investment. Gina wants to hear more; it's as though, having been given the moral of the story before learning what happens to Lucia, Gina needs to hear it told again. After all, the story is about the intimate relationship between a father and daughter, one that continues after death.

In telling his tale, Nino is able to offer his own interpretation of the father-daughter burial. As folktales function to guide behavior, Nino offers his opinion of what the villagers should have done: "'I've always thought they should have buried Lucia alone. A child has to make its own way. . . . If the child finds the right way, it finds its own road back to where it belongs'" (190). Nino's interpretation grants his daughter personal autonomy and insists on the ineluctable bonds of the culture of heritage. Nino's warnings to Gina after he tells the story parallel the Puritan jeremiad of the seventeenth century in its exhortative tendency to caution the next generation against possible declension: "'Don't look forward to my dying too much. Nothing will be different when I'm dead. . . . Listen, Gina. Be careful. There is no cure for what you've got'" (190–91). Nevertheless, through this folktale, Gina has been nourished, but she must engage regularly in the telling of stories from her culture in order to guard against losing her identity as an Italian American. As Leslie Marmon Silko says about her own Pueblo culture's curing ceremonies:

> They are all we have, you see,
> all we have to fight off
> illness and death.
> You don't have anything
> if you don't have the stories. (qtd. in Minh-ha 136)

Gina's adulthood is enriched by the cultural traditions of her past, however imperfect those traditions are. Like Niobe in *A Cup of the Sun*, Gina realizes that her family and community are more than a place; they are an index that she will carry with her into her future. Her Italian American ethnicity is more than a designation; it is a way of life.

# 3 *Remembering Their Names*

## *The Developmental Journeys in Diana Cavallo's* A Bridge of Leaves *and Dorothy Bryant's* Miss Giardino

Either you will
go through this door
or you will not go through.

If you go through
there is always the risk
of remembering your name.

—Adrienne Rich, "Prospective Immigrants Please Note"

Diana Cavallo and Dorothy Bryant radically depart from representing Italian American family culture. In both Cavallo's *A Bridge of Leaves* (1961) and Bryant's *Miss Giardino* (1978), any ostensible representation of family and family life is remarkably attenuated. The focus in each novel is on the individual's experience as he or she struggles to understand his or her role in the world. What sounds precisely like the qualifications delineating the traditional bildungsroman is modified by each novel's focus on ethnicity as a source and subject of character development.

Much has been written in the past twenty years on the ways in which the genre of the bildungsroman has expanded and redefined its traditional limits.[1] Most critics agree that two of the distinctive features of the genre include a belief in a coherent self and the possibility of developing that self (Abel, Hirsch, and Langland;

Felski). The genre is also fundamentally optimistic because it subscribes to the belief, as Felski writes, "in a possibility of meaningful development" (138). This belief is especially problematic in light of the post-structuralist challenge to a unified subject and its criticism of the realist text, which purports to represent reality with authenticity.[2] Nonetheless, feminist critics tend to agree that the wealth of literature depicting women's emotional and social development is a legitimate and significant enterprise, "a necessary cultural strategy for a marginalised and oppositional group" (Felski 146). Lazzaro-Weis adds that "nostalgic bereavement of loss, always a part of the definition of the form, takes on a new relevancy in the more recent manifestations of the genre" (24). While Lazzaro-Weis is primarily thinking of women's literary characterizations of the mother-daughter or father-daughter conflict, the genre increases in scope if we take into account the variable of ethnicity.

Feminists have thus been instrumental in bringing to discussion the ways in which gender modifies and challenges literary representations of development. Abel, Hirsch, and Langland's previously mentioned edition, *The Voyage In*, discusses how female characters typically develop later in life after fulfilling traditional expectations of marriage and motherhood. Such deferred maturation, Abel suggests, has more to do with the limiting social options for women than it has to do with any personal failure on the women's part. Often, too, because women have been socialized to work within the private sphere of the home, they have found it more difficult to sever family ties than men (7, 8). As we will see, both protagonists in Cavallo's and Bryant's novels experience similar difficulties, even though neither is traditional in the sense of meeting the conventional expectations of being married and having children.

Cavallo's protagonist is male, thus enabling his growth in ways closed traditionally to women: he "comes of age" fairly early in manhood and has the prerogative of education and separation from the family of origin. Nonetheless, his relationship to his grandmother challenges the Freudian paradigm in much the same way that female developmental novels do: instead of seeing his connection to his maternal ancestor as a contrast to his own, one that he must separate from, he defines himself in relation to her. The fact that the *male* protagonist identifies with his grandmother as his earliest and most important caretaker compels a reconsideration of the ways ethnicity itself challenges traditional interpretations of male and female development.

In Bryant's novel, the female protagonist reaches the age of sixty-eight before she discovers the psychological space that will assist in her development. As much as Anna Giardino experiences the painful soul-searching common to the male bildungsroman,[3] she ultimately chooses to accommodate herself to the world in an active way, thus paralleling other novels of female development. Both protagonists come to realize that complete withdrawal from the outside world will lead to further illness, if not death. However, both characters suffer from emotional crises that enforce temporary isolation. This time of painful meditation is necessary for both protagonists to grieve for their losses and finally to retrieve parts of themselves that will provide them with the materials for a healthier future.

As important as the lens of gender is for illuminating the crises of each protagonist, it is also necessary to take into account the lens of ethnicity and its equally pervasive influence on the development of both protagonists. Though fewer articles have focused on how not only gender but also ethnicity complicates development, it is a subject of great concern to Cavallo and Bryant.[4] Like gender, ethnicity also affects the characters undergoing transformation. They suffer in ways uniquely related to their cultural backgrounds; their individual agency is highly influenced by their understanding of themselves as Italian Americans. Such concern with the past may signal a loyalty to utilizing a traditional narrative structure and theme, but Cavallo and Bryant stretch the boundaries of the traditional immigrant saga by writing stories that only peripherally recall the transatlantic crossing and the early years in America for immigrants of Italian descent.

Cavallo and Bryant restructure the Italian American text in such a way that the topic of ethnicity itself gets aligned with modernism, not traditionalism. Both writers utilize modernist narrative strategies such as the nonlinear plot, the interior monologue, dream sequences, and fractured grammatical form. Conspicuously absent from both texts is the traditional realist plot of immigration and assimilation so frequently seen in both Italian American autobiographies and the four novels examined in the first two chapters. Sollors aptly suggests that too often ethnicity gets equated with tradition, thus preventing critics from analyzing the more innovative aspects of ethnic writing (*Beyond Ethnicity* 244, 240).

While it is true that both Cavallo's and Bryant's novels can be categorized under the rubric of bildungsroman, they stretch the boundaries of that genre both thematically and structurally. In both novels, the goal of the protagonists is not to achieve individual autonomy as much as it is to reconnect the self to the past in order to move into a healthy and rewarding adulthood. To achieve such a reconnection, the movement into memory is necessary, painful, and illuminating. As Susan Fraiman explains in her article on the bildungsroman, two imperatives—individuality and mobility—are inherent to the genre. However, the movement, she writes, "is not necessarily a literal journeying, say, from country to city; it may involve mental travel to a higher moral or emotional ground" (139). Both *A Bridge of Leaves* and *Miss Giardino* reflect a shift in Italian American narrative traditions away from the painstaking reenactment of the immigrants' journey to the new world. On their emotional voyages, however, both protagonists recall their ancestors' earlier journey and thereby legitimate the enterprise of emigration. Crucially, the protagonists recognize that their identities have been shaped by the formidable and often perilous movements of their ancestors. The suffering that ensued later in America affected the ways in which the protagonists thought about themselves as Italian Americans and as individuals within the larger cultural milieu.

As discussed in the introduction and the previous two chapters, the topic of illness is central to Italian American literary traditions. Narratives about illness and death pervade the saga of immigration, especially because the majority of immigrants lived in overcrowded and unsanitary ghettos. Cavallo and Bryant move away from representing illness as solely a narrative about poor working conditions and bad housing. Because they focus on the single character's struggle to achieve a coherent identity, the narrative of illness becomes specific to one person, not to the Italian American family. Yet, this minimalist tendency allows each author to explore the complex relationship between the protagonist and his or her family. What begins as a narrative of quest for individual autonomy ultimately ends as a compelling narrative about family relations.

Cavallo and Bryant use the topic of illness to explore the psychological confusions of the protagonists. Thematically, the authors' concern is to trace the characters' progression from temporary illness to a reintegration of the self. The specific illnesses from which the protagonists suffer symbolize their struggle to understand and integrate the painful scenario of the family of origin into their present lives. Such a narrative is similar to the women's developmental text in that women have traditionally been required to tolerate the confusions and demands of the family while their own development went unattended. In her analysis of Clarice Lispector's novels, Marta Peixoto describes the female protagonists' attempts at recuperation as leading to dissatisfaction, rage, or even madness: "[T]he stories present the dark side of family ties, where bonds of affection become cages and prison bars" (Abel, Hirsch, and Langland 289).

However wary they are of the potentially imprisoning nature of family ties, Bryant and Cavallo examine how the family is the locus for the development of their protagonists. The pain from which the protagonists temporarily suffer is closely related to the literary madness Lilian Feder describes in *Madness in Literature*. Feder necessarily distinguishes between actual clinical madness and the representation of madness in literature as a vehicle of self-revelation. If indeed it is true that writers have been fascinated by the ways in which madness reveals the "processes of the human mind" (xi), then they have been equally committed to the belief that madness is an attempt at *recovery*, or, as Feder explains, quoting Freud, "a process of reconstruction" (25).

Both Cavallo and Bryant incorporate narratives of temporary illness to explore the anguished psyches of their protagonists. Feder offers several descriptions of potentially mad behavior, three of which lend insight to Cavallo's and Bryant's characters. First, the combined feelings of love and aggression and their symbolic expression are "the surest clues to the mind in confusion or conflict" (19). Second, suffering from violent hallucinations, for example, is a means by which, as Freud explains, forgotten material "forces its way into consciousness." Turning away from reality may actually be a process of regaining memories long repressed in the unconscious (26).

Third, in their attempt to recover themselves, the mad may "distort reality," but in doing so they "create an emotional environment for the reconstruction of a self image" (27). The environment of amnesia and recurring dreams in which Anna Giardino is submerged in Bryant's text and the environment of the asylum in which David willfully exiles himself in Cavallo's text provide them with the emotional space to regain the memories that, in their absence, haunt and agonize both characters. In each of these descriptions of mad behavior, the psyche struggles for autonomy, which aptly parallels the purpose of the bildungsroman: to depict the protagonist's struggle to achieve independence and mobility.

Both Cavallo's and Bryant's protagonists ultimately acknowledge that they were not well during their psychic journeys to achieve wholeness.[5] Each character has been educated and enjoys the ambiguous freedom of living alone, eventually accessing the repressed memories that have led to mental suffering. In *A Bridge of Leaves*, the thirty-year-old narrator, David, reenacts an extended period in his life when he was unknowingly mourning the losses of his grandmother and his twin brother, Michael, who died before David could consciously remember him. His intense relationship with Laura, a college friend and actress, leads David briefly to work in an asylum, where he tries to join Laura, who is suffering from catatonia. Before succumbing to the lures of the asylum, David extricates himself from the environment of illness by invoking and confronting his cultural heritage and the losses therein.

In *Miss Giardino*, Anna, a sixty-eight-year-old retired high school teacher, suffers from amnesia. During her recovery, Anna is compelled to recall the past through recurrent dreams and long stretches of old memories, both functioning as "psycho[ses] of short duration," to use Freud's terminology. These lead to her eventual recall and restitution of self. Both David in *A Bridge of Leaves* and Anna in *Miss Giardino* experience epiphanic moments of self-realization. Their ability to overcome their suffering depends upon a self-discovery, a modern-day *anagnorisis.* That Anna is entering old age when she comes to understand herself further highlights the impediments a woman—in Anna's case, an unmarried second-generation Italian American—faces when trying to achieve a satisfying maturity. Because of their strong familial bonds, both characters are connected to female ancestors who aid in their transformation. David and Anna meet the challenge of family and by doing so remember their names.

Much of Diana Cavallo's novel was written in New Hampshire at the MacDowell Colony, to which she was awarded a fellowship. Cavallo's interest in incorporating a madness narrative within the book may very well be due to her brief work as a psychiatric social worker.[6] The novel traces David's thoughtful ruminations, giving the story the sound of the confessional or the autobiography. The narrator's probing words sound much like an extended monologue, and his progression into adulthood might be called an intellectual drama. The generic slipperiness of *A Bridge of Leaves* compares with other novels in which issues of ethnic identity are part of the focus.[7] Although Cavallo's novel is perfectly structured, it nonetheless has the quality of being "asymmetrical, irregular, or uneven" (Newman 9). Cavallo's ambiguity regarding David's actual illness reflects this unevenness, or "disease," in the tone of the narrative. In this way, Cavallo parallels Waldo in her attempt to probe the uneasiness undergirding her protagonist's development. Like Niobe in *A Cup of the Sun*, David will come to learn, through suffering and mourning, that his past is a way of life—the index he will carry with him.

The narrative is divided into three parts. Part 1 might be called the family narrative; part 2, the education narrative; and part 3, the illness/madness narrative. Although the sections are separated and purportedly focus on David's life as a youngster, a college student, and a worker in an asylum, respectively, they regularly recall the narrative of family origins through the use of what I will call "ethnic symbols," those recurring images that reveal and highlight the conflict within the character and also have a direct relation to his or her ethnic identity.[8] In Cavallo's and Bryant's texts, ethnic imagery functions as an addition to and/or a replacement of actual representation of the immigrant family in America.

Though he never categorizes himself as a third-generation Italian American, David begins his narration by describing his decrepit and increasingly senile grandfather, who at eighty-six is nonetheless aware of and mourning the fact that he is the only one left of his generation. David's language of declension to describe, ironically, his own lack of spirit in the face of death parallels the traditional generational rhetoric of the early Puritans: "It seems young people like myself have less of everything—less contentment, less pain, . . . less pride of achievement" (6). That David is disturbed by this perceived weakness of his generation reveals his abiding concern with his identity as the grandchild of a more fulfilled type of man. David describes himself as "overlaid with what I have become," and to uncover the means of ordering his various "selves," he must return to the past. Without knowing it yet, David is choosing to reconstruct what Sollors calls "a modern identity in the name of ethnicity," thus typologically functioning as "the antitype, the redemptive fulfillment of types, of original ancestors" (*Beyond Ethnicity* 230).

Outwardly, *A Bridge of Leaves* is a traditional bildungsroman that depicts the development of a young man's rite of passage into adulthood. Cavallo nonetheless interrogates this paradigm through David's description of his relationship to his twin, Michael, and his Italian grandmother, whose emigration from the homeland provides a gloss on David's later self-imposed exile in the asylum. Each of these relationships informs David's development into an adult who is neither entirely independent nor separated from his origins. Rather, David's experience of fragmentation and alienation underscores the modern condition and his own choice to accept rather than to repress his confusion. Both his negotiation with his reflection in the mirror and the discovery that he is a twin enable David to recognize the doubleness of his identity.

In the first line of the novel, Cavallo describes David looking in the mirror, a gesture revealing his desire to understand his identity. Such references to mirrors recur throughout the narrative to reinforce the process of David's identity formation. Jenijoy La Belle explains that "since the self . . . is never fully achieved, it is necessary to look in the glass to see how one is doing in the process of constantly reinventing the self" (17). David's reconstruction of a modern identity "in the name of ethnicity" is a process of constantly reinventing the self, especially because his actual ancestors can no longer provide a lens through which the narrator can perceive and formulate his identity.

Further symbolizing David's keen awareness of his dual nature is his discovery that he is a twin. As a result of this knowledge, David embraces the position of ethnic dualism, thus challenging the notion of a single, unitary identity. Sollors calls those ethnic characters acutely aware of the duality of their identities "double-consciousness characters," who, like David, may be "attracted to mirrors, reflecting windows, or smooth-surfaced ponds" (*Beyond Ethnicity* 249). Having experienced the sensation that he was "two persons at once," David reveals to the reader that he is a twin. In early childhood, David was accidentally mistaken for his dead brother. As a result, he loses the ability to reflect himself without intense awareness of the looming presence of his dead brother: "Out of this submersion for an instant came consciousness of that other dead self, the lost blood stream, the complementary nervous system, the dissolved will, my brother" (11). David believes that the "world of human memory" will reclaim the unborn, offering Michael "one, vast rebirth" (12). However, his deeply repressed guilt and grief over the loss of his brother prevent him from mourning his separation from Michael and accommodating himself to the realization that he is fragmented as a result of such loss.

Cavallo examines David's loss throughout *A Bridge of Leaves*, but one scene in particular anticipates his ability to be healed, not destroyed by his grief. In part 2 of the novel, David walks home one night with his college friend, Laura, and they begin to talk about the crowds of stars in the sky. After pointing out Castor and Pollux to Laura, who unknowingly instigates further discussion with her comment, "'Oh, Gemini, the twins,'" David further explains their story, thus reaffirming the irresistible connection between himself and Michael:

> "Well, their devotion was the main thing. Inseparable to an unbelievable degree. Far from the ordinary bond. They were each other's complement . . . if that explains it. . . . To make the story short, death spared one and took the other. For the survivor, life was unbearable, '*he* living, Castor dead.'" (italics mine, 83–84)

The single quotations around the final words suggest that David is quoting another source, but the unidentified pronoun "he" also suggests that David has in mind himself. Furthermore, by "reading" the meaning of the stars, David constructs himself as a text, one that he, however, feels control of, despite his inability fully to grieve. By engaging Laura in the story, David shares the significance of his suffering and at the same time reveals his fragmented identity. David continues the story by telling Laura that each brother would live on alternate days, "'one life divided between the two,'" to which Laura replies, "'[S]o they were placed there side by side across the sky . . . always together . . . symbols of devotion'" (84). For David, embedding the story of his loss in another story places him squarely within literary and historical traditions of love and loss. Although he is yet unable to identify himself fully within those traditions, he has offered himself a vocabulary of loss in which to contain his grief. For Laura, as will be seen, no such language exists to allow her to control her confusion and maintain a duality of selves without succumbing to irreversible madness.

As if to reinforce the many manifestations of duality in *A Bridge of Leaves*, Cavallo juxtaposes David's early realization that he is a twin to the narrator's empathy for his grandmother's immigration experience. Seduced by a narrative of romance, the grandmother makes the journey to America for the love of a handsome man "of inconstant attentions and little means." Having betrayed her dreams "to this half-life of reverie," the grandmother's exile from the Mediterranean shore leaves her a divided and anguished self in the new land. In the space of one paragraph, Cavallo reenacts the immigrant voyage and makes an implicit connection between the grandmother's irretrievable loss and the narrator's search for an identity (14). David venerates his grandmother; his dedication to her throughout the novel offers an example of the way a young Italian American male formulates and sustains an identity that depends upon the strength of ancestral ties. In this way, the grandmother functions in much the same way as Mister Tiff of *Like Lesser Gods*, whose guardianship becomes the model of successful mentoring in the Italian American works under consideration. Despite her sorrow over leaving the old world, the grandmother recalls and transmits the narrative of leave-taking to her grandchild, who carries the story of homesickness into his adulthood.

The figure of the grandparent resonates in many narratives written by Italian American women. In Helen Barolini's multigenerational novel *Umbertina* (discussed in the next chapter), Marguerite, an agonized third-generation Italian American, is advised to begin her search for self-understanding with her grandmother, whose name inspires the title of the book. Tomasi, Benasutti, Cavallo, and Tina De Rosa all "begin with the grandparent," joining other texts that focus on a significant ancestor who often functions as the transmitter of the familial and cultural history to the generations that follow.[9] As Helen Barolini explains in *The Dream Book*, the figure of the grandparent—whether real or imagined—"is as far as a present-day Italian American can trace his or her descent" (100). The Italian who immigrates to America may be able to claim a family history stretching back for thousands of years, but the grandchild can only trace his or her descent to the grandparent, who thus comes to embody age-old traditions, customs, and stories from the homeland.

That David identifies his relationship to his grandmother as intimately symbiotic—"I felt her pulse before I knew my own; lying against her chest I could hear the rhythm of her life in the crease of her neck, and I took it for my own" (14)—accords well with the revisionist theory of the mother-infant bond explained by Nancy Chodorow in *The Reproduction of Mothering*: "[T]he basic feminine sense of self is connected to the world, the basic masculine sense of self is separate" (169). In discussing the different ways in which boys and girls formulate identity, Abel, Hirsch, and

Langland summarize Chodorow's pre-Oedipal theory, suggesting that such a different interpretation of development is not inferior to traditional masculine formation but rather an alternative to it (10).

David identifies himself not by contrast but by relation to his grandmother, thus implicitly challenging the masculine paradigm that perceives the self as separate and the masculine experience of autonomy as the criterion for fulfilling adulthood. Early in his childhood, however, David loses his grandmother and is not fully able either cognitively or emotionally to grieve for his loss until adulthood. Just as he tries to rescue his twin by imaginatively reconstructing him as a conscience, David tries to reenact his early days with his grandmother through his relations with two friends at college. Though he is not fully aware of the symbolic significance of his actions, David maintains a connection with his family history when he is separated from the cultural trappings of his ancestral home: its rich Italian dialect; the rattle of pots and smell of garlic; his grandparents' high-bolstered bed; the last photograph taken of his grandmother, "her sad eyes and the old tales of sickness and death that I heard from her" (46). Only partially aware that his grandmother's death symbolizes the death of his culture of origin, David leaves home, feeling bereft of a heritage and a past. To preserve his own history/self, David reenacts the memories of his familial past during the second phase of his mental career at college—part 2 of the novel.

David's identity remains confused and unresolved because of its dualistic nature, one that stands "midway between the ancient forms" (his grandparents, his heredity) and his "entranced, startled self" (37). The university setting of part 2 replaces the family orientation typical of many immigrant narratives in part 1. As a third-generation Italian American, David chooses the American routes of education and alienation, both of which lead him to intense introspection, thus paralleling the traditional bildungsroman as much as the female novel of self-discovery in which the protagonist's search for self-knowledge leads her "from alienation to authenticity" (Felski 133).

The narrator's education is internal and psychological, encouraged both by the solitary setting of his dorm room and his intense friendships with two characters, Phil and Laura. In his attempt to "extend a bridge" between the ancient forms and his "entranced" self, David reenacts family relationships with these friends, who might usefully be interpreted as vicarious and potentially dangerous selves of the narrator. By the end of his journey, David loses both friends; Phil disappears and Laura goes mad, both trenchant forms of alienation that David ultimately must reject. Each loss recalls the death of David's twin and his grandmother, thus compelling him to recognize and mourn those losses.

Laura's eventual descent into madness provides the most poignant and disturbing commentary on David's struggle for autonomy. Laura's incarceration in an asylum (part 3) provides David, ironically, with the emotional environment for the reconstruction of his self-image (Feder 27). As if to reinforce David's feelings of spiritual and emotional instability well before he enters the asylum, Cavallo introduces an image that has particular relevance for the Italian American: the Madonna. During a brief pilgrimage to St. Anne de Beaupré, whose monastery is located in upper Quebec, David struggles to find spiritual solace in the modern-day trek. David and Phil drive through the coastland of Canada and stop to take a swim in the clear mountain water. Though the narrator had earlier admitted that he could not be redeemed by Catholic rituals, his description of their swimming reads like a baptism of two lost souls, each mirroring the other's movement and feelings. Jointly, they are arrested by a statue of earthly succor: "a black-draped figure with raised fingers—the Black Virgin of the Rocks that Canadian farmers placed everywhere to invoke a blessing." Although David explicitly denies the efficacy of the Virgin's prayers—"she tried in vain to stay the river and to keep us rooted by her side"—he invokes her presence at one of the climactic moments of the narrative, when he later sees Laura transfixed in front of a three-paneled mirror (73).

The fact that Cavallo chooses in this section to represent the Madonna as black may also reinforce the subversive nature of her power. Lucia Chiavola Birnbaum interprets the presence of black Madonnas as a metaphor for the "popular hope for liberation of the poor, the marginal, and the suppressed of the earth" (*Black Madonnas* 12). David's denial of her effectiveness is concomitantly an affirmation of her presence in his psyche. Because she is a *black* Madonna, as Carlo Levi notes, she "was no sorrowful Mother of God, but rather a subterranean deity" whom it is necessary to adore (qtd. in *Black Madonnas* 18). In this way, David further aligns himself with his "ancient forms." During times of great want and grief, the Italian peasant would invoke the aid of the Madonna, "the primary female figure in Italian Catholicism" (Gambino, *Blood of My Blood* 150).[10]

Unfortunately, Laura is more aligned with the white Madonna of church doctrine, thus embodying the characteristics of "obedience and patience" (*Black Madonnas* 3), which may partially account for her lack of subjectivity in the narrative. In addition, Laura is an actress who is unable to divorce herself from the roles she plays on stage. In dramatizing the character Signora Frola of Pirandello's *It Is So! (If You Think So)*, Laura cannot distinguish between herself and the mother in the play, who tragically seeks her daughter who has been dead for four years. David's attraction to such a woman stems less from sexual desire than from a primordial need to retrieve that part of himself that he feels he has lost. The narrator's sexual consummation with Laura and his later discovery of her mother's past give David the kinds of revelations he is unable, during college, to provide for himself. If indeed Laura is part of the narrator's agonized self, then David is providing himself with a way to cope with his painfully subjective experience.

The scene of their lovemaking occurs in an abandoned lookout near the ocean, one of David's childhood haunts. The scene resonates with the past and David's memories of his grandmother; it allows David to return to and reenact a time in his life when he felt sheltered and secure. After lovemaking, David observes that Laura's gesture of lifting her damp hair away from her face recalls his grandmother nimbly plucking back

> strands from her forehead . . . hands moving in rapid strokes, kneading, crocheting. Out there was the sound of the sea. She sat on the sofa, . . . off in thoughts of another sea, blue and faraway. . . . She smiled and curved the same fingers that lifted hair—to beckon me. . . . I sat on the

highest seat in the world, the warm curve of lap that took me up, clearing off for me my place in the world, my shelter. The ocean reclaimed the wave. (115–16)

In Laura, David is temporarily able to recover the maternal. Their consummation signals the union of David's ancestral culture and the part of himself he feels he has lost. Throughout the narrative, David experiences successive returns to his familial culture; gradually, he learns how to return to the past through memory no longer vitiated by fear or confusion.

Laura remains a disturbing character in David's journey to achieve authenticity. Laura seems at first to function as a mirror image of the narrator: both have lost beloved family members; both refuse to discuss their pasts with each other; both feel unanchored because of their tragic losses; and both are searching out their selves. However, when David discusses the sense of dualism inherent in the identity of the Pirandellian character Signora Frola, Laura *denies* that the character has an identity at all. While Laura proclaims that her character is "no one," David strongly feels that she was "not just *one*" but rather a composite identity (81). Cavallo aptly chooses the Pirandellian play to showcase Laura's inability to authorize herself as an identity outside of the role she plays. Laura cannot accept the possibility of the character having a multidimensional self. Her nihilistic interpretation of Signora Frola parallels her self-denial and her refusal to recognize that she might be able to develop an identity.

Such abrogation of the self is most apparent during the consummation scene. Just as Laura regularly annihilates herself into the roles of the stage, she abrogates her individuality during their lovemaking with "a joyousness of abnegation" (114). What ultimately destroys Laura is her inability to recognize an identity that is distinct from her mother's without denying the fact of her mother's madness and subsequent suicide. David learns from Laura's father that he suffers from the same "melancholia of spirit" that his daughter does. Discovering further information about Laura's mother, David learns that she became "mind-ill and incapable" after bearing her daughter (171–72).

Because her mother suffered from depression, Laura was compelled to play the adult prematurely, entertaining her mother by play-acting for her. After the mother commits suicide, Laura submerges herself in the roles she plays onstage, never developing what Chodorow calls an internal "*core* of the self" (67).[11] Furthermore, the fact that Laura's father, without malicious intent, calls his wife "mind-ill" serves to designate her as different, as "Other." That Laura remains silent on the subject of her mother's "madness" further privatizes the experience and subsequently pathologizes Laura's own suffering.[12]

Laura's loss symbolizes David's search for a viable self, but he dangerously assumes that Laura is his complement, his "other part at last," his lost and grieving self (191). Felski explains that women's position vis-à-vis men's development is one of support: "Men, and a society in which men hold power, objectify women as Other, as supplementary to and supportive of male identity" (133). Given the alienating form of passivity to which Laura ultimately succumbs—catatonia—Cavallo may very well be suggesting that David's gender contributes as much to his development of self as it does to Laura's loss of subjectivity.

David is brutally shocked into revising his belief that Laura is his complement when he comes upon her "transfixed, riveted, bewitched, before the mirror, no longer of the world" (191). Cavallo again incorporates mirror imagery in this scene but distinguishes between Laura's descent into actual clinical madness and the narrator's ongoing negotiations with his image in the mirror. In front of a three-paneled mirror, Laura stands in her blue nightgown, the color appropriately symbolizing the Virgin.[13] David utilizes metaphorical language to describe Laura's stasis: "The full-length mirror, . . . held her form like some great, life-sized triptych, the Virgin, and she, Byzantium-blue" (192). That David depicts Laura as a life-sized triptych suggests her inability to negotiate multiple selves before her; her statue-like appearance not only signals her catatonic state but also David's burgeoning realization of the illusory nature of his quest to formulate his identity through another. To signal Laura's profound psychological disturbance, Cavallo suggests that Laura's relationship to the mirror is "a psychic killing" rather than an intense identification (La Belle 128).

While David returns to the mirror in an effort to negotiate the dimensions of his self, Laura gets captured by the mirror. To signify Laura's psychic death, Cavallo ends part 2 with David's description of Laura's immobility in front of the mirror. The fractured grammatical form indicates David's intense recognition of the mirror's power as an instrument of self-destruction as much as self-possession:

> . . . and which one am I? . . . Three, separate, contending . . . "yes" to the right, "yes" to the left, "yes" to the very center, "yes" everyone, yet hold me, stop me, fix me in one, "no" to the shifting, the moving, "no" to the flitting, the fleeing, the in and out of me, stay hold close fix end and the stop of me (193)

The madness narrative that encompasses part 3 of *A Bridge of Leaves* completes David's restitution of self. David must enter the "walled city" of the asylum in order to clarify his identity and end his search for a complete self through another person. What David learns within the confines of the institution is ultimately useful to him, allowing him to determine his role as an individual with a future in a world outside the static environment of the asylum.

Nonetheless, when David enters "Laura's city," he is vaguely filled with the excitement that guides an initiate, hoping, if not to save Laura, then at least to join her in stark exile from the world. To convey the riskiness of such a journey, David describes himself as a modern-day Dante, accosted on the threshold "of the Inferno. . . . With as much foreboding, I entered the first circle" (199). Echoing his cultural ancestor, the narrator invests Dante's odyssey with modern meaning: madness is a kind of psychological hell in which the inhabitants are wholly circumscribed by their ceaseless suffering. Like Laura, they are stopped in time and unable to shape any form of a future around the past.

When David describes the elderly inhabitants in the asylum, he employs generational rhetoric, referring implicitly to the necessity of cultural origins: "[H]ad they drifted off from everyone, out of touch with relatives and friends for over a generation already?" (201). Without a sense of continuity—whether rediscovered or imagined—David will not be able to formulate a coherent identity in the future. David needs to accept a dynamic definition of ethnicity, one that can sustain loss. Without continuity, David realizes, there is only death—spiritual, psychological, actual.[14]

In his desire to return to cultural origins—to "early grandmother-swathed time" (203)—David initially sees only one route, the world of madness, where he can both obliterate and dramatize his loss. Invoking once again the memory of his ancestors' voyage to America, David wishes to make "a crossing" into Laura's world in order to "anchor again a life set adrift by her going" (217). Just as his grandmother was unable to retrieve a part of herself that was lost by coming to a new world, David will be unable to erase his loss by willing himself mad.

Cavallo reinforces the ineffectuality of David's desire in the penultimate event of part 3, the mad lawn party scene that concludes the narrator's stay in the asylum. The conversations that ensue among the inmates on the lawn of the asylum reveal their inability to converse with each other in the present, trapped as they are in their mental anguish. The inhabitants increasingly submit to what Feder calls a "Dionysiac frenzy"; however, they do not return to "primordial psychic freedom," only to their present and ceaseless suffering (10–11). Throughout David's attempt to join their saturnalia, there remains within him some consciousness of being, some "oneness" that withstands "even the swirl, a tongue of fire dancing the waters, undrowned. There was no sucking me in" (238). Appropriately, Cavallo's use of water imagery regarding David reconnects him to the ancestral transatlantic crossing; to his own successful negotiation through his mother's birth canal; to the maternal relationship enjoyed with his grandmother; to the Black Madonna of the Rocks protecting the farmers' crops from flooding; and, finally, to his consummation with Laura near the ocean.

Realizing that he has irrevocably lost Laura, David achieves what I earlier called a modern-day *anagnorisis*, a discovery not only that Laura was "beyond recall" but also that he had never overtly mourned his other losses: "Tears unshed by my grandmother's bier; I knew she was dead. Unshed by the mirror; would I never say: she is gone, nothing to save her? . . . I said it now" (239). David's withdrawal from the outside world enabled him to incorporate the knowledge of his loss into a future decidedly part of the social world. Through his close encounter with madness, moreover, David reveals to himself the very psychic processes that accounted for his necessary withdrawal and return.

To describe David's return to the outside world as an achievement of "oneness" within himself is potentially misleading. David's recognition and acceptance of his losses signal his consciousness, but to be conscious, as Robert Scholes explains, "and, above all, to be conscious that one is conscious—is to be split, differentiated, alienated" (74). The final chapter of *A Bridge of Leaves* solidifies this idea. David clarifies that he is writing in the very present as if to position himself in a historical context, in which his new self-knowledge provides "the endpoint from which all aspects of the text gain their significance in terms of the developmental plot" (Felski 139). Having come to accept the death of his beloved ancestors, David infuses his final ruminations with rebirth imagery, comparing the natural processes of the earth to his own connection to origins.

Of the healing nature of rain, David writes, "between sky and earth no margin; all has become one moist descent" (240). The operative word—descent—reinforces both the narrator's acceptance of the past and the retrospective nature of the bildungsroman itself. David begins the narrative "within months of [age] thirty" and ends his story on the threshold of a new beginning, revitalized by the memory of his cultural past. Recognizing the fragility of identity and ethnicity, David observes the ash tree struck by lightning. His interpretation of this sudden death is overwhelmingly affirmative: the ash tree "remained rooted in earth, . . . still of its world, though less tree" (242). Such a description indicates the optimism underlying the genre itself: the belief in the possibility of meaningful development, despite struggle and anguish.

David's final reference to nature signals his awareness of the dynamic enterprise of discovering identity "in the name of ethnicity." He refers to the common "rosemarie," who knows it grows more beautiful when an approaching foot "crushes its life juice. . . . I am that berry, that sturdy rosemarie, . . . that tender root, that lofty ash. . . . We have loved what we have been. There is no terror in becoming" (243). That David ultimately alludes to the symbol of remembrance is not surprising. But his struggle for identity requires a "(re)-invention and discovery of a vision, both ethical and future-oriented" (Fischer 196). David's memories will not cause stasis; they will allow him to continue developing his varied selves. Thus, David's transformation is affirmative.

Like David, Anna Giardino also emancipates herself from her terror of becoming in Dorothy Bryant's *Miss Giardino.*[15] Bryant's earlier female novel of development, *Ella Price's Journal* (1972), attends to the deferred maturation of the protagonist. Such a narrative pattern has been described by Abel, Hirsch, and Langland as the awakening novel, in which the protagonist develops significantly only after fulfilling "the fairy-tale expectation that [she] will marry and live 'happily ever after'" (12). In her third novel, *Miss Giardino*, Bryant offers a more complex account of development by examining the intersection between gender and ethnicity in the emotional development of an Italian American high school teacher, Anna Giardino. Though this novel does not trace the protagonist's emancipation from the yoke of marital bonds, it does align itself with both the underlying precept informing the traditional bildungsroman and the female novel of development. Both the evolution of a coherent self (central to the bildungsroman) and the deferred growth of the protagonist (central to the female developmental novel) occur in the character of Anna Giardino. Abiding by familial expectations and discovering that she remains neither fulfilled by those expectations nor emotionally and spiritually developed, Anna Giardino's mental journey requires her to invent methods by which to heal herself. In doing so, she becomes the quintessential autodidact: she teaches herself to reread and rewrite the script of her life.

Bryant's novel traces Anna Giardino's recuperation from amnesia to full memory. Just as David's entering the asylum revealed the confusion of his identity, Anna's two-day stay in the hospital and her loss of memory compel her to reexamine her life as a family member and as a teacher. What may be called Anna's "new" memory is at the same time tempered by her recognition of the contumacious if not dangerous patterns of behavior to which she had succumbed in her years of retirement. The novel begins with sixty-eight-year-old Anna waking up in a hospital, unable to remember what put her there. Her amnesia is less a reflection of the fact that she was allegedly terrorized by an attacker than a symbol of Anna's despair, her will to forget. Having worked as a high school teacher in the Mission District of San Francisco, Anna Giardino has been retired for three years when she is apparently robbed one night on one of her midnight walks near Camino Real High School, her place of employment for forty years. Found unconscious, Anna is hospitalized for two days in the same hospital where her mother died, eight years before.

Her mother's severe suffering throughout Anna's early adulthood partially influences Anna's decision to remain unmarried. Anna does not want to repeat the agony of her mother's life. Bryant's novel further aligns itself with conventional nineteenth- and twentieth-century narratives in which the female protagonist refuses heterosexual romance and marriage. According to Marianne Hirsch, the woman's "singularity" is based on a "dis-identification from the fate of other women, especially mothers." Jettisoning traditional constructions of femininity, as Anna does, makes her mother, conversely, "the primary negative model for the daughter" (*The Mother/Daughter Plot* 10–11).

What becomes increasingly apparent to Anna is the many ways in which she *has* reproduced the life of her mother in her own life. Moreover, Bryant's rebirth motif with regard to Anna Giardino's reconstitution of self connects her irresistibly to her mother, who becomes by the conclusion of the narrative her most cherished mentor. Finally leaving the home she shared with her mother symbolizes Anna Giardino's autonomous flight, the image of rebirth inscribed in the nomenclature "Phoenix Street." Sudden and unexpected, Anna's departure is not motivated by fearful memories of the violent living conditions suffered in her childhood because of her father's viciousness, to which her sisters fell victim. Rather, Anna realizes that a shift in location is central to the process of her self-discovery (Felski 134).

By identifying with her mother's words at the end of the narrative, Anna Giardino successfully lives/writes "beyond the ending" of the punitive plot reserved for "rebellious" autonomous women (DuPlessis 5). Not surprisingly, Anna seriously reconsiders the school's earlier proposition that she write a history of Camino Real. Having attended the original school as a high school student and having invested forty years there as an English teacher make her an optimal candidate for such a venture. Anna's transition from the speechlessness that comes with loss of memory and real despair to the recuperation of herself as a talented woman allows her to authorize herself as a teller of *her story.*

Although the novel's structure parallels the traditional bildungsroman in its chronicling of seven days through which Anna is portrayed as processing her memories, the novel nonetheless incorporates modernist narrative strategies in its use of dream sequences and lengthy italicized sections of memory. The narrative is both chronological/linear and spatial/circular, suggesting, like *A Bridge of Leaves*, the generic diversity of its form. As Lazzaro-Weis says, of the genre's theme and purpose, the bildungsroman represents conscious human self-formation, but the protagonist must undergo "a process of alienation in order to achieve self-consciousness" (26). Anna Giardino's amnesia, an illness specifically suitable to her personality, functions as an appropriate form of alienation for the protagonist. Confused and disoriented at first, Anna's need for control and mastery over situations encourages her to begin to recall her past and restructure her life emotionally. Memory loss acquires positive value as it aids in Anna's psychic struggle for autonomy. Forced to reconsider her life, Anna Giardino gains a changed perspective on her family, friends, sexual relationships, and teaching career.

Bryant incorporates lengthy episodes of memory and recurrent dreams about fire in order to bring Anna to a painful but necessary discovery of self. Anna's earliest memories recall the immigrant narrative in the United States, a plot that writers such as Tomasi and Benasutti make central to their texts. Bryant's inclusion of the narrative of Italian Americans struggling to survive in an apparently hostile world reinforces the centrality of this story to the protagonist's development of self. Bryant's dedicatory note to her parents, Giuditta Chiarle Calvetti and Joseph Calvetti, suggests the various applications of the journey motif: Bryant's parents' immigration to the United States; Anna Giardino's mother's journey with three children from the Piedmontese village; and finally and centrally, Anna Giardino's internal and psychological voyage from a repressed fury that has made her unaware of herself to a fully recovered older woman who discovers the freedom that comes with understanding the uses of memory. Although Anna's psychic journey is given the fullest treatment of the three, it does not diminish the sustaining importance of the parental trip to the new world.[16]

In one of her first long stretches of memory, Anna recalls the family's successive moves and ongoing failures to achieve a modicum of prosperity in America. Coupled with this memory is the deathbed confessional scene with her father, an enraged immigrant whose dreams of America were methodically destroyed throughout his struggle in the new world. Embedded within the memory of her violent childhood, Anna recalls the theme of loss common both to the earlier novels of family life in America (Tomasi, Benasutti, Savarese) and to the later novels that focus on psychological suffering resulting from the effects of self-loathing and discrimination (Waldo, Barolini, Hendin, Maso).[17]

Like Cavallo, Bryant implicitly equates America with illness, further refining the ways in which Italian American writers have characterized the process of emigration. When Anna first remembers her mother, she recalls the hospital scene where her mother died (3). When Anna first remembers her father, she recalls the physical suffering he endured because of inhumane working conditions in the coal mines. To understand her own development, Anna must remember her mother's "always accepting her powerlessness" and her father's "fury, his cruelty" (3, 17). As a child, Anna tries to deny her lack of power by refusing to let her father bully her into crying. Her determination to remain impassive during his violent outrages—"I will die first"—becomes an iron pattern in her development into adulthood. Anna's ability to control her emotions and to repress her own anger increasingly stunts her emotional life, depriving her of feeling anything at all. Like Octavia Waldo in *A Cup of the Sun*, Bryant similarly explores the psychological ramifications of illness and how that illness is insidiously transferred onto the children, who are further removed from the aspirations and failed dreams of the first generation.

Anna Giardino's father violently projects all the bitterness he feels onto his equally disenfranchised family. His psychological burden is all too familiar in narratives of failed transplantation. Hurling the fury of his life onto his frightened children, Anna's father provides another image of the *paterfamilias.* Neither benevolent (Tomasi's Pietro Dalli) nor ineffectual (Benasutti's Papa), nor insisting on the strength of *l'ordine della famiglia* in a new world (Waldo's and Hendin's fathers), Anna Giardino's father represents the illusory nature of the American dream and the anger and violence that may ensue as a result of constant suffering. Succumbing to lung disease, Anna's father experiences a slow death from having inhaled noxious fumes from his earlier coal-mining days. Though his disease recalls Pietro Dalli's death from tuberculo-silicosis in *Like Lesser Gods,* Anna's father is never gentle, nor does he ever find meaningful work or a sense of place in America. While Pietro Dalli's life is given full development in Tomasi's immigrant narrative, Bryant is dedicated to examining the ongoing effects of the immigrant parent's behavior on the children, a strategy Waldo uses in *A Cup of the Sun.* The fact that Anna's earliest memories return her to her childhood suggests the unreconciled nature of her family life and her need to rethink her childhood in light of her present predicament.

Anna Giardino's desire to escape the illness and violence associated with the narrative of family relations takes her to what she perceives to be Anglo values of orientation: education, reflection, and individualism. Because of their virtual ineffectiveness, Anna was compelled to replace the religious superstitions and old-world faith of her mother with the rational atmosphere of the library and schoolroom. Reading becomes an avenue of freedom, though Anna chooses the language of her mother's culture to describe her access to the world outside her home: "I am worthy to enter this quiet hall with its sacred smell of old bookbindings and glue, a smell that gives me the sense of peace and safety that Mama gets from the candles and incense of the church" (12).

For Anna, taking the escape route through education replaces and supersedes the routes taken by her mother and sisters: marriage and motherhood. As the youngest child of four and the only child born in America, Anna learns English without an accent, reserving the lilting sounds of Italian only for her mother. For this acquisition, she earns the appellation "'the American'" from her father, who increasingly saves all his anger for Anna, whom he identifies as "other," as useless and selfish, reading too much, making herself "'no good for anything else'" (10).[18] As discussed in previous chapters, the father has transported the fear from Italy of making his children better than himself—*Fesso chi fa i figli meglio di lui*—thereby diminishing his control as *capofamiglia*. As a child, Anna Giardino suffers from a kind of "double jeopardy" in which she is denigrated for being an American in the family home and perceived as an object of suspicion by the "sharp, pale ladies" in the library.[19]

When her older sister Victorina visits Anna in the hospital, she exemplifies the old-world mentality that Anna fought against as a young girl. The seventy-five-year-old slot-machine junkie provides Anna with a mirror into her self, though Anna is still blind to the full implications of her father's effect on her. Victorina tells her sister that Anna resembles the father not only on the outside but also on the "'inside. I don't know what it is. Something driving you. It makes you not need people, makes you do things, like going to college, to make a place for yourself above us'" (16). Victorina's comment echoes the father's jealousy of his daughter's departure from the family's traditional norms; any deviation from familial insularity is met with distrust and scorn. Nonetheless, Victorina assesses that her sister's behavior in the family accords with Anglo-American values of orientation. The emphasis on doing, achieving, and succeeding as an individual distinct from *la famiglia* was interpreted in many Italian American households as treasonous behavior.

Having found peace in the solitude of reading and studying, Anna Giardino works hard to forget her father. Nevertheless, alongside the childhood memories of tumultuous family life is Anna's memory of her return from college to sit at her father's deathbed. In her later years, Anna supplies the paradox of her father's existence as an immigrant in America. Unable to die for years, her father thrives "in the air that strangles him" (13). At fifty-three, however, Anna's father is dying, ironically without anger or rancor, only asking to see Anna, formerly described as "the deserter, the American, dead to him" (17). Between gasps of breath, the father names her back into the home, calling her by her birth name, "'Anna.'" Relinquishing bitterness and hatred, the father finally admits that he loves his daughter, though he can only whisper through blue lips, "'I . . . like you.'" Unable to respond with the impossible words, "I love you, Papa," Anna remembers that gesture of restraint as "more cruel than anything he has ever done to me" (18–19). Though she does not hate him anymore, Anna Giardino has learned to repress her anger and her love toward her father for his envy, abuse, and resentment of his youngest daughter.

In order to reassess her subsequent behavior as an educator, a lover, a friend, and a family member, Anna Giardino turns to sleep, which she believes will further reveal the hidden memories that she has consciously chosen to forget. She courageously turns away from the outside reality of the hospital and the doctor's diagnosis in order to regain memories long repressed in the unconscious (Feder 26). In doing so, Anna Giardino learns that her seeming impassivity and control were merely cloaks to disguise her increasingly virulent feelings of aggression (symbolic of the mind in confusion), resulting from years of being the sole support of her mother, of being disadvantaged in the workplace, and of feeling powerless to effect change. In each of her "fire" dreams, Anna Giardino reconstructs her emotional past, leading her to understand why she attempted to burn down Camino Real High School on the night that she staved off an attempted robbery.

An analysis of the recurring fire dreams that Anna has and her ultimate reenactment of the scene of the crime will illuminate the process the protagonist undergoes to allay and resolve her fears. Throughout Anna's reconstruction of her emotional past, she functions as a modern-day Oedipus, deciphering the code that offers her insight into her future, without which she will die. Moreover, Bryant recasts the Oedipal plot by having her protagonist embody features of both the enigmatic Sphinx and the traditionally powerless Jocasta. Solving the riddle of her past *herself*, Anna does not succumb to the traditional Sophoclean plot: she does not kill herself but rather experiences a reawakening central to women's developmental novels.[20]

In each of her fire dreams, Anna Giardino watches Camino Real burning while she unsuccessfully tries to save others, including her mother, her friends, her students; everyone "seemed to be waiting for her to do something" (49). Throughout each sequence, her pleas fall on deaf ears, forcing her to risk dying herself to save the others. In her final fire dream, Anna forgets that she is watching her dream and is reduced to screaming frantically to students who ignore her. Nonetheless, conditioned to seeing herself in the role as saver and firmly believing in education as the means to effect that salvation, Anna yells, "'Fire! Stop playing and let me get you out of here. You'll all die in this place!'" (108). Anna's dreams reveal her own longing to be rescued, and she is willing to play witness to her lost memory in order to retrieve the part of herself she has lost.

Particularly illuminating is Anna's second fire dream, which returns her to the original Camino Real High School, the one that in actuality had burned down shortly before Anna graduated in 1922. Standing next to the principal, Anna is given a coded message that she will have to decipher in order to understand herself. Mr. Simpson explains to the young Anna that "'the fire is all inside and the outer shell shows nothing. . . . Cold fire, that's the worst kind.' . . . He pointed at her and then at the brick wall, and she saw that he meant for her to tear it down, brick by brick" (21–22). Anna eventually realizes that the oxymoronic descriptive "cold fire" is self-referential; she must claim the identity in order to heal from her suffering.

Uncovering the layers of repressed rage is a frightening and exhausting activity, but it must be done in order for Anna fully to retrieve her memory. In one of her long stretches of memory shortly thereafter, Bryant reinforces the connection between Anna tearing down the brick walls constructed to protect herself and her high school teacher's survival book, a book that "'will tell how to survive in the world as a refugee. . . . Escape techniques. Disguises. A very useful book in the days that are coming'" (32–33). During the subsequent years of their friendship, Anna knows that Mr. Ruggles is still writing his survival book. After he dies in 1934 and his wife the following year, no trace remains of the manuscript. Just as David "read" the stars to understand the profound depth of his loss of Michael, Anna's script reads much like her high school teacher's survival book, replete with escape techniques and disguises. The fact that the manuscript is not found bodes well for Anna Giardino, as she can create her own text in order to accommodate a diverse understanding of herself as a woman and an educator.

In attempting to escape from her mother's life of marriage, motherhood, and overarching powerlessness, Anna Giardino fell victim to another kind of disenfranchisement within the educational system. Viewing education as a means of freeing herself from the frustrations inherent in being ignorant and vulnerable, Anna remained throughout her life passionately committed to the belief in salvation through education.[21] In 1928, the year Anna graduated from college, a white woman with a B. A. was severely limited with regard to career choices. Once the depression came, Anna Giardino was the sole support of her ailing mother. Anna's fire dreams represent her own incapacity to effect change: to save her mother from a violent household; to save her students from the frustration and fear that come with ignorance.

In order to protect herself from the desperate realization of such vulnerability—in order to survive as a refugee—Anna Giardino controlled her reality by dying emotionally:

> She had learned long ago to protect herself, to live behind a shield. She could not remember exactly when it was that she began to build the shield. Not at first, not in the beginning of her teaching, for if she had, she would never have loved Stephen. She was now very different from the woman who loved Stephen. Not less passionate. Just better, she thought, at control, at defense. (47)

Anna's fire dreams and lengthy memory sequences compel her to put down the shield. She needs to become helpless in order to become well. In feeling helpless and frightened, Anna becomes more aware of her capacity to attain a new kind of power, a power no longer motivated by anger and desperation.

To secure a complete transition from a state of helplessness and pain to a revitalized understanding of her identity, Anna Giardino chooses to reenact the night that she was attacked. She can no longer depend on her fire dreams, because her "conscious mind had now moved ahead of her dreams," forcing her to complete her journey in full consciousness (139). Anna Giardino's illness—in her case, amnesia—generates within her what Sander L. Gilman calls "the Other whom we have feared, whom we have projected onto the world" (2). Having throughout her long tenure as a student and teacher adopted a belief in one's ability to solve problems, Anna must now succumb to her own vulnerability in order to discover "what it was that seemed to be frightening her to death" (141). The self that Anna Giardino discovers is both terrifying and illuminating. Anna learns that the other whom she has feared and projected outside of herself is indeed within herself.

Although Anna initially chuckles at the thought of returning to the scene of the crime, her actual reenactment ushers in the epiphanic moment in her life. Stopping across the street from the high school, Anna believes that her extreme fear might cause her to die. When she reaches into her pocket and discovers a key and matches, Anna recognizes those to be the visible testaments of her desire to burn down the high school. Crying out in shock and pain, memory surges through Anna "like an electric charge," triggering full recall of what happened that night. In her confession to her former lover and old-time friend, Arno, Anna explains how her repressed fury finally explodes (like the coal mine did years before, killing her only brother, Mike) in uncontrollable anger and violence toward her would-be mugger, Booker T. Henderson. Booker turns out to be a former student:

"It wasn't that I was angry because he tried to rob me. . . . It was because I recognized him. It was because I hated him so. Or not really him. He was everything I hated, everything that had gone wrong, everything about the school, about my life, everything I hated was . . . Booker. I hated him the way he hated me when I was his teacher. I was . . . insane with hate." (143)

Anna acknowledges the fact that her anger was a form of madness, receiving "the accumulation of injury and frustration, ignorance and fear, from so many young people" throughout her long career as a teacher (145). Such a recognition further allows Anna to reestablish her identity with her familial past, without which she will die. In doing so, Anna realizes that her madness has been insidiously transferred from her father's generation onto her own. Having miserably endured the "horrible wrench of the emigrant," Anna's father in turn brutalized his family (146). Having internalized the anger her father imposed on her, Anna mistakenly thought she was successfully controlling her increasing frustration as an educator. However, during her tenure as a teacher, Anna observed in her students the same exchange of fury, the "trading of destruction" that her father exhibited at home. Realizing the incontrovertible connection between her Italian American heritage and the African American and Mexican American students, Anna is finally able to express and understand disempowerment without the anger that earlier fueled her thoughts:

"If I told [the student] my father was a slave destroyed by The System, would he listen? If I told him we are both victims? If I told him he is enjoying this [gathering up all this fury and aiming it at me, the one simple, easy, accessible target] in order to avoid the harder work of doing something about it?" (130)

Although Booker T. Henderson repudiates the symbolic significance of the name his mother gave him and scorns the teacher whom he perceives as representing the establishment, it is he who unknowingly defuses the stored-up rage of Anna's whole life. It is he who saves his teacher from reenacting her father's past. Anna's journey is incomplete without her former student, who unwittingly pushes her back into her mind, the mind that "she had misplaced . . . and had found . . . again." Anna Giardino's journey through madness is homeopathically cured by its own "violence of energy exchange," leaving her able to acknowledge the intimate connection between identity and ethnicity: "And how had she differed from her father? At first she had hated him; then she forgot him. Now, finally, she understood him. She had learned to understand him by becoming him" (145–46).

In claiming "a modern identity in the name of ethnicity," Anna Giardino wisely dismisses Arno's advice to "'forget it,'" assuming that she could start her life with a clean slate. Having the luxury of understanding her father's tormented life, Anna asserts a right to an important distinction from her parent: "It was a difference in what they knew. . . . She must not forget what she now knew about herself. If she forgot, if she dulled her consciousness, she would die in the same despair as her father, without even his hope of a new generation to benefit from his sacrifice" (146). From her father's sacrifice, Anna Giardino learns an essential truth that is incumbent upon her never to forget. In this regard, she parallels the achievements of other protagonists of the bildungsroman, producing substantive changes in her life.[22] Anna's newfound memory, cleansed of anger but not the memory of her anger, allows her to function as the modern-day "antitype" of her ancestors. She fulfills their aspirations to find comfort and a sense of self in the new world.

Earlier in the narrative, the protagonist's tenant, Lori, compares Anna's amnesia with a tabula rasa: "'like you're new-born, starting all fresh.'" Well before Anna reconstitutes herself, she corrects her tenant's misperception, because her mind, however much lost, has been indelibly marked by the experiences of her life. In answer to the question of what it feels like to have no memory, Anna responds, "'Not like being new-born. Because, although I don't remember, it's still all there. Like being in a house suddenly made invisible. Not seeing the walls, one still . . . bumps into them. And then they're visible . . . suddenly'" (68).[23] After she bumps back into her memory, Anna Giardino emancipates herself, not from the past—to do so would be vain and destructive—but from the impediments of her present.

In the span of one day, Anna sells her house on 22 Phoenix Street to her young tenants, who have longed to refurbish the old place; she leaves behind all her mother's belongings, not in an attempt to obliterate her mother's memory but rather to reinvest her own life by recovering her repressed identity. Having been prematurely old at the age of thirteen, Anna early on recognized the impoverishment of her home life and was compelled to find work as a helper in the home of a middle-class Jewish American family who lived on 22 Phoenix Street. Her later move with her mother into that same house was an upwardly mobile gesture on Anna's part. Her ultimate decision to leave that house symbolizes "an act of separation from familial and sexual ties," allowing Anna to learn what freedom means to her as a result of her "changed consciousness" (Felski 133). Though she *consents* (Sollors's term) to a new life, one stripped "down to essentials," Anna knows the damage done to the emotional self in repressing or trying to erase the past (156).

Perhaps the finest testimonial to Anna Giardino's growth into peaceful maturity is her psychic reunion with her mother at the end of the narrative.[24] Earlier in this chapter, I suggested that female protagonists of the bildungsroman disidentify with the mother in order to escape the maternal plot of marriage and motherhood. Anna reproduces the maternal in her passionate desire to save her students from the fate of ignorance and violence from which her mother (and teachers) helped her escape. In "writing beyond the ending" of a narrative that would have her survive as a refugee disconnected with herself or as a powerless woman in the face of discriminatory behavior in the work force and the social milieu, Anna Giardino chooses the language of poetry and the route of imagination to begin her new voyage.

In her first memory, Anna recalled the final days of her mother's life. Interspersed with her mother's early memories of the voyage to America is her final vision before dying, one that has "'all colors. Like angel wings.'" Her mother's vision recalls the panoramic radiance of the old country. Lacking what she considers the imaginative force to see the past or the future, Anna comes out of her reverie repudiating her own creative capacities, having neither the patience, the saintliness, nor the faith of her mother (4–5). After Anna's recuperation, and aware of her potential autonomy in light of her newfound freedom, Anna embraces her mother's view of the world: raising her eyes to the wet rooftops, Anna notices that the skies have cleared and spontaneously identifies with her mother's vision by exclaiming, "'[A]ngel wings!'" (160).

Both protagonists, David of *A Bridge of Leaves* and Anna of *Miss Giardino*, take excruciating journeys in order to claim the legacy of their pasts. Only then can David say unflinchingly of his past, "We have loved what we have been. There is no terror in becoming." Similarly, Anna Giardino can become the unaccommodated woman at sixty-eight who can gratefully leave her old house of books and papers and say, "'I'm through with the past, but I mustn't lose it'" (155). David and Anna discover creative ways to reinvent their cultural pasts, knowing their ancestors, long dead, cannot provide them immediate access to help them formulate or sustain their identities.

# 4 *A Process of Reconstruction*

## *Recovering the Grandmother in Helen Barolini's* Umbertina *and Tina De Rosa's* Paper Fish

Helen Barolini and Tina De Rosa demonstrate their allegiance to the familial narrative of Italian America from the perspective of the third generation. They return to the family novels of development so ably portrayed by Tomasi and Benasutti, but they complicate their efforts in specific ways: Barolini writes out of a distinctly feminist awareness, explaining that her novel *Umbertina* is "as much feminist as it is ethnic" (Interview, tape 2).[1] De Rosa's interest in modernism aligns her closely with Bryant, Cavallo, and Carole Maso, but her focus unwaveringly remains on the family, recalling the novels of Waldo and Hendin. What makes both *Umbertina* (1979) and *Paper Fish* (1980) so compelling is their devotion to the figure of the grandmother.

Examining David's development in Cavallo's *A Bridge of Leaves* in chapter 3 required only brief information on the figure of the grandparent in Italian American literature and culture. Because Barolini's and De Rosa's texts have as a central focus the imaginative recreation of the grandmother's life, three ideas about this recurring narrative bear further commentary. First, in order to maintain a viable connection with one's Italian American ancestry, Barolini and De Rosa reshape through fiction the grandmother's life both in Italy and America. It is as though each author entrusts her imaginative life to the figure of the grandmother, claiming her as totem, as wise seer. Much of what is written, then, is imaginative recreation rather than documentary-like reconstruction.[2] The fact that Barolini in her childhood could not literally understand the Calabrian dialect (or any Italian, at the time) of her grandmother reflects the Americanizing tendency of some second-generation parents who, in their desire to be accepted rapidly as *American*, did not transmit the Italian language to their children.[3]

Second, for writers like Barolini and De Rosa, the concept of generations becomes central to the construction of their novels. Sollors has been instrumental in articulating in detail the American fascination with the idea of generations: "Though it defies measurability, the generation is first and foremost a mental concept which has been experienced as well as used to interpret experience throughout American history" (*Beyond Ethnicity* 210). Such rhetoric serves each author's creative purposes well: the third-generation granddaughter functions as the "redeemer" of the first-generation immigrant grandmother, endowing her with all the strength and goodness putatively lost in the second generation. However ahistorical generational rhetoric might be, such an alliance between "first" and "third" generations produces narratives about fulfillment, not about loss and degeneracy.

The conclusions of both *Umbertina* and *Paper Fish* are affirmative, further aligning themselves with the tradition of arduous but fulfilling development represented by the bildungsroman. Whether or not the third-generation granddaughters could literally speak to their first-generation Italian grandmothers, each is devoted to reconstructing the cultural past of the grandmother in an effort to value herself as Italian American. Barolini describes her writing about Italian American themes as helping her discover "almost imperceptibly, my own validity" ("Becoming a Literary Person" 271). Of the American tendency to employ generational rhetoric when speaking of lineage, Sollors writes, "Apparently talking about lineage, they [Americans] are actually inventing not only a sense of communal descendants . . . but also a metaphoric ancestry in order to authenticate their own identity" (*Beyond Ethnicity* 234).

Third, in their quest to receive legacies of selfhood from their grandmothers, the granddaughters, according to Gardaphé, reinvent *italianità* by fashioning "a usable past in which they can locate the cultural elements needed to create integral selves."[4] Gardaphé explains that the grandparent serves as the "mythic *figura* who is the source of the ethnic stories created by the third generation" (*Italian Signs, American Streets* 121). The grandparent figure comes to represent the original source, the third-generation's sole connection to the ancestral past. Recalling the past is as much a literal activity as it is a metaphorical undertaking, the process of reconstruction becoming a journey toward ethnic selfhood. Though Marcus Lee Hansen's perspective on generational rhetoric has not been immune from criticism, his belief that "what the son wishes to forget the grandson wishes to remember" finds its equivalent in Barolini's *Umbertina* and De Rosa's *Paper Fish* (495). Barolini and De Rosa write novels that focus on discovering what contentment means to the descendants of real and imagined grandparent figures. At the end of her long life, Umbertina recalls the meaning of *benessere*: "well-being of the total person—not just money, but spirit, too" (138). Both authors recognize that their creative reconstitution of the grandmother is necessary for the spiritual fulfillment of their protagonists.

In the authors' approaches to storytelling, Barolini is more traditional than De Rosa. The third-person narrator in *Umbertina*, for example, functions much like a historian, recording in detail the economic and social forces compelling Italians such as Umbertina, the goat girl from the mountains of Calabria, to immigrate to the United States. Imagining the physical features of Umbertina, Barolini writes out of an awareness of oral traditions, as though overhearing neighborhood gossip: "She had hazel eyes, fair skin where the sun did not reach, and a strong chin. In the village people said of Umbertina that she had character right from the womb. 'She'll be the man of her family,' they said" (23). It has been said that where history is insufficient, myths are created (De Vos, "Ethnic Pluralism" 21). If Barolini's history becomes mythologized, it does so because it is concerned with the social and spiritual value of origins. Recreating the ancestral past endows the grandmother figure with the strength and potential that will be reinterpreted by granddaughters and great-granddaughters in order to structure and give purpose to their own lives.

De Rosa's narrative style is less overtly historical than Barolini's, presenting not the external drama of migration but the internal thoughts of an Italian American family. As a modernist, De Rosa is more interested in the perceptions of her characters than she is in observing their outward behavior. Though De Rosa tells her story as a modernist would—by using multiple perspectives, overlapping narratives, and interior monologues—*Paper Fish*, like *Umbertina*, is also embedded in oral tradition, the first line of the novel mimicking the traditional beginnings of story:

> This is my mother, washing strawberries, at a sink yellowed by all foods, all liquids, yellowed. This is my mother scalping the green hair of strawberries. . . . These are my mother's hands, skin that has touched thousands of things now touches strawberries. . . . (8)

At the outset, De Rosa employs traditional storytelling techniques such as straightforward chronology, repetition, and present tense in order to embrace and record her culture of origin.[5] *Paper Fish* is filled with the grandmother's stories, De Rosa using both a linguistic transcription of the Italian into English and poetic diction, embracing oral and literary traditions.

Both Barolini and De Rosa incorporate a journey narrative in their texts, creating a female character who longs to recapture and maintain an indelible relationship with her Italian heritage. Such a quest necessitates the kind of exploration reminiscent of Niobe's search for self in Waldo's *A Cup of the Sun*. Like Niobe, Tina of *Umbertina* and Carmolina of *Paper Fish* develop out of their relation to the family, without which they would not achieve a cohesive self-identity. In this way, neither Tina nor Carmolina is the central focus of either novel; the family unit is. As Carmolina's rhetorical question in *Paper Fish* suggests—"They won't ever let us go, will they?"—her ancestry is as immediate and germane to her life as is the ostensible present in which she speaks (125). Though Tina of *Umbertina* travels to her great-grandmother's native village, Castagna, in hopes of discovering her ancestor's secret strength, she needs to return to her living family—in Italy and America—to complete her quest.

Barolini represents Tina's fulfilling growth into adulthood as one that combines an acceptance of her Italian and American backgrounds with her career as a Dante scholar. Having received the direction that she sought from her great-grandmother, Tina returns to New England, planning her wedding for November, exactly one hundred years after her great-grandmother Umbertina Longobardi was married. Planting the rosemary in commemoration of her ancestor, Tina is reminded of the story behind the gesture: "'It's the family women's quaquaversal plant—wherever one of Umbertina's clan descends, there also will be rosemary planted, for where it grows, the women of the house are its strength'" (403). The operative word—"quaquaversal"—is defined as dipping or pointing in all directions from a central point or area. Tina's future may take her many places, but her sense of herself is rooted to her identity as an Italian and an Italian American woman.

In the penultimate scene of *Paper Fish*, De Rosa redefines the meaning of a traditional marriage ceremony in her portrayal of the symbolic communion between Grandma Doria and Carmolina, reinforcing the granddaughter's role as the transmitter of family stories and traditions. The final scene of the book comprises a series of vignettes, De Rosa's narrative version of snapshots that mourn and invoke the loss of an Italian American neighborhood.[6] The epilogue functions doubly, both as a commemoration of and eulogy for the Italian American ghetto of her childhood. Both authors know that invoking what is lost is a process of reconstruction, the central concern of these novels.

Helen Barolini's first novel, *Umbertina*, was written in bits and pieces until 1976, when Barolini received a grant from the National Endowment of Arts to complete the book.[7] Combining interviews with immigrant women, archival materials, actual visits to southern Italy, residence in Rome, and family history gleaned from her mother, whom she calls "the storyteller" in the dedicatory note, Barolini provides a historically accurate account of the poverty and political oppression in the last half of the nineteenth century that drove southern Italians across the sea.[8] In a seminal essay from which *Umbertina* was born, Barolini reveals the close autobiographical links between that novel and her own family story:

"My grandmother died in 1939; it took thirty-seven years for me to get to her grave. It was a going back, reascending time to the places of my youth and to an awareness of where the end of my own journey will be" ("A Circular Journey" 121). Visiting Calabria in 1969 brought back in full force the vision of her grandmother, a "mysterious, impenetrable figure." Barolini recognized the imperative nature of her writing this story, which she has called "a heartful thing," written with a "kind of passion and compulsion" (Interview, tape 1).

*Umbertina* is a multigenerational saga that spans four generations of Italians in America and in Italy, covering the years 1860 through approximately 1975. Though the novel is divided into three sections, each one focusing on a particular generation, Barolini suggests by her development of fourth-generation Italian Americans that the confusions of identity continue well beyond the third generation. Sollors explains that generational numbering is "always a metaphoric enterprise and generational identity a matter of potentiality." While the American paradigm of generations focuses on the third generation, which typologically speaking represents the antitype, the fulfillment of one's ancestors, Barolini extends the sequence of grandparent (foundation), parent (declension), and grandchild (fulfillment) to include the great-granddaughter, Tina, who continues the reconstruction initiated but not completed by her mother, Marguerite (*Beyond Ethnicity* 220, 230).

In *Umbertina*, Marguerite, the granddaughter, and Tina, the great-granddaughter, return to the places of their southern Italian ancestors and to varying degrees achieve success in their ventures. *Umbertina* chronicles the life stories of Umbertina, the Calabrian goat girl, who comes to America as a young, married woman with children; Marguerite, the granddaughter of Umbertina, who remains fascinated by the memory of her grandmother in black who speaks an unintelligible language and sits motionlessly, "peering through spectacles like a solemn owl"; and Tina, who is christened Umbertina for her maternal great-grandmother "to give her strength in life" (144, 273).

The way in which Barolini organizes her saga parallels the structure of the narrative trilogy outlined and examined by William

Boelhower in his essay "The Ethnic Trilogy: A Poetics of Cultural Passage." Boelhower's analysis sheds light on the separate but interrelated sections of *Umbertina*. Part 1, "Umbertina, 1860–1940," constitutes the first part of the saga that Boelhower paradigmatically calls construction (or book 1 of a trilogy) in that the ancestors dominate the section; the immigrant journey to the new world assumes mythic proportions and the primary orientation is on the future. In writing the novel, Barolini has explained that she was thinking in terms of a trilogy (Interview, tape 1), its central ordering principle being "fundamentally generational" (Boelhower, "The Ethnic Trilogy" 7). That the "connecting tissue," as Barolini calls it, should be the character of Umbertina further reinforces the central role that the foundational character plays in the lives of future generations (Interview, tape 1).

Part 2, "Marguerite, 1927–1973," moves from exclusive focus on the children of immigrants (the paradigm of deconstruction, according to Boelhower) to a concern with the grandchildren. Tangentially, there is evidence in part 2 of *Umbertina* of the deconstructive phase of immigrant/ethnic trilogies: Marguerite's parents, Carla and Sam, are governed by the present, influenced by the American culture and its emphasis on accruing wealth and appearing to be happy (belonging to the right club, living in the right neighborhood, buying the right clothes). As Boelhower points out with regard to the second phase of ethnic trilogies, the imagination no longer controls the characters; they settle for what can be done within defined limits, coming up against a "commonplace world, . . . against its fallenness" ("The Ethnic Trilogy" 14–15). The narrative logic in this section is ruled by conflict, including Marguerite's aggressive rejection of her parents' devotion to the trappings of American success.

Much of the Marguerite section and part 3 ("Tina, 1950–") form part of the final narrative program of trilogies: the reconstruction of "an original lost world" through the process of interpretation and interrogation (Boelhower, "The Ethnic Trilogy" 17). The primary orientation, then, is on the past as it is projected and recovered by the memory, thus enriching the present and future. Characterizing Umbertina as the original ancestor suggests the role of myth in the construction of families, each generation reconstructing through memory and imagination the potential of the grandmother to provide strength and to offer wisdom.

In part 1, Barolini charts Umbertina's emigration from Castagna (the mountainous interior of Calabria) to the ghettos of New York. In America, Umbertina is practical, hard working, and determined to make good, that is, achieve material wealth. In time, Umbertina and her husband, Serafino, develop a lucrative business as owners of a local grocery store. Such determination and success come with a price tag that Barolini captures by introducing two central symbols: the tin heart and the matrimonial bedspread. Both of these objects gain symbolic value for Marguerite and Tina, who reinterpret and extend their meanings. First, the tin heart hangs from Umbertina's waist in Castagna, a crudely shaped holder in which the goat girl places her knitting needles when her hands are occupied with other work. This object is given as a "courtesy" to Umbertina by Giose, a charcoal maker from a neighboring village, who is about to be conscripted by the army. Because he is poor and uncertain of his future, Giose refrains from speaking to Umbertina's father about marriage. Though she warily accepts the gift, Umbertina longs for a different life, the one her future husband, Serafino, will provide her by taking her to America. The tin heart that Umbertina wears as a girl still hangs in her kitchen when she is an old woman, stirring the imagination of her youngest child, Carla, the future mother of Marguerite. Occasionally, Umbertina wonders what it might have been like to have married a younger man (Serafino being several years older), having never experienced passionate feelings for her husband, only "the warmth of affection" (46).

Never one to submit to sentimentality, Umbertina tells Carla, who is curious to know if her mother was happy with Poppa, about the importance of *place* to one's sense of *benessere*: "'The important thing . . . is to find your place. Everything depends on that. You find your place, you work, and like planting seeds, everything grows'" (133). For Marguerite and her daughter Tina, the tin heart comes to represent, as Boelhower puts it, "the world of concrete space, of objects, of the self as being-in-the-world" (*Through a*

*Glass Darkly* 126). Though Umbertina inevitably lost the potential for another kind of life in Italy, she embraces her decision stoically and perceives the tin heart as a kind of testimonial to the suffering and loss endured when transplanting from one culture to another.

The second object, Umbertina's matrimonial bedspread, comes to symbolize the project of ethnic trilogies: in order to escape from the poverty of tenements, Umbertina sells her *coperta* to garner enough money to move to upstate New York. After she unsuccessfully tries to buy back the spread, realizing its significance to her life, Umbertina learns that the loss of her treasure symbolizes her sacrificial entry to a better life in Cato, New York. Umbertina thus fulfills the narrative of construction, discovering an "ideal habitat," which is part of the "utopian impulse of the emigrants" (Boelhower, "The Ethnic Trilogy" 12). Nonetheless, Umbertina's deathbed vision recalls Pietro Dalli's of *Like Lesser Gods* in its evocation of the old country, symbolized for Umbertina by the intense colors and intricate designs of her bedspread. Though she purportedly never looked back on her early years in Italy, Umbertina's final request for a cup of water from the spring in Castagna belies her stolidness.

On her quest to discover her ancestral place, Tina visits Castagna, Umbertina's tin heart fastened on her shoulder bag. Though she drinks from the village fountain, recalling her great-grandmother's final request, Tina leaves Calabria still confused and unfocused. It is no irony that Tina feels Umbertina's presence when she later visits the Museum of Immigration on Ellis Island. Tina sees displayed a matrimonial bedspread along with other materials collected from immigrants on the Lower East Side during the time of Umbertina's young adulthood in New York. Unbeknownst to Tina, the *coperta* was brought to America by her own great-grandmother. Perhaps it is appropriate that Tina indirectly rediscovers her great-grandmother in America, for Umbertina, like most forward-looking immigrants, fiercely believed in the future of the new world. Furthermore, Tina's return to New York enables her to complete the reconstruction of the narrative trilogy initiated by her mother, Marguerite. Both symbols—the tin heart and the matrimonial bedspread—resonate in meaning for Marguerite and Tina as they creatively interpret the past.

Toward the conclusion of part 1, the long-widowed Umbertina reassesses her life, wondering whether she made the best decisions regarding her female children, whom she loved but treated as inferior to and less capable than her male children. Strong herself, Umbertina disallowed that kind of assertion for her daughters, who end up chained to custom and often abused by their husbands. At the annual family picnic, Umbertina sits "regally under her tree like an old Indian squaw," peering at her children and grandchildren and reconsidering her life (135). Knowing bitterness as well as contentment, Umbertina sees troubling signs ahead for her family, who are increasingly detached from her and view her as a foreigner, an exotic creature from another culture. She feels loss as she asks herself, "'Who do I have to tell my story to?'" (138). Unlettered like so many immigrant women of her provenance and generation, Umbertina Longobardi must depend on future generations to rediscover and write her story.

Though Barolini has constructed the first part of her saga along fairly conventional lines, she does not literally begin with the Umbertina section. Rather, the prologue provides a reinterpretation of the immigrant journey from Marguerite's perspective as an Italian American woman married to an Italian poet and living in Rome. The close juxtaposing of grandmother and granddaughter highlights their distinct but equally difficult forms of survival, reinforcing the radical change in living standards between immigrant grandparent and Americanized granddaughter. The prologue presents in miniature the marked difference between Umbertina and Marguerite. Despite her worries in old age, Umbertina found her place; in contrast, Marguerite, married for eighteen years with two living children, is plagued by doubt.

In the prologue, Marguerite Morosini attends her regular session with the Sicilian psychiatrist Dr. Verdile. Married to the Venetian poet Alberto Morosoni, Marguerite examines her decision to separate from her husband, hoping from that to discover her own needs. Marguerite learns that her problems are just as much connected to her Italian American identity as to her identity as a woman. Barolini integrates issues of ethnicity and gender to emphasize the immense difficulty for an American from Marguerite's generation to find a secure sense of place in the world without regularly succumbing first to the needs of others.

In the first visit, Dr. Verdile encourages his analysand to reject her tendency to avoid problems, explaining that her favorite escape hatch is self-punishment (4). What perhaps was perceived as necessary self-sacrifice and moral good for the Italian immigrant mother, who subordinated all personal needs to the welfare of her family, is now reinterpreted by the children of immigrants, who question the morality of self-abnegation. *La via vecchia* has been replaced by the security that material prosperity brings to the children of immigrants. Irresistibly, however, the allegiance to family still surpasses all other loyalties, particularly to oneself.

Marguerite is torn not only by her situation as a third-generation Italian American but also by her role as a mother and wife in the 1950s and 1960s. No longer limited by the need to survive and attain material comfort, Marguerite early on attempts to break away from what she perceives to be the narrowness of her parental home by traveling to her grandmother's country. There, she marries a northern Italian, an option open to her only because of her American status. As Alberto arrogantly explains to Marguerite: "'It's a good thing your Calabrian grandparents emigrated to America and made it possible for a northern Italian like me to marry you. Not many northerners would let themselves in for a marriage with a *terrone*'" (170).[9]

Marguerite's decision to marry abroad and launch her future in Italy is reminiscent of the actions taken by a heroine of a century before, Isabel Archer. Marguerite's recognition of the parallel is evident in her wry substitution of James's title *The Portrait of a Lady* for "Portrait of a Loner" (201). Though a century separates them, both Isabel and Marguerite share problems unique to their positions as women "out of place" and therefore susceptible to male control. While Isabel Archer goes to Italy to *affront* her destiny, Marguerite returns to her ancestral homeland to confront her *destino*, both women finally recognizing the ineluctable pull of circumstances that circumscribe their lives.

The dream that Marguerite relays to her therapist at their next meeting further demonstrates the interrelation between ethnic and gender issues. The fact that Marguerite usefully interprets her dream suggests her potential to achieve a satisfying maturity. In the dream, Marguerite is the only foreign teenager in an Italian classroom where the teacher is strict and demanding about assigning the students permanent seats. The students are required to write an essay on a particularly "low, animal, shameful" word: "grossness." Though she tries to appropriate the power and confidence of her therapist by putting on his big black glasses, Marguerite remains anxious and feels disadvantaged. Because she is given less ink than the native speakers, Marguerite wonders whether she will run out before completing the assignment: "'I keep thinking: But I am a foreigner, I already have a disadvantage'" (14).

Remaining after eighteen years of marriage a self-conscious "American transplant filled with fears and desires" (5), Marguerite has failed to overcome her negative feelings toward her hyphenated status, that is, both as an Italian American and as an American in Italy.[10] She has not with ease moved beyond the self-loathing typical of her parents' generation. Her reason for marrying the poet may have more to do with wanting safety and affection, which Alberto supplies, than with achieving a fuller evolution of self. In this way, Marguerite repeats the nineteenth-century narratives of both her grandmother Umbertina and the fictional Isabel Archer: like Umbertina, Marguerite marries a much older man, who introduces her to another country. Like Isabel Archer, Marguerite may very well be marrying more out of maternal than passional need.[11]

Marguerite's dream reveals a profound anxiety about her identity as an American, as an American abroad, and as an Italian American. As a young girl in upstate New York, she felt "foreign" in the American classroom, as many ethnically identified children do. Her parents' wholesale rejection of their *italianità* negatively affects Marguerite, who feels different and trembles "in a confusion of roles." As a youngster, Marguerite is repelled by the way her parents have adopted an ascetic and unemotional way of life, symbolized by the unlit birch logs in the fireplace, serving no purpose other than show (147). At the same time, she is confused by and attracted to Grandma Umbertina's "large, motionless, black figure" (144). In analysis, Marguerite interprets her parents' behavior, realizing that their separation from their Italian identity has produced in them unresolved conflict and bitterness. Of her father, Marguerite says, "'[H]e couldn't be either Italian like his father and mother or American like his models without feeling guilty toward one or the other side'" (18). Unfortunately, Marguerite's second-generation parents passed on to their inquisitive, thoughtful daughter a legacy of confusion. Her formative years left her without a sense of a secure identity. Perhaps that is why Marguerite longs for the kind of permanent place the teacher of her dreams assigns to her.

However, from her dream, Marguerite learns that everything keeps changing, except for her own deep anxiety. When she comes to interpret the word "grossness," it admits no unitary definition. The fact that in her dream Marguerite could not see the word clearly on the board reinforces the skittishness of language itself, its potential for multiple meanings: "'[M]aybe it was *grossese* in the French sense of pregnancy, or *grossolano* in the Italian meaning of coarseness. In any case, a sense of roughness, earthiness, elementariness. . . . Being pregnant, giving birth, growing'" (16–17).[12] Being bilingual and a translator of her husband's poetry, Marguerite knows that language is elusive and associative, the word "grossness" suggesting a return to the primordial, before the birth of language.

Appropriately, Marguerite feels and hears a connection between "gross" and "grocery," for that brings her back to her ancestral roots, epitomized by Umbertina: "'My grandmother had a grocery store—and that would really be getting back to the base of everything. That's it!'" (17). Longing to recover the kind of primitive strength the grandmother possessed, Marguerite is in a position to move beyond the "entropic conditions of the cultural crisis of the second paradigm," represented by her parents' generation (Boelhower, "The Ethnic Trilogy" 18). Analyzing this part of her dream leads Marguerite to the possibility of pursuing her origins further, having always suspected that it was Umbertina who brought her to Italy in the first place: "'But I've never even taken the time to go see where she came from. I've never found her'" (17–18). To fulfill her quest, Marguerite must accept her ideal role as the third-generation antitype, recognizing her identity in the name of ethnicity. What prevents Marguerite's completion of her goal has much to do with her role as a wife and mother.

Marguerite regularly submits to the demands of her parents, husband, and children. As a result, she never finds the time to rediscover her origins and reconstitute her identity as a third-generation Italian American woman. Early in their marriage, Alberto pledges a life of art with Marguerite, easily forgetting such an alliance when the children come. The implicit condescension involved in Alberto's statement to Marguerite—"'I will make a real human being out of you'"—suggests his inability to see his wife as fully human when he marries her (169–70). Like Pygmalion, Alberto threatens to fashion his ideal woman, denying Marguerite her own will to create herself. That he never fulfills the threat reveals his own classic position of "detachment," leaving Marguerite to find her own way (170).

Recognizing her mistake in expecting Alberto to fulfill all of her longings, Marguerite nonetheless realizes that her husband offered no support for nurturing her inner life:

> Life centered around Alberto; even her hopes and aspirations focused on him. These were the years she was also occupied with the two little girls, and Alberto left them and the management of outward life completely to her—forgetting somewhere, like an umbrella it's a nuisance to pay attention to when skies are so clear, the inner life in her he had also pledged himself to support. (173)

When she does try to increase her knowledge about Italian culture, Marguerite is ridiculed by Alberto for her "helter-skelter accumulation of . . . the merchandise of culture" (168). Marguerite's own comments about her learning fall into the tradition of Americans in Italy, who feel that Europe epitomizes intellectual and moral experience unavailable in America.[13] Marguerite says to Alberto:

"[T]hese things [of culture] were part of your background from always. . . . We don't even know who we are any further than my grandparents, and you've got family trees right back to the thirteenth century. It's only with my parents that reading and writing and speaking correctly began for us. That's the difference between us!" (170)

Like Anna Giardino, Marguerite must become a student of her own life, investigating her desires and dreams in order to develop herself. Finally taking control of her theme on the multiple meanings of the word "grossness," Marguerite must have faith in her ability to overcome her fear of running out of ink: "'Don't worry that you're not given enough to write your theme. No matter how little you seemed to have been given, it will be enough'" (18). Dr. Verdile's assurances encourage Marguerite to write her way home to her grandmother. Beginning with the grandmother assures Marguerite of the necessity of retracing her lineage through the female line. Directly following the imperative of the prologue—"'[S]tart with your grandmother'"—Barolini literally begins with her section on Umbertina, holding off Marguerite's story until part 2. The novel attests to Barolini's personal decision to recreate her grandmother's existence, but she does not allow such success for her fictional character Marguerite Morosini.

Had Barolini not written *Umbertina*, perhaps she might have lost her way and remained uncommitted to her artistic goals.[14] Though analysis provided Marguerite time for reflection about inner strife, she was unable to apply her moments of powerful lucidity in any sustained manner in her daily life. She neither attained the kind of permanence of place that her parents maintained by staying home nor the kind of internal harmony that Alberto possessed, despite frequent moves between Italy and America.

Marguerite's failure may be attributed to internal weakness of character and to a marital and familial situation indifferent to her needs. Failing to internalize the injunction to recover her past and find her place in the world, Marguerite instead reverts to an iron pattern in her life: defining herself against another's needs. Her final years (she is in her forties) are filled with the passion she has for a lover much younger than Alberto, a writer whose aspiration for the Strega Literary Prize supersedes every other consideration in his life.[15] Marguerite strayed from her goal of understanding her life by recovering her grandmother. Defining herself solely through another, Marguerite lends painful truth to her daughter's realization that her mother "wasn't strong enough to be herself" (341).

Only in part 3 does the reader discover the profound significance of Marguerite's memory of the "pursy-mouthed refrain of her convent-school days. 'Who pays the fiddler? . . . The girl pays the fiddler'" (267). After Marguerite's lover has lost the coveted Strega Award, the fundamental meaning of the convent-school warning comes to fruition, reinforcing Marguerite's gendered position. Pregnant with Massimo's child, abortion dangerous and illegal in Italy, Marguerite's death in a car crash driving over the mountains is less accident than suicide. In Marguerite's life, the fallen woman dies and her "favorite escape hatch" of self-punishment is less a choice than a pattern reinforced by the culture.

Tina's coming-of-age rests on her ability to resume her mother's failed journey. Marguerite's death represents what Rachel Blau DuPlessis calls the "rightful end" of women in romance plots: "*Bildung* and romance could not coexist and be integrated for the heroine at the resolution." Though DuPlessis is referring to nineteenth-century fiction, Marguerite's narrative scenario parallels the nineteenth-century plot in that her quest is "set aside or repressed" by marriage and ultimately by death (1, 3, 4). Barolini focuses her final section of the narrative trilogy on Marguerite's firstborn daughter, Tina, integrating both feminist and ethnic projects.

First, like other twentieth-century women writers, Barolini creates a character who is able "to solve the contradiction between love and quest," thereby revising the negative ending of her mother's life (DuPlessis 4). Second, by doing this, the daughter is concomitantly able to rediscover her cultural heritage and reconstruct her mother's fractured and incomplete life. Barolini's final section represents, then, the reconstruction of the ancestral past in which "the bare present is redeemed through genealogical enrichment," satisfying the project of ethnic trilogies (Boelhower, "The Ethnic Trilogy" 18).

In order to rediscover the originating source represented by her great-grandmother, Tina must reconnect with her mother, who has left her with an inheritance of confusion about her identity as an Italian American and as a woman. On the one hand, Tina recognizes how desirous she was to be just like her mother—"be like her, look like her"—but on the other hand, Tina recognizes well before she learns of her mother's pregnancy that she must not "end up" like her mother, tragically dead in her forties (276, 281). To discover her future goals as an Italian and an Italian American woman, Tina must solve the problems of her mother, revising Marguerite's decisions in her own life choices.

Just as Laura of *A Cup of the Sun* unknowingly sought her mother throughout her brief life, Marguerite searches for maternal sustenance in her husband and lover, though she never finds this. As Phyllis Chesler points out, "[M]ost women have 'lost'—or have never really 'had'—their mothers," and perhaps this feeling accounts for Marguerite's continual movement from one house to another, in America and in Italy (44). Her seeking takes her outside rather than inside the self; had Marguerite sustained her desire to reconnect with her grandmother, she might very well have identified her mourning as attributable to her search for the mother. Marguerite's search stems from a feeling of being "wildly unmothered," having grown up in a "male-controlled world" without the express support and approval of her mother (Rich, *Of Woman Born* 225). Though she momentarily identifies herself as the "Sicilian Persephone," it is *her* daughter Tina who goes down to Hades (southern Italy, specifically Calabria) and ultimately wends her way back to both mothers: Umbertina and Marguerite. Tina is able to articulate her confusion and thereby clarify it: "At the bottom of it all was her mother; her beloved, foolish, dead-and-gone mother" (357).[16]

When Tina reads the final entry of her mother's diary after Marguerite's fatal car accident, she learns that the probable cause of her mother's death was self-inflicted. Marguerite writes:

*Is this paying the goddam fiddler? Now I'm pregnant and it's Massimo's child and who else but me is going to pay? Now what? Ask him to leave his wife? . . . A backroom abortion? . . . What could I tell A.? What do women do in Italy . . . or anyplace? What is this terrible thing that happens to us in our bodies where we grow our own punishment, this living thing in our guts which is the proof of shame, guilt, sin, anger, frustration, lust.* (296)

Marguerite's suicide arises from the severity of her desperation. Though she claims a right to expression, she privatizes the experience within the diary. One might assume that Marguerite's Italian American heritage with its ingrained belief in *destino* would strongly dictate against suicide. However, Marguerite's lack of power as a woman further results in self-denial, this time to the point of annihilation. Female suicide attempts constitute "an essential act of resignation and helplessness" (Chesler 49). Marguerite's avenue of freedom from her body costs her no less than death.

As Marianne Hirsch explains, "nothing entangles women more firmly in their bodies than pregnancy, birth, lactation, miscarriage, or the inability to conceive" (*The Mother/Daughter Plot* 166). Marguerite pays the fiddler in order to disentangle herself from her body. Though no such generalization is finally possible, Adrienne Rich speculates that the choice of abortion, "legal or not, is harder psychically on women who have borne children than on a woman who has borne none" (*Of Woman Born* 268). Marguerite's "choice" to inflict punishment on herself reinforces her inability to claim an existence that embraces maternity without the conventional restrictions of marriage and monogamy.

Aware of the facts of her mother's tragic death, Tina is able to offer a "new reading" in light of her position as interpreter of the previous generations (Boelhower, "The Ethnic Trilogy" 16). Tina ironically describes her mother's death and subsequent cremation as her belated "walling off her own dependency on any man who would keep her from the fullness of her own life and expectations" (320). At first, Tina unthinkingly wants to destroy her mother's diaries. She fails initially to realize that in them is the history of so many women's lives, providing Tina with a story to interrogate and change. In order to fulfill her desire to "come out alive and whole," Tina rewrites her mother's life in three principal ways: she chooses abortion over an unwanted pregnancy; she marries outside her ethnic group without relinquishing her professional goals; and finally, she reunites with her great-grandmother, completing the narrative impetus of reconstruction.

Tina's own unwanted pregnancy recapitulates her mother's, but Tina's choice to abort calls into question what Carol Gilligan describes as "the opposition of selfishness and morality" (134). Seeing herself as capable of choice, Tina feels responsible for the abortion without feeling morally reprehensible. Marguerite could never completely separate self-assertion from selfishness, having internalized the notion that morality for women lies in self-sacrifice. Unable to accept her pregnancy as the positive fruition of her elemental dream about the word "grossness," Marguerite interprets her pregnancy in moral terms, that is, as a punishment for her infidelity.

Tina chooses to abort her child, thereby rewriting the script of self-sacrifice that determined her mother's actions. At the same time, during the procedure of abortion, Tina feels that she is "sharing with her mother for the first time the communion of womanhood" (327). Aware of the fact that the fiddler is the patriarchy, Tina recognizes her own female body as subjected to male authority. Paying the physician who performed the operation with money instead of with her life, Tina asserts her right to be a self divorced from the conventional role of motherhood. Barolini defines womanhood not only in terms of pregnancy and motherhood but also in terms of choice and responsibility. Tina learns that making a decision to have an abortion does not preclude her from experiencing the joys of passion or the virtue of responsibility.

Ultimately marrying an Anglo-American man, Tina overcomes the agonized conflicts that beset her mother when Marguerite chose to marry outside her culture. Waiting to marry until she launches her academic career, Tina enters a "mixed marriage" without feeling inferior or uncertain. In this way, Barolini rewrites the text of one of her sister writers, Mari Tomasi. Tomasi felt it necessary to disable her Anglo-American male character before he married Petra Dalli of *Like Lesser Gods*. In contrast, Barolini enables her female character, reinforcing Tina's strength by reuniting her with her maternal ancestor. Tina's coming-of-age is symbolized by her reconnection to her great-grandmother, begun in southern Italy and continued in her trip to Ellis Island. The matrimonial bedspread that Tina sees hanging at the Museum of Immigration augurs well the success of Tina's future: it symbolizes the beauty of the past and Tina's ongoing interpretation of its many pieces.

Barolini's *Umbertina* reiterates many of the concerns of the earlier novels by Italian American women writers, especially Tomasi's *Like Lesser Gods* in its dedication to exploring the first-generation immigrants who came to American shores. Committed to a thoroughgoing analysis of the impact of gender on women's development, Barolini extends and complicates the exploration of women's lives, aware of how each generation struggles in ways unique to their economic and social positions. The canvas on which Barolini writes is wide, traversing two countries and spanning four generations of Italian Americans. Umbertina's ubiquitous presence illustrates what Barolini explains is "the role of mythmaking in a family" (Interview, tape 1). The third-generation ideally reinterprets and reconstructs original ancestors, assuring parents of their virtuous intentions: "I am not swerving, Dad (or Mom). I am fulfilling Grandpa (or Grandma)!" (Sollors, *Beyond Ethnicity* 230).

Tina De Rosa's first novel, *Paper Fish*, provides another example of the way in which the grandmother figures so largely in the construction of a third-generation self. *Paper Fish* received the Illinois Arts Council Literary Award in 1980 for earlier published portions of the book.[17] De Rosa's novel represents a departure from the realism undergirding Barolini's text to the modernist strategies of nonchronology, interior monologue, and multiple perspectives that are more closely reminiscent of Bryant and Cavallo. Although De Rosa's complicated narrative structure differentiates it from such earlier novels as *Like Lesser Gods* and *No Steady Job for Papa*, *Paper Fish*, too, fictionalizes the world of Italian immigrants. Like Tomasi, Benasutti, Waldo, Hendin, and Barolini, De Rosa explores the meaning of being an ethnic American, but *Paper Fish*, like *Miss Giardino*, emphasizes to a lesser degree the desire to Americanize and instead concentrates primarily on accepting an Italian American selfhood as a final status. In narrative strategy, then, De Rosa compares more to Cavallo and Bryant, though De Rosa *maintains* the familial focus and the immigrant enclave throughout her novel.

Though she does not traverse two countries or structure her text around the operations of a trilogy as Barolini does, De Rosa innovatively employs many of the recurring themes basic to Italian American women's novels: the journey to America; the immigrant as literary protagonist; the Italian American enclave as setting; the relationship between generations; the young girl seeking an identity; and finally, the manifestation of illness within the family. The depiction of the excruciating voyage from homeland to new world is not literally documented in *Paper Fish* but nonetheless is emphasized as part of the ethnic memory of the eldest character in the novel, the paternal grandmother. Like Cavallo and Bryant, De Rosa skews the journey sequence in *Paper Fish*, making the grandmother's recollections serve a different purpose in her old age. Grandma Doria has already lived out to some extent the immigrant dream of achieving material comfort and autonomy. The fact that De Rosa intersperses the grandmother's memories with present events reinforces the usefulness of the past for Grandma Doria's granddaughter Carmolina, who uses her grandmother's memories of the homeland as the subjective topography for her own fertile imagination.

Examining primarily the ethnic neighborhood that is the setting for her novel, De Rosa deemphasizes the struggle to gain American status, muting this concern of so many immigrants. Instead, the characters in *Paper Fish* focus on accepting an ethnic selfhood as a final status. The tension between the immigrant family's quest to become American and their desire to retain Italian customs is often resolved in the third (or fourth, in the case of *Umbertina*) generation's allegiance to more than a symbolic ethnicity.[18] Unlike, for example, Waldo's *A Cup of the Sun* and Hendin's *The Right Thing to Do*, De Rosa's *Paper Fish* explores the connection between generations rather than, as often occurs, the conflict between immigrant parents who hold tenaciously onto Italian mores and the American child whose education often forces compliance with another set of standards. *Paper Fish* avoids this characteristic confrontation between *la famiglia* and public education by deflating the importance of the American culture's claim upon the unassimilated immigrant. De Rosa achieves this primarily through a nonchronological narrative that tells crossing and intersecting stories from the perspectives of four generations of characters, including the great-grandparents in Italy, entirely imagined by De Rosa.[19] De Rosa reconstructs a family history that reflects and reiterates its own poignant connections to one another. Unlike Barolini, De Rosa did not travel to Italy or examine archival materials for her novel. Of Italy, De Rosa says, "'I still haven't been there. I could always imagine Italy because I heard so many stories about it from my grandmother and from the people in the old neighborhood'" ("An Interview" 23).

De Rosa incorporates a journey narrative, exploring a young girl's search for an identity. Novels written by Italian American women have often challenged the emphasis on the individual quest for an identity that necessitates exclusion from the family. De Rosa's *Paper Fish* is no exception. Her ancestry as immediate and vital as her present thoughts, Carmolina hungrily listens to her grandmother, who has given her, as De Rosa puts it, "an entire mythology" ("An Interview" 23). De Rosa's third chapter, "The Family," conflates familial events from several generations of the BellaCasa clan, but not in an attempt to paint a happy picture of the unity of their lives, for happiness is foreign to them. Rather, De Rosa demonstrates structurally the interconnectedness and interpenetration between generations, weaving a complex pattern, which the characters cannot fully comprehend.

It will be Carmolina's responsibility to decipher the complex code of the BellaCasa family, her grandmother passing down the family heritage to her granddaughter. Although such inheritors sometimes feel incapable, the young characters in De Rosa's *Paper Fish*, Barolini's *Umbertina*, and Cavallo's *A Bridge of Leaves* are empowered by their ancestor's strength and enter adulthood with the legacy of memory from which they gain sustenance and the power of words. The reader participates in *Paper Fish* as though decoding a palimpsest, a multilayered text in which all the events are revivified and transformed by the characters' memories, each memory to be read vis-à-vis the memory before, the memory after, and the memory within the memory itself.

Recurring with disturbing frequency in the novels discussed thus far is the manifestation of illness. Writers such as Tomasi, Waldo, and Hendin incorporate the topic of illness both as a realistic comment on the prevalence of suffering in poor communities and as a metaphor for the immigrant experience of living in a world indifferent or hostile toward newcomers. De Rosa fits into this tradition of using illness as an actual and metaphorical element in the text, but she diverges from the tradition because the suffering character in *Paper Fish* is not shunted off to a sanatorium, nor does the character get well or die as the sick characters do in *Like Lesser Gods*, *A Cup of the Sun*, and *The Right Thing to Do*. Though it is true that immigrant Italians in America were traditionally resistant to the idea of institutionalizing family members,[20] ill characters in the above novels do not *remain* an insistent influence on the developing formation of a girl character. In contrast, the first daughter, Doriana, remains a compelling influence on her younger sister, Carmolina, in *Paper Fish*.

As we have seen, Cavallo's *A Bridge of Leaves* and Bryant's *Miss Giardino* use the topic of illness to probe into the psyche, but their works' emphasis, unlike De Rosa's, is on reintegrating the self by expelling, even exorcising, the illnesses that afflict their characters. In De Rosa's novel, Doriana does not get well or die. She survives. She is not weak because she is sick, nor is she strong. *Paper Fish* explores how Doriana's illness affects every family member and how illness is not peripheral to their lives, to be cast out at all costs. De Rosa seems to be suggesting, powerfully, that illness *is*.

*Paper Fish* revolves around the lives of the BellaCasa family, second-generation Italian Americans living in an Italian ghetto on Chicago's west side during the mid-1940s. The novel is divided into six parts, with a prelude and epilogue framing the sections. The prelude is told from the voice of the BellaCasa's second daughter, Carmolina, who has not yet been born: "I am less than a fraction, the smallest fraction of time, of moment, of memory" (8).[21] The narrative then shifts to third person in part 1, though the voice might very well be a matured Carmolina, who has "solved the mystery" of her ethnicity advanced in De Rosa's epigraph:

> Our images and our memories
> face each other,
> bewildered,
> in a mirror.
> Who is to solve the mystery?

As discussed in several of the novels (*No Steady Job for Papa*, *A Cup of the Sun*, and *A Bridge of Leaves*, especially), the mirror is used as a metaphor for ordering the confusions of the self and the family within the Italian American household. As an ethnic symbol, the mirror functions to legitimate and reinforce the struggles of the developing character, who is painfully aware of the demands inherent in maintaining a dual heritage.

Jenijoy La Belle explains that looking-glass scenes in women's writing reveal "an intimate and significant relationship between the mirror and a woman's conception of what she is, . . . and what she will become. . . . [I]t is necessary to look in the glass to see how one is doing in the process of constantly reinventing the self" (2, 17). La Belle's employment of the word "reinventing" possesses special meaning for De Rosa's *Paper Fish* because of the novel's emphasis on Italian American identity. De Rosa's use of the pronoun "our" in her epigraph complicates the mirror scene for Carmolina because her reinvention of the self is not only connected to her growth into womanhood but also to her acceptance of *la famiglia* as integral to her Italian American identity. An "instrument for self-possession and creation," the mirror as it is portrayed through the lens of ethnicity deepens and complicates the puzzle of identity (La Belle 20). De Rosa's use of the mirror in her epigraph imposes order upon the confusion at the same time that it reinforces the meaning(s) of being Italian American.

Although the multidimensional narrative of *Paper Fish* resists simple summary, basic details are needed for an overview of the narrative. Part 1, "The Memory," recalls the marriage and the lives of Sarah and Marco BellaCasa, parents of two daughters, Doriana and Carmolina. The chapter also chronicles the childhood memories of the paternal grandmother, Doria, who presently lives in her own home across the alley. In part 2, "Summer, 1949—Late July," Carmolina has run away from home. The efforts of the neighborhood people, from the street vendors to the old Italian women dressed in black, constitute a metaphorical search party for the lost eight-year-old girl. The section concludes with a family meeting in the kitchen of Sarah BellaCasa, though Grandma Doria most dominates the scene. Part 3, "The Family," recalls and further develops Grandma Doria's early married life, Marco's marriage to Sarah, and the fire that burns down the BellaCasa home, forcing pregnant Sarah to jump out of the two-story bedroom window.[22]

Part 4, "Summer, 1949—Early June," details the lives of the neighborhood people and Carmolina's interest in the wandering gypsies. Doriana's illness is dramatized by stubbornness, fits, and violence, which precipitates a family meeting about institutionalizing her, though financially and emotionally this proves to be impossible. The occurrence of the family discussion is threatening to Carmolina, since she does not fully recognize the extent of her sister's illness. Carmolina only believes that what might happen to her beautiful, doll-like sister might also happen to her. To prevent their conversation from continuing, Carmolina forces herself to get sick, breaking up the family meeting "into little pieces" and beating her "fists against the toilet seat" (80).

Part 5, "Summer, 1949—Late July," focuses chiefly on Carmolina's actual journey on the streetcar alone. She runs away from home and ends up in an unfamiliar neighborhood, unfriendly to Italians. Doriana, as though cognizant of Carmolina's absence, suffers from a high fever. While gone, Carmolina recalls conversations that she and Grandma Doria have had, which clarify her understanding of herself and Doriana's illness. When returned to her home by the police, Carmolina is suffering from a fever akin to her older sister's.

Part 6, "Summer, 1958," moves ahead nine years and ends in a ritual ceremony between the aged Grandma Doria and seventeen-year-old Carmolina. This scene symbolizes Carmolina's coming-of-age and suggests her acceptance of the legacy of selfhood bequeathed to her by her grandmother. Early in the novel, De Rosa anticipates Carmolina's continuing struggle to negotiate her connection between her adult self and the family by depicting the future estrangement between Carmolina and her mother, Sarah:

When the child grew to be a woman, she never let herself get sick, but stayed enormously healthy . . . because the mother was no longer there to comfort her. . . . [T]hat mother would die when the child grew up, that magical lady with the wonderful hair who cared so much would die when the child grew to be an adult and a strange old woman would take her place, . . . a strange old lady who had . . . mysterious old eyes would kill the young mother with the wonderful black hair and the child would never see its mother again, its mother would never again tiptoe oh so softly into the bedroom with the magical barley soup to make her well again and the little girl, oh how the little girl would miss her all of her life. (23–24)

As Adrienne Rich writes, "this cathexis between mother and daughter—essential, distorted, misused—is the great unwritten story" (*Of Woman Born* 225). By including this scene early in the narrative, De Rosa reinforces the continuous nature of Carmolina's journey, for the adult woman will search for the mother—through memory and reinvention of ethnic identity—into her future. In *Paper Fish*, De Rosa concentrates on developing a crucial strand of the mother-daughter cathexis, that between grandmother and granddaughter. The narrative impetus of reconstruction for Carmolina is to carry forward her grandmother's stories and, through the power of language, recover the mother.

The journey motif is interwoven with other themes in *Paper Fish*: Carmolina's personal development; the relationship between generations; and Doriana's illness. Used metaphorically in the novel, the motif of the journey deemphasizes the literal migration to the new world and instead legitimizes the uses of memory in retelling the tale of beginnings. Like Grandma Doria's people in Italy, memory in *Paper Fish* has its "own way of remembering" (25). The grandmother's memories of the booted country serve as a running commentary on her allegiance to the imagination. Along with the old-world cultural objects surrounding Grandma Doria's life in America is the keen memory of the past with her sister, Sabatina, and her parents in a small Neapolitan town. This memory is as present in the grandmother's mind as is her immediate life as a widow in America. Doria reinvests memory with new meaning when she tells stories about her past to her granddaughter Carmolina. The prevalence of storytelling in Doria's southern Italian family is affirmed by Carmella, Doria's mother, who tells tales of the roaming gypsies in Italy. Doria's appreciation of the beautiful but terrifying outsiders is not lost on Sabatina, the frightened recipient of Doria's storytelling.

The potency of this old-world image of the potentially dangerous but fascinating gypsy is carried on in the third generation of the BellaCasa family through Carmolina, whose own interest in gypsies is fired by her grandmother's stories and by their appearance in empty storefronts in her neighborhood. What precipitates Carmolina's decision to run away is both her reenactment of Doria's girlhood wish to join a circus and Carmolina's own fear of being sent away as she thinks her sister, Doriana, will be. Carmolina thus metaphorically and literally resumes the journey that her grandmother longed to take as a young, imaginative girl. Just as Tina continues her mother's unfinished journey in *Umbertina*, so, too, will Carmolina reconnect with her mother on her journey away from home.

Surely Doria's literal voyage to America far exceeds in scope her youthful yearning to join a circus, but it does not diminish the significance of telling tales of wandering gypsies, a tradition that is passed down generationally from mother to daughter:

> The unborn, the never-seen, populated the trees, the small stone paths, and the stories of these astounded Doria. Creatures which had never existed lurked in the tales of her mother, Carmella, lurked in her words, in the catches of her voice. They peered out of their red eyes at the small child listening. (28–29)

The spectacular creatures of Grandma Doria's tales are quintessentially marginal but compelling in their mystery, their wandering natures, and their capacity for survival. The grandmother passes on these stories to Carmolina, who is imaginatively sustained by them: "And Grandma was making the world for her, between her shabby old fingers. She was telling Carmolina about Italy, about the land that got lost across the sea" (21). De Rosa affirms the importance of storytelling to the illiterate peasants of the *Mezzogiorno*, whose memories are sharpened by the repeating nature of their oral traditions.

Carmolina resumes the journey begun by her grandmother, but De Rosa initially undercuts the actual occurrence of Carmolina's disappearance by placing the event early in the text with minimal development or commentary (part 2). Of greater concern in part 2 is De Rosa's description of Carmolina's precocity as a seven-year-old whose adeptness with language allows her to use words as a defense against being misunderstood: "When Carmolina was seven years old, she read about Leonardo da Vinci, how he wrote everything backwards" (36). In this section, De Rosa introduces another activity in which right and left are reversed, like looking in a mirror. Both types of signs, La Belle explains, "are difficult to decipher and show an unsettling dissonance between signifier and signified" (121).

Carmolina mimics the Italian artist's literary strategy by writing words in reverse on a white bag of bakery bread, an action suggesting her access to literary creativity in the midst of everyday reality: bringing home fresh bread after Sunday mass. Her parents, at first, cannot read the text: "You have to use a mirror," Carmolina teaches them, "and when they read the message, This bread brought to you courtesy of Carmolina BellaCasa, their smiles were uneasy" (36). Carmolina's deliberate inscrutability makes the parents of Doriana uneasy, but the "dissonance" apparent in her coded writing reveals important dimensions of Carmolina's young character.

Carmolina betrays an early awareness of the capacity of words to strengthen the self. This emerges not only from her hearing stories told but also from reading about a northern Italian artist. Like Barolini, De Rosa embraces both northern and southern Italian cultures, imaginatively connecting written and oral traditions. Carmolina's development as a writer occurs through listening to and reading about her culture of heritage, not about what the American public school dictates. Intuiting her parents' fear of her difference, Carmolina paradoxically protects herself from being misunderstood by writing in code. Fearing that close proximity between the sisters will negatively affect Carmolina's developing consciousness, the parents begin to talk about separating the children, who share a bedroom: "[T]hey were afraid . . . that she was spending too much time with her sister, that the disease would spread" (36). The fact that Carmolina writes in reverse on the paper bag suggests her need to protect herself from being known by others, including her parents, who might too readily identify her with her older sister, an identification perceived by the family negatively. The BellaCasa's use of the word "disease" can be interpreted to define not only Doriana's mental debilitation but also their own enormous feeling of uneasiness about Doriana's illness.

That Carmolina unequivocally accepts and loves Doriana does not make her immune from her parents' surveillance or from the neighbors who say that "Carmolina had stolen the brains of her sister, who ever heard of a four-year-old girl making up stories the way she did" (62). Recognizing early in life that something is "wrong in the house" (18), Carmolina is deprived of the regular forms of childhood play, such as talking out loud to herself and to her dolls, activities perceived with trepidation by the confused parents of Doriana (77–78). As a result, storytelling becomes Carmolina's plaything; she begins to tell "herself the stories her mind made up. Her mind made stories like toys, she could wind them up and watch them, they buzzed and jerked and made music" (77). As La Belle explains, "almost any type of crisis, but particularly a personal loss or even fear of loss, seems to initiate in many female characters a powerful need for literal, as much as mental, reflection" (100). Both activities—storytelling and mirror gazing—reveal Carmolina's fear of losing her sister and her desire to control that fear. The mirror metaphor clarifies Carmolina's reality: she writes words in reverse both as a protection and as an elucidation of the self. Her parents must decipher Carmolina's text/self in order to understand that she is *not* ill like her sister, but they sometimes misread her needs.

For example, although Carmolina's father is a policeman trained in seeking out clues to solve problems, he cannot find his lost daughter.[23] Though he thinks he spots her in his rearview mirror "waving at him from behind her dark eyes," Carmolina, out of her fear of being sent away, has made herself untranslatable: "She was talking backwards to him in the mirror, he could not understand the words" (38). De Rosa extends the mirror metaphor to include Marco's extreme vulnerability in the face of loss: his throat is made of "glass" as he shouts out Carmolina's name in the dark; "the houses staggered past him broken and backward in his eyes" (36). More often than not in *Paper Fish*, the glass is broken, thus indicating the broken lives of the family and the Italian community at large, whose men dig their hands into the dirt beside the curbstones to find "no olives, only chips of glass" (49). For Carmolina, the mirror acts as a metaphor for ordering what she accurately perceives to be the disorder in her family, originating in and exacerbated by her sister's illness. Carmolina bravely imposes order on a fragile identity as a protection against losing it altogether. The inverse imagery acquires fuller significance when Carmolina leaves home.

During Carmolina's journey away from home, she invokes her grandmother's presence when creating stories about the strangers she encounters. For example, the old man with a white pushcart "probably built the wagon at night, after the death of his wife, to save himself from loneliness, Grandma would say" (101). Carmolina's kind of creativity parallels the internal thoughts of another ethnic character of high modernism: David Schearl of Henry Roth's *Call It Sleep* (1934). In his introduction to the republication of Roth's novel, Alfred Kazin describes David Schearl as "the artist as a very small boy" (xviii). In De Rosa's novel, Carmolina is the developing artist, the small girl who uses stories to explore and legitimate her life. Like David in *Call It Sleep*, Carmolina runs away from home and delves below the everyday, reconstructing reality from the inside out. In contrast to Roth's novel, however, *Paper Fish* does not limit the scope of perception to one character; rather, each character's perception of reality, however confused and indeterminate, is the thrust of this novel. Carmolina's imaginative capacity gives her the courage to continue her exploration into the self.

Toward the end of her journey away from home, Carmolina, now hungry and feverish, enters a surrealistic realm represented by the italicized section of staccato-like prose that mimics Carmolina's increasingly confused state of mind:

> *Night. A blink. An eye moving. Whose eye? A twist of the hand, fingers grip the dark, the dark has the hands of a skeleton. Hair falling into her eyes. Flash of red tennis shoes on hot pavement. . . . The eyes blink. Head jerks upwards. . . . The eye shifts. Streets weave. . . . Someone turned the world upside down and shook out all the people. Nowhere to go. . . . Dawn. The sun is an eye, staring through sun-blood. A cobweb moves in the air. . . . It is a very fine cobweb. . . . The rain slashes down like tiny knives and cuts apart the cobweb in her hands.* (104)

Carmolina's world has been reduced to a grim, mechanistic activity, where nature itself is indifferent to the beauty of the cobweb described at the end of the excerpt. The spider's web is destroyed by rain that "slashes down like tiny knives," an image of pain and vulnerability, much like Carmolina's own position as a displaced person. The scene also recalls an episode with Doriana crawling in a closet "under dead dresses," snatching and eating spiders, to the horror of her mother. In both instances, something beautiful has been destroyed: Doriana, although lovely, has been damaged by a debility that renders her voiceless and misunderstood. Carmolina's nightmarish trek in an unfamiliar neighborhood makes her susceptible to her own fears of being sick and sent away: "[I]t seemed to her that her mind just blinked away sometimes and forgot to listen, but it always came back, so no one could say it was gone for good" (104). The destroyed cobweb suggests each girl's fear of imminent separation from the other at the same time that it reinforces their interweaving lives.

It is no accident that after this nightmarish episode, Carmolina enters a drugstore, mesmerized by "her own reflection in the apothecary jar" (105). The mirror metaphor here solidifies the connection between Carmolina and illness and, as a result, the impossibility of discussing Carmolina without emphasizing Doriana's impact on her younger sister. In the drugstore, Carmolina recalls two revelatory childhood memories. Both illuminate the extent to which illness has pervaded Carmolina's young life. Moreover, both memories also demonstrate Carmolina's need to gain emotional distance from the family in order to understand her placement within it, a quest akin to Niobe Bartoli's in *A Cup of the Sun*. Both writers portray female characters who develop into mature adults; aware of the crises that beset them as children, they are also capable of maintaining their devotion to the family. Neither Niobe nor Carmolina desires utter emotional detachment from the family; rather, they gain the perception that comes with private reflection and the use of memory.

In her first memory in the drugstore, Carmolina recalls her violent act of destroying her stuffed doll, Maryalice, in an uncontrollable frenzy of anger (109).[24] Carmolina's attempt to kill the doll reveals her subconscious desire to obliterate Doriana's illness, which renders her doll-like with a face "like porcelain, like the face of a porcelain Madonna" (73). The fragility apparent in this image is doubly reinforced, first by De Rosa's recurring image of glass easily shattered and second by the image of the Madonna, the central figure of Italian Catholicism in the *Mezzogiorno*.

In her state of catatonia, Laura of *A Bridge of Leaves* is compared to a life-sized Virgin just as Doriana's face resembles the Madonna, though the comparisons in both cases are not quite exact. Like Laura, Doriana is a broken doll, a sick Madonna, perhaps another reflection of the diminished efficacy of Catholicism for Italians in America. Doriana cannot be discarded or put back together again like Carmolina's doll, Maryalice. On her hands and knees, Sarah silently picks up the stuffing from the doll, perhaps thinking, as she does in another context with Doriana, "[Y]ou look into your pockets, and there is only a spool of thread and some needles" (107). Sarah is a mother who mends without materials. Though she is Lithuanian in ethnicity, like her Italian husband and family, she, too, has become a specialist in survival.[25]

To reinforce Sarah's inability to offer sustenance of healing value to her sick daughter, De Rosa's third-person narrator recalls a scene of breast-feeding during one of Doriana's high fevers, when she is nine years old:

> She hauled the weight of the sleeping child into her arms, moved across the floor like a cripple, locked the front door, pulled the chain across the door. . . . "This is a secret," she whispered to Doriana. "You are never to tell anyone." . . . Doriana opened her mouth again, closed it over her mother's breast. . . . In her sleep, Doriana sucked the dry breast. (108)

De Rosa's inclusion of this scene within the chapter on Carmolina's journey away from home further reinforces Sarah's centrality as a nurturing figure, despite the futility of her gesture. Like her mother, Carmolina will have to learn how to love and nurture her sister without hoping to make her well. Carmolina's several uncompleted phone calls to her mother during her absence anticipates Carmolina's future investment in the efficacy of memory to sustain the love the daughter once felt from the mother, despite its absence in adulthood. The adult Carmolina will be able to recall the mother's voice, filling her "like warm water" (108).

The destroyed cobweb, the mangled doll, and the broken glass all emphasize the physical and psychological pain in the BellaCasa family. The family's confusion about Doriana's illness and Carmolina's disappearance is illustrated by another example of the mirror-image employed in the prelude: "My family was left with glass eyes." This image verges on the grotesque in another scene where Carmolina watches Mrs. Schiavone at the butcher shop decapitate a chicken, whose "lifeless head stared out of its baffled eyes, . . . like a doll with eyes of glass" (8, 68). These images suggest the family's inability to understand the disorder affecting their lives. Grandma Doria, however, orders the difficult reality by telling stories to explain the confusion, reinstituting her longtime allegiance to oral traditions. Carmolina's second memory, in fact, recalls a conversation that she has with her grandmother. Their talk serves as a commentary on Carmolina's first memory and a clarification of Doriana's position in the family.

De Rosa again uses the journey motif as Grandma Doria's method of explaining her first grandchild's illness: "'Doriana she get lost in the forest. . . . We no know where. We try to find her. We still try to find her. . . . We never stop looking'" (111). Grandma Doria retells the story of beginnings for Doriana by using an extended metaphor of the forest. De Rosa translates the grandmother's Italian by using an Italian American dialect:

> "In the forest the birds are. Ah, such beautiful birds. . . . Blue and pink. Doriana she go into the forest to look at the birds. The birds they sing in the trees, they sing, they turn into leaves. Doriana she have a key to the forest. It a secret. Only Doriana know where she keep the key. One day Doriana go into the forest. She forget the key. She get lost in the forest." (112)

Although the family never knows precisely how Doriana becomes sick, they each have their own perceptions. Grandma Doria attributes her granddaughter's illness to the fire in the BellaCasa house when Sarah was pregnant with Doriana. Sarah attributes her daughter's illness to the severe fever that turned her baby's face blue. Either way, Doriana's "'face it turn hot like a little peach and she scream and try to get out the forest.'" Doria uses the image of the forest to reinforce her namesake's internal struggle to "come home." The forest, located "behind her eyes," also parallels the experience of the Italian immigrants themselves who struggle to find a sense of place after leaving the homeland: "'When you fight to come home, you beautiful'" (112).

The scene between grandmother and granddaughter is so deeply etched in Carmolina's memory that when she comes out of her second reverie in the drugstore she blinks and feels "Grandma sitting in her eyes" (112). Carmolina's journey away from home cements her relationship with her sister; each girl suffers from an illness in each other's *absence*. Sarah correctly interprets Doriana's high fever as a reaction to Carmolina's disappearance, a voiceless plea for her sister's company. Sarah's comment "'I think she knows Carmolina's gone'" is dismissed by Marco's painfully ironic reply: "'That's crazy. . . . This whole family has gone stark staring nuts'" (114).

When Carmolina is returned home by the police, disoriented and feverish, she is convinced that they have taken Doriana away. Her ostensibly illogical thought—"they had sent the real Doriana away a long time ago"—reflects Carmolina's burgeoning understanding of her sister's illness, an understanding that sounds much like Grandma Doria's (118). In reuniting the sisters, De Rosa recognizes the vital significance of family in forming Carmolina's identity. Though the sisters suffer a similar illness in each other's absence, they are not mirror images of each other. Carmolina's ability to mature will of necessity separate her from her older sister, but such independence does not signify Carmolina's lack of acceptance of her sister. Carmolina's coming-of-age depends primarily upon her connection to her ancestral past, especially to her aging grandmother.

In part 6, De Rosa creatively depicts an immigrant marriage that highlights Carmolina's growth into adulthood. Although the ritual of marriage has been conventionally portrayed as a heterosexual union, De Rosa redefines its meaning from an ethnic and feminist perspective. Grandma Doria, aware that she is dying, realizes that she will not live to see Carmolina married. As a result, Doria requests to see Carmolina dressed "in the gown of a bride, but she was not a bride" (124). De Rosa is parodying the traditional wedding ceremony, but she is doing so as an experimental writer, not as a satirist. The ensuing private ceremony between grandmother and granddaughter poignantly depicts Carmolina's painful acceptance of her grandmother's imminent death and her future calling as the artist of reinvention: of her Italian American family and the dying Little Italy in which she was born and raised.

De Rosa reinforces the vital relationship between generations by employing a series of parallels that focus on Grandma Doria's and Carmolina's final preparations before the ceremony. The author once again employs the image of the mirror to emphasize the similarities between both women, who talk to themselves in front of it. For Grandma Doria, the mirror shows her the face of a paper fish—"'and all the scales, they fall'" (123).[26] Images of age and decay are also present when Doria sees the face of her mother, Carmella, in the mirror, thus forecasting her coming death and her reunion with her own mother.[27] At peace with the idea of dying, Grandma Doria warns her reflection that death will have to wait—"'First I go see Carmolina,'" her mother's namesake (124).

Carmolina's image in the mirror reflects the confusion she feels as a young woman who will inevitably enter adulthood without her cherished grandmother. De Rosa describes the mirror as "soundless" to suggest that the young woman cannot yet name her confusion. When the procession begins outdoors—Doria's two sons carry her in her mahogany chair because of the pain in her feet—the neighborhood people witness the ceremony and validate its significance by their very presence.[28] During the outdoor procession, Carmolina remains inside her parents' home, looking at herself in the mirror in an attempt to negotiate an acceptable identity. In a small portion of the mirror sits Doriana, holding a doll with a porcelain face, symbolizing the reality of her life. The fact that the older sister can be seen only out of a small corner of the mirror suggests Carmolina's growth as an individual distinct from Doriana, but Carmolina needs the intercession of a stronger, though failing, Madonna figure to complete the image she has of herself.

The significance of memory remains integral to this chapter as Grandma Doria stands back and "remembers" Carmolina's girlhood and ends her reverie by giving her granddaughter a reminder of the impetus that allowed Carmolina to take the journey away from home on the streetcar: "Grandma slipped the handkerchief with the coins knotted into it into Carmolina's hands. 'My little gypsy,' she whispered" (128). The coins symbolize Carmolina's journey into a future without the actual presence of her grandmother, a fact that she initially denies by saying, "'You're not dying.'" In the final gesture of letting go, Grandma Doria, like the father at a wedding ceremony, gives Carmolina away, not to someone else, but to herself. The grandmother forces Carmolina to look at herself in the mirror with the final injunction, "'Now it you turn. You keep the fire inside you.' Carmolina looked into the mirror's silver face. It gave back to her her own face" (130). By doubling the possessive pronoun, De Rosa signals a transition into adulthood that will always include the duality inherent in Carmolina's position as an Italian American.[29]

Grandma Doria's final words to Carmolina reaffirm what De Rosa has called "the passion, the heat, the vitality, the love, and fierce pride of who we are at heart," qualities De Rosa believes are rare commodities in a country "where the highest emotional charge comes from the falling of the Dow Jones average" ("An Italian-American Woman Speaks Out" 39, 38). Like David in *A Bridge of Leaves* and Tina in *Umbertina*, Carmolina has been given her grandmother's life force. The fact that Carmolina's own face is reflected in the mirror (without the shadow of Doriana or the reflection of her grandmother, who had stood next to her) reinforces Carmolina's acceptance of death and her role as an Italian American woman who will keep the fire inside her through the process of reconstruction.

Though they differ in their stylistic approaches to the topics of ethnicity and gender, Barolini and De Rosa are committed to reinterpreting the past through the third-generation daughter, who speaks for the original ancestor. The principle of recovery governs both novels and the Italian American novelistic tradition in general, for all the writers in this book are dedicated to historicizing and thereby legitimating their cultural pasts.

# 5 *Recent Developments in Italian American Women's Literary Traditions*

The topic of ethnicity has continued to inspire the writers of the 1980s and 1990s. The ways in which they inscribe ethnicity in their works reveals the resiliency of the topic itself. For example, the relationship between cultural and sexual identity becomes thematically relevant to such novels as Dodici Azpadu's *Saturday Night in the Prime of Life* (1983) and Rachel Guido deVries's *Tender Warriors* (1986). The paucity of literature about homosexual existence in Italian American families reveals an acceptance of normative heterosexual relations as the viable area of investigation. Historians and sociologists of Italian American folkways and behavior have tended to categorize as deviant and unacceptable all behavior not in keeping with family honor.

As late as 1985, Colleen Leahy Johnson examined the Italian American family in Syracuse, New York, discussing areas such as aging, marriage, intermarriage, and family conflict, but never once did she broach the subject of homosexuality (*Growing Up and Growing Old in Italian-American Families*). Harriet Perry earlier analyzed the most identifiable roles of Italian immigrant women: girl-child, spinster, wife, widow, nun, and whore. Each role is "culturally prescribed and proscribed, with a relatively narrow intermediate area of optional behaviour" (223). Because Perry limits her examination of behaviors to what sociologists recognize as roles available to females, she omits discussing behaviors that are not merely unacceptable but also are in direct defiance of patriarchal norms.[1]

Literary treatments of disturbing topics such as mental illness, incest, and family violence have made their way into the novels of Italian American women. In the 1980s, writers such as Azpadu and deVries further broke the imposition of *omertà* by incorporating into their family narratives a lesbian daughter who is forced to leave the Italian American household because of her love of women. These novels are distinct from the lesbian coming-out novel in their devotion to the Italian American family. The lesbian daughter is either reintegrated into or remains marginalized by the family of origin.

Another way writers have maintained an interest in cultural identity without making the Italian family the impetus of their narratives is through the continued inclusion of features of *italianità*: the *Pietà* at the 1964 World's Fair and the submerged Italian American ethnicity of the grandparents in Carole Maso's *Ghost Dance* (1986); the father's six-inch bust of Verdi and sibling solidarity in Agnes Rossi's *The Quick: A Novella and Stories* (1992). These texts are multidimensional in their focus on thematic worlds outside the Italian American family. Nonetheless, both Maso and Rossi mourn the loss of parents and relatives; in doing so, features of Italian American culture rise to the surface. Perhaps one of the recurring themes of the 1980s and 1990s in the writings by Italian Americans is the elegiac note they sound for first- or second-generation parents and grandparents who have died or are now quite old. Both Maso and Rossi write from the perspective of third-generation daughters; like De Rosa and Hendin, they mourn the loss of a grandparent or parent, who represents the culture of the ancestors.

Finally, an interest in the viability of ethnicity as a source and subject of American literature can be seen in the recent publication of short story collections, especially Rita Ciresi's *Mother Rocket* (1993), Anne Calcagno's *Pray for Yourself and Other Stories* (1993), and Renée Manfredi's *Where Love Leaves Us* (1994). In each of these books, references are made to things Italian, such as food, the Madonna, the saints, *il mal'occhio*, *l'ordine della famiglia*, and *il destino*. Also, the use of puns and repeated references to mirrors reinforce the thematic importance of cultural identity in the characters' lives. Each collection features at least one story that focuses either directly on Italian American ethnicity or on cultural identity as a means to understanding the self in the modern world.

Ethnic identity continues to influence the narratives written by Italian American women. Having broken through the code of silence, the writers neither cast off cultural background as a provocative area of literary treatment nor solely utilize the story of Italian America as the means to explore the development of the self. The following discussion will offer ways of reading cultural identity as inscribed in the works of recent writers.

## Coming Out as Lesbian in Italian America

In her introduction to *Inside/Out: Lesbian Theories, Gay Theories*, Diana Fuss explains that sexual identity is "less a matter of final discovery than perpetual reinvention," an explanation that parallels the porous nature of ethnicity itself (7). Italian American writers have at times characterized father figures as incapable of accepting the changing nature of their positions as Italians in America, imposing inhibitive rules on their children that only serve to alienate them further. Deviations from prescribed behavior have the potential to isolate a person from the family, especially a woman. Laura of *A Cup of the Sun*, Gina of *The Right Thing to Do*, and Marguerite of *Umbertina* are each separated from their families of origin and risk further isolation from the community because of their unacceptable behavior according to the standards of *la famiglia*: having sex before marriage, getting an abortion, being unfaithful, for example. Although Gina in particular faces physical abuse from her father, what becomes more problematic for these characters is the family's and community's potential ability to ignore their existence, to isolate them from society. When this happens, as it does for Laura, the family and community effectively "kill" her symbolically. According to ethnologist Maureen J. Giovannini, such a symbolic killing is "often a more effective deterrent to deviance than is violence" (329).

Italian American lesbians risk such a symbolic killing when they act upon their desires. As much as they want to be nurtured by their ancestral legacies, characters depicted as lesbian in Italian American texts learn that they must revise the patriarchal norms that guided their development. For Italian Americans, codes of *omertà* and *onore* in support of *l'ordine della famiglia* require subordination of the individual to the family and of any member deviating from family solidarity. Motherhood, within the bounds of conventional heterosexual marriage, is the expectation placed on Italian American women. To pronounce *viva voce* that one is a lesbian not only places one outside the perimeters of the family but also effectually locks one out. For gays and lesbians, however, "coming out," announcing their gayness, has become "conventionalized as a personal rite of passage" and as such has become a process of discovery and recovery of their sexual selves and of their relationship to more than one family: to the Italian American family and to a community of gays and lesbians, to which there are varying degrees of loyalty and connection (Gever 195).

Like other gay persons, Italian American lesbians experience the ongoing intersection between two images that relate to gay positioning in Western culture: the image of coming out and the image of the closet. In "Epistemology of the Closet," Eve Kosofsky Sedgwick explains that the process of coming out is not unidirectional; the revelation has the potential for serious injury to both parties involved—gay and straight.[2] Coming from a patriarchal familial culture, Italian American lesbians recognize the potential damage such a revelation will incur. Aware of the fact that coming out of the closet is never purely a "hermetic" act, the Italian American writer's decision to depict this social process is a profoundly courageous gesture of independence (Sedgwick 53).

As much as the act of coming out is liberating and euphoric, the writers regularly depict the closet as a "shaping presence" in the lives of their lesbian characters (Sedgwick 46). For Italian American writers, exploring the process of coming out is an attempt, in effect, to place their characters as sexualized beings inside Italian American houses. As Diana Fuss explains, "[T]o be out is to be finally outside of exteriority and all the exclusions and deprivations such outsiderhood imposes. Or, put another way, to be out is really to be in—inside the realm of the visible, the speakable, the culturally intelligible" (4).

For the lesbian characters in Dodici Azpadu's *Saturday Night in the Prime of Life* and Rachel Guido deVries's *Tender Warriors*, coming out to the family means the emergence of further alienation: the lesbian characters are excluded from family matters, and a veil of silence shrouds their existence. Azpadu and deVries conclude their novels differently, offering contrasting options for the continued development of their Italian American lesbian characters, whether or not they are welcomed back into the family. In both novels, the characters hope to recover a space in which they are allowed to be visible as lesbian *and* Italian American. Both identities—sexual and cultural—modify and inform each other in these novels, suggesting the pliable nature of identity itself.

Before examining how the Italian family narrative informs the plots and themes of Azpadu's and deVries's novels, it is necessary to take notice of their relationship to what Bonnie Zimmerman identifies as lesbian writing. In *The Safe Sea of Women: Lesbian Fiction 1969–1989*, Zimmerman explains that certain factors comprise lesbian writing: lesbian novels have a central, not a marginal, lesbian character, "one who understands herself to be a lesbian"; lesbian novels place passional love between women at the center of the stories; and lesbian texts place men "firmly at the margins of the story" (15). Closer to the classic bildungsroman than the feminist novel of awakening, the lesbian novel of development utilizes the basic narrative form by focusing on the heroine's adolescence. Tracing the girl's growth from adolescence into adulthood, lesbian novels depict the protagonist's "educational process" as inextricably linked to her "discovery of love and sexuality" (Zimmerman, "Exiting from Patriarchy" 247).

Neither Azpadu's nor deVries's novel fully corresponds with the salient features of the lesbian developmental novel, perhaps because they are insistently engaged by the intersection between sexual and cultural identities. These novels begin where traditional lesbian novels leave off: after the awakening process, after the acceptance of a lesbian identity, and after the affirmation of one's lesbianism to the outside world (Zimmerman, "Exiting from Patriarchy" 245). For Azpadu and deVries, being a lesbian is a continuous process of recreating one's relationship to the Italian American family. While both authors utilize various features of the lesbian developmental novel, such as depicting a lesbian character as the central protagonist in Azpadu's book and incorporating features of the bildungsroman in deVries's work, they do so in the service of *la famiglia*, not solely to depict an individual coming-of-age by revealing her sexuality.

Marianne Hirsch has defined the bildungsroman of the twentieth century as "the most salient genre for the literature of social outsiders, primarily women or minority groups," a genre regularly utilized by the Italian American women examined in this book ("The Novel of Formation" 300). Azpadu and deVries reformulate the developmental novel to include the possibility of the family's growth if they are able to overcome their homophobia and accept the lesbian daughter. The Italian American family's ability to affirm the lesbian daughter's decision to love women crucially determines the daughter's capacity to develop a coherent "ethnic" self, one that includes both the family of origin and the gay community.

*Saturday Night in the Prime of Life* is Dodici Azpadu's first novel.[3] Azpadu's protagonist, Neddie Zingaro, never returns home, although her family, especially her mother, haunts her life. The novel revolves around the twenty-six-year estrangement between mother and daughter. Neddie and her longtime partner, Lindy, painstakingly compose a letter of invitation to Neddie's mother, who has expressed feelings of loneliness in old age in one of the rare letters written to her daughter in a quarter of a century. Fifty years old herself, Neddie recognizes the fear of aging and invites her mother to come live with them. Neddie's letter is followed several weeks later by a phone call in which Concetta repeats all the invectives of the earlier days, reducing the conversation to a one-way string of epithets hurled against her only daughter and eldest child. The novel ends with Neddie and Lindy pondering the course of their own uncharted aging.

As much as the novel revolves around the lesbian history between Neddie and Lindy, it is a history that is highly informed by Neddie's Sicilian, widowed mother. Azpadu does not depict Neddie's engagement with culinary traditions, holidays, and the Sicilian dialect, which Neddie knows but uses only when her mother calls. Evident in this novel is the absence of such nurturing traditions. Instead, the presence of Concetta looms ubiquitously in Neddie's and Lindy's lives, even though the mother herself has practiced a "studious and long-standing avoidance" of her daughter (16).

*Saturday Night in the Prime of Life* examines how lesbian identity interpenetrates with Sicilian family culture, highlighting the marginalization of both mother and daughter. Barolini's description of the Italian woman's diminishment of power in America parallels Concetta Zingaro's situation in Azpadu's novel: "[S]he was quickly dethroned into the image of the old woman in the kitchen, stirring the sauce, heartwarming, maybe, but actually a figure of ridicule, a caricature" (*The Dream Book* 12). While she is no longer the vibrant figure that she was as a young mother, Concetta Zingaro continues to wield power in manipulative and effective ways. The novel portrays her life as a widowed grandmother, whose two sons perform their filial duties without complaint or enjoyment. Never challenging any of Concetta's outmoded and destructive beliefs, both sons ignore the fact that their sister has been ostracized from the family for decades. As a result, their silence reinforces the will of the mother and symbolically kills their sister.

Concetta, like her husband before her, harbors all the patriarchal assumptions regarding proper male-female relations: husbands are served by wives; men work outside the home, women inside; sons are more prized than daughters; and divorced women are *puttane*. Refusing to accept the fact that her son Bernardo is married to a divorced woman with children and that her youngest son, Carmello, regularly cooks and serves his family, Concetta finds herself at seventy an old woman dressed in black, feeling lonely and separated from her family. As much as her family's Americanization pleases Concetta, she realizes, like Umbertina of Barolini's novel, that she has little in common with Carmello's "golden"-skinned children, the result of intermarriage: "She frequently suffered a racial vertigo, the consequence of gradually bleeding to death—

not from the public wound, but from one secretly self-inflicted" (4). Concetta's firstborn child, Neddie, remains the one family member left who speaks the Sicilian dialect. Incapable of admitting in any sustained manner that the only person in her life who reaffirms her Sicilian cultural identity is her daughter, Concetta circumscribes her life by adhering to beliefs and behaviors that are either ineffectual or damaging.

That Azpadu describes Concetta's and Neddie's Sicilian heritage as racial and not ethnic deserves commentary. Before Italian unification, Sicily was invaded by a host of foreign groups from Africa, Greece, Asia, and Spain. Azpadu's repeated references to skin color—olive—suggest that neither mother nor daughter considers herself "white." Although historically, racial minorities in the United States have experienced qualitatively harsher discrimination, Azpadu's use of the term "racial heritage" reveals what John Bukowczyk has called the phenomenon of the "not-yet-white-ethnic" (qtd. in Roediger 184).[4] In *Towards the Abolition of Whiteness*, David R. Roediger includes Italians in the immigrant population who were "historically regarded as nonwhite, or of debatable racial heritage, by the host American citizenry" but whose duration of "'not-yet-whiteness', as measured against that of racial oppression in the US, was quite short" (184–85).[5] Both Concetta and Neddie are comforted by their "common racial heritage," and each tacitly recognizes that their fragile connection continues to exist because of a shared cultural background.

Neddie's partner, Lindy, reveals her own racism when she and Neddie thumb through photographs of the Zingaro family: "Concetta's nose, eyes and mouth epitomized an unpleasant racial mixing which only in Neddie did Lindy find attractive" (29–30).[6] As distasteful as Lindy finds the Zingaro's family features, she cannot avoid feeling threatened by what Concetta can give her daughter that she cannot: "racial comfort" (62). The maternal attraction that Neddie feels toward Concetta has more to do with their Sicilian background than it has to do with their personal feelings toward each other. The mother's denial of the daughter at the end of the novel injures both of them. Unwilling to overcome her fear and disgust toward her daughter's lesbianism, Concetta will enter old age without the comfort of a shared cultural identity. Unwilling to leave her relationship to tend to her mother, Neddie will continue to countenance her mother's calls, if only to hear and speak Sicilian.

*Saturday Night in the Prime of Life* honors lesbian existence as a means to achieving a coherent identity but also mourns the loss of the family of origin to reanimate cultural identity. Like several other novels by Italian American women, Azpadu's novel is elegiac, grieving the loss of ancestors who represent cultural traditions, with all their flaws and misapplications. Azpadu suggests that Neddie is not fully able to develop a sexual and cultural identity that will allow her to go peaceably into old age. When the family of origin ostracizes a member because of her movement away from prescribed sexual norms, that person suffers a crisis of cultural identity, as Neddie does. The resolution of the novel is hardly optimistic, though it realistically portrays the potentially ruinous results of coming out as lesbian in Italian America.

Rachel Guido deVries's *Tender Warriors* treats the issue of lesbianism from the vantage point of a woman who is reintegrated into the Italian American family. Unlike Azpadu's novel, *Tender Warriors* has as its protagonist a straight male whose illness serves to reunite other family members who have been estranged since their mother's death. The death of Josephine DeMarco initiates a quest for Rose, the eldest child and a lesbian; Lorraine, a reformed drug addict, now married; and Sonny, the protagonist, the youngest and only son, whose brain seizures have partially blocked the memory of his mother's death. The novel revolves around each family member returning home, where Dominic DeMarco, an often violent and angry father, still lives. Together, Rose, Lorraine, and Dominic search for Sonny. Toward the conclusion of the novel, Sonny remembers to attend the two-year anniversary mass of his mother's death. Once there, he falls unconscious to the floor. By the novel's conclusion, deVries suggests that the twenty-seven-year-old Sonny DeMarco will achieve health again and claim an adult existence without the solicitous ministrations of his saint-like mother.

That Rose DeMarco is neither the center of the novel nor its narrative consciousness reinforces deVries's interest in the interdependence of the Italian American family. Despite her brother's illness and her sister's drug habit, Rose DeMarco, at age thirty-seven, still tortures herself with the knowledge "that everything about her was different from them" (71). On her own journey to locate her brother, Rose returns to the parental home where she and her father eat fusilli and meatballs, feeling "as though the meal had given them back something familiar" (106). "*Mangiando, ricordo,*" Barolini writes in her book, *Festa*; "by eating, I remember" (13). Rose's response to sharing a meal with her father recalls a sense of comfort when Josephine, the undisputed center of the family, was alive. Directly following this scene, Sonny makes a phone call home, asking for "Momma," symbolically recalling a time when the family's unhappiness was soothed by Josephine.

*Tender Warriors* functions more as an ethnic or communal bildungsroman along the lines of Tomasi's *Like Lesser Gods* than it does a traditional lesbian text. Before the family attends the anniversary mass for Josephine DeMarco, they congregate in the kitchen, the mother's traditional domain. As inviolate as her position as the center of the family was, Josephine was "powerless in the world beyond her home" (54), much like Maria, the mother in Tomasi's novel. At the grave site, Rose believes that her mother's road to liberation was death itself—"I guess you got out the only way you could" (21). Unable to control her husband's infidelities or violent tirades, Josephine spent her time protecting her children, especially Sonny, from Dominic's insistence that they live "their lives the way *he* thought they should" (56). Much like Aldo Bartoli of *A Cup of the Sun* or Nino Giardello of *The Right Thing to Do*, Dominic DeMarco vainly tries to maintain what he considers his undisputed title of *capofamiglia*. Having been tormented in boyhood by ethnic slurs such as "greaseball" and "guinea," Dominic believes that wielding power is the only way to earn respect. Any opposition from his children signals a deviation from *l'ordine della famiglia* and incurs his scorn and abuse. After the mother's death, the grown children no longer visit the father because his rigidity prevents them from being who they are, especially Sonny, whose sickness confuses and angers Dominic. Without the centralizing influence of the mother, this Italian family disperses, making continued development impossible without the ministrations of each family member.

One of the predominant themes on which deVries focuses her novel is equally pervasive in the writing on southern Italian culture: the elevation of the maternal role. Josephine DeMarco's maternal function in the family parallels that of many immigrant mothers, who often mediated between the demands of the Italian father and the needs of each of her children. Despite dissension, mothers were often able to maintain a semblance of family solidarity. Josephine's death brings each member of the family to a crisis of ethnic identity. Sonny's illness symbolizes the fact that the family's very existence is threatened by her death. In order to revitalize their relationship to the family, each DeMarco member prays to Josephine, as though she were the Madonna or a treasured saint. Josephine's favorite saint was Lucy, the patron saint of Syracuse in Sicily, invoked by those whose sight is diseased or failing.[7] Although she has died, the power of the mother to act as an intercessor remains vital. Each of the characters believes that Josephine provides them with the vision needed to shape their futures.

Each of the DeMarcos must clarify their relationship to the family of origin before attending to their personal development. For Rose, caring for her mother's grave and involving herself in Sonny's return to the family brings her back to the parental home. Rose assumes the maternal role by acting as a mediator between her father and Sonny, notably without relinquishing her relationship to her partner, Deborah. As a result of Rose's efforts, the DeMarco family unites as one in order to locate Sonny. The family makes its headquarters at Dominic's house, and Deborah assists in helping Rose and her family contact Sonny. For the Italian American family to remain an integral part of the children's continued development and negotiation with their cultural identity, the older generation must countenance difference.

*Tender Warriors*, similar to *Like Lesser Gods* and *No SteadyJob for Papa*, is highly optimistic in its belief in the sustaining nature of the family. Its pages reveal the possibility of older family members accepting the different life choices of younger members without seeing in those choices the diminishment of cultural identity. While the image of the closet may continue to be a shaping presence for the lesbian characters in these books, the Italian American household also continues to shape their lives.

## Narrative Strands of *Italianità* in Maso and Rossi

The key to unlocking the confusions and anguish of the present lies in the stories of the past. Carole Maso and Agnes Rossi subscribe to the importance of memory to reconstruct the past in order to make living for their characters meaningful. Maso's *Ghost Dance* and Rossi's *The Quick: A Novella and Stories* are insistently concerned with the ways developing characters make sense of the silences pervading their ancestry. In both texts, the submergence of ethnicity in the name of an American identity must be reevaluated by both the characters who have repressed their cultural identity and by the first-person narrators who are trying to understand themselves.

In *Ghost Dance*, Carole Maso incorporates Italian American identity as one of the interlacing strands that comprise the complicated identity of Vanessa Turin, the first-person narrator, whose losses inform the movement of the novel.[8] A child of German and Armenian ancestry on her mother's side and Italian ancestry on her father's side, Vanessa Turin probes the silences and explores the possible reasons informing her parents' unusual reticence about their pasts. In an interview, Maso explains that all her books play with questions like "[W]ho am I? How does one construct a self?" ("Interview by Nicole Cooley" 33). Other questions that Vanessa must ask throughout her journey into adulthood include "Where did Mom go?" and, ultimately, "Where is my family?" as she is left alone, without her father or brother, both of whom have disappeared before the narrative begins. In order to answer these questions, Vanessa must heed the imperative that she hears and invents throughout the novel: "Tell me a story."

Italian American women's novels often portray family members learning the stories of the past in order to "fight off illness and death" (Leslie Marmon Silko qtd. in Minh-ha 136). Although

Maso explores the development of the self through multiple narrative strands, they all focus on one theme: loss. Comprised of a multidimensional narrative and bits of seemingly disconnected information, *Ghost Dance* captures the fragmentation that occurs when ancestral traditions are silenced, submerged, and repressed. Stylistically parallel with De Rosa's *Paper Fish* in its technical virtuosity, Maso's *Ghost Dance* reconstructs family traditions by assembling the broken pieces into, as Robert Orsi explains, "new patterns according to a complex and multi-levelled logic" ("The Fault of Memory" n. 38, 145).[9]

*Ghost Dance* is divided into five parts. Part 1 begins in the recent past when Vanessa is returning to college at Vassar—her mother's alma mater—for the second semester. Her mother, Christine Wing, is an extraordinarily gifted and famous poet and works with a ferocity bordering on the unbearable, believing that "there is no rest from perception" (49). Christine's struggle with mental illness—manic depression—is captured immediately in the text through Maso's creation of the magnificent image of the "Topaz Bird." Invented by Christine for bedtime stories to help Vanessa and her younger brother, Fletcher, cope with her "inexplicable sadness or rage or joy," the image acquires many meanings throughout the novel. Like her mother, Vanessa also understands that the Topaz Bird is the "wild, brilliant Bird of Imagination. The Bird of Great Invention" (8, 16). Vanessa's belief in the healing capacity of storytelling, which the Topaz Bird symbolizes, will help her uncover the reasons for her mother's suffering and for her father's deep-boned silence. It will also help Vanessa develop into an artist of what Maso calls "lyrical fiction," which she describes as "the desire of the novel to be a poem" ("An Essay" 26). Vanessa will piece together the stories, through image patterns and narrative fragments, of her family's sorrow.

At the time that Maso begins the narrative, Vanessa does not know that she will be seeing her mother for the last time, waiting for her "under the enormous clock in Grand Central Station where we met briefly, she on her way back from Maine and I on my way to college for the second semester" (41). (We learn in part 5 that Vanessa's father's 1973 Pinto is rear-ended at a toll booth; the gas tank ruptures and the car bursts into flames. Christine is sitting in the back seat and is said to have died instantaneously. Vanessa's brother, Fletcher, and her father, Michael Turin, receive second-degree burns but manage to get out of the car.) As much as Vanessa wants to come home with her mother, Christine insists that she leave for school. Before they depart in different directions, Vanessa uncrumples a piece of paper to find a list of her mother's "New Year's Resolutions." The resolutions compel Vanessa to reconsider not only her mother's fierce work ethic but also the American emphasis on setting goals and achieving dreams. One wonders what Benjamin Franklin or Jay Gatsby would have made of "Enjoy life more"; "Work fewer hours. Relax more"; "Spend more time with the children" (9). That Christine is not given the opportunity to enjoy life more fully *and* to continue her artistry is one of Maso's strategies for critiquing the definitions of American progress and success.

Another way in which Maso interrogates American beliefs in progress and modernization is through her inclusion of ethnicity as a means of maintaining a viable identity in a world where mass production and commercialization are valued more than the individual and community. In parts 2 and 3, Maso explores the potential reasons undergirding the silences of Vanessa's mother and father. Christine's mother is bedridden with heart disease throughout Christine's and her sister's childhood. Sarkis Wingarian, their father, shortens his name to "Wing" in an attempt to gain American stature and perhaps to gain the acceptance of his disapproving in-laws.

Working tirelessly at the silk mill in Paterson to pay for his wife's medicines, Sarkis further compels his beautiful American daughter Christine to model at commercial studios in New York. Vanessa imagines that her mother later fails the MGM screen test in Hollywood, refusing to function as an invented "product" of the new country. Years after his wife has died and his two daughters are college-aged, Sarkis leaves America, disillusioned by its false promises, aware of the fact that his old age brings him scorn, not respect, in the new country. Taking back his name—Wingarian—Sarkis reanimates his relationship to his Armenian identity, but he leaves his two daughters alone to accommodate the memories of their parents' suffering. Believing words to be "medicine, too," Christine tries to make her mother well through the language of storytelling and later through poetry (111). Likewise, Vanessa imagines a relationship with Grandpa Sarkis—whom she has met only once—that is as close as touch:

> In the old country you can grow silk on trees. In the old country you are worth your weight in gold. In the old country his people were slaughtered like sheep. . . . When I get older and begin to gain weight myself, I know I will think of him. I will watch my hips turn to gold. (212)

In Vanessa's imaginative recreation of her father's past, she constructs scenarios based on actual relationships to her Italian paternal grandparents, on observations of her father's suffering, and on specific events that she and her family attend, especially the 1964 New York World's Fair. Throughout *Ghost Dance*, strands of *italianità* intersect with three narratives: Christine's family's narrative; Vanessa's college friend Marta's longing for home; and the Native American traditions that Vanessa's Italian grandfather adopts after the 1964 World's Fair.

Michael Turin suffers in ways unique to his position as a second-generation ethnic. Like Marguerite of *Umbertina*, Michael's relationship to his immigrant parents is attenuated by *their* deliberate suppression of *italianità* in the name of achieving an American identity. A stockbroker by profession, Michael's remoteness causes his children to invent homework assignments just to hear him speak. Refusing to provide them with any information about one of their fabricated assignments—learning their "family history"—Vanessa and Fletcher must create and construct a past that clarifies their father's silence. As Maso herself says of *Ghost Dance*, "[T]he way to resist [silence], to speak against silence, is very much what [the] book is about. To live next to silence, but to speak" ("An Interview by Nicole Cooley" 34). In one of the earliest references to the puzzle of her father, Vanessa imagines the possible reasons for his refusal to tell her the family's story. Vanessa constructs a tale about her paternal grandfather, who destroys all the tomato plants while the young Michael freezes the scene in his mind. Vanessa imagines her father trying to forget his father's insistence that they are Americans now, not Italians:

> Did his father announce that there will be no more Italian spoken in his house? No more wine drunk with lunch, as he burned the grapevines? Did he tell his wife there would be no more sad songs from the old country? How much she must have wept, hugging her small son to her breast! (74)

Vanessa's imaginative recreation is buttressed by her father's rare but highly emotive responses to things Italian. For example, on a walk at a wildlife center with her father and Fletcher, where they pick up leaves from the ground, Vanessa is witness to her father's ecstatic memory of the leaves that his grandmother in Italy would dip into egg and flour and fry: "This was one of the happiest days of my life: clutching his hand, holding close the story of how his grandmother, who had never lived before this day, changed simple leaves for a young boy into veal" (93). This rare glimpse into the father's cultural past offers a gloss on Michael's reaction to observing Michelangelo's *Pietà* displayed at the 1964 World's Fair. Although Italy no longer interests his father, both of Michael's parents accompany him to see the sculpture. "Standing between his parents, hugging them to his side on the moving conveyor belt," Vanessa's father cries, affirming his daughter's speculation that he had earlier dreamed of "a grieving mother [who] cradled her dead son's body in silence" (124, 123). His parents' decision to suppress all traces of Italian identity emotionally kills Michael, who longs for an affirmation of his cultural roots. In an inversion of the image of the *Pietà*, Maso suggests that Michael Turin is the perpetually dolorous son, holding his parents in his arms and grieving his loss of them.[10] Michael is moved to tears that day and spends the entire morning with Vanessa in front of "that sad sculpture" while the rest of the family goes elsewhere (124).

The 1964 World's Fair is a turning point for Vanessa's paternal grandfather, Angelo. Arrested with his grandson, Fletcher, at the civil rights demonstration in front of the Ford Pavilion's Progressland, the grandfather's belief in America as a promised land is thoroughly crushed. Feeling "betrayed at the core," Angelo spends his final years journeying "back through time, to a simpler place, where he would live the last years of his life" (130). That he replaces his Italian culture with Native American beliefs reaffirms the grandfather's love of heritage and his awareness of its necessity to give meaning to his final years. Angelo's repeated trips to the Black Hills of South Dakota constitute a search for his suppressed past and a strategy for finding a way to maintain some hope for what America might have represented before modern technology and white men obliterated the Indians and the land. Able to communicate with the Native Americans because he is fluent in the "language of hands," Angelo's relationship to Native American traditions is abetted by his Italian background and his love of an ideal America (78). Forecasting a terrible drought, the grandfather spends his final years searching for water: "It was the fear he had held in check for nearly seventy years; in Italy as a little boy, then as a young man, his whole life, it had been the same fear" (87). A farmer by trade, Angelo's search might very well recall residual boyhood fears in Italy, where water supplies were scarce and water often insalubrious. Fruitlessly trying to find the secret of rain, Angelo's response to his failure sounds much like *la miseria* mentality and *contadino* despair: "'We are at the mercy of a God who does not really care if our children are thirsty or our crops die'" (87).

As much as the grandfather feels that he has cast off his Italian culture for good, it seeps back into his life as he is dying. "Babbling in some troubled dialect," Angelo slips back into Italian on his deathbed when he says goodbye to his wife (90). Hearing for the first time "the forbidden language," Vanessa realizes that her grandfather's cultural heritage can never be fully denied. Like his search for water, the grandfather's journey home takes him back to his first language: "[T]he language that he had given up in this country now came streaming back. My grandmother squeezed his hand. She talked back to him" (139).

The grandfather ultimately leaves his grandchildren a complex legacy, which includes both his culture of heritage and his adopted Native American traditions. No longer acting as a mediator between homeland and new-world cultures, as other godparent figures in Italian American novels have done, Angelo nonetheless functions as a guide and mentor to his grandchildren. Leaving the children with the history and rituals surrounding the Ghost Dance and specific directions for the after-death ritual to ensure "the proper relation between the living and the dead," Angelo effectually aids in their ability to understand both familial loss and the losses incurred in the name of American progress (92).[11]

Part 4 probes more fully the effects of having suppressed one's ethnic identity. In particular, Vanessa's paternal grandmother, Maria, has denied her Italian ancestry, not out of a sense of wanting to assimilate American ways, but out of deference to her husband. Fully schooled in the discipline of *serietà*, Maria Turin's immersion in her role as the stabilizing force within the family ironically deprives her from reconceiving her Italian culture in America. Visiting her grandmother during the summer, Vanessa regularly associates Maria with consistency, good sense, and order. Whether or not she yet appreciates her grandmother's respect for the concrete—"the observed life"—Vanessa is given a legacy from Maria that is all about living well in the physical world. Repeating in rotelike fashion the kinds of information her granddaughter should know—"like when to sow vegetables"—Maria stands over Vanessa's bed at night, hoping that such useful knowledge sinks below the conscious (175).[12]

When Vanessa, Fletcher, and their father visit Maria years later at a nursing home on the Bicentennial, they discover that the grandmother's national allegiance is not to the American flag but to her homeland village in Italy. Just as Angelo returned to his native tongue before dying, Maria, too, no longer beholden to her husband's command, returns to her beloved country, dancing the tarantella on her last day of life. In some cases, July 4 was the assigned time for the fulfillment of the Ghost Dance prophecy (Mooney 19). That the grandmother's final dance occurs on this day connects her to her husband and to the idea of reuniting with her people in the Italian homeland.

While Fletcher later denies that his grandmother ever danced on the lawn (248), Vanessa constructs a narrative that will account for Maria's bitterness and resentment, particularly toward her son, after Angelo's death. Disconnected from *italianità*, Maria is not allowed to transmit her culture—which she equates with love and nurturance—to her child. Such cultural loss causes Maria to feel bitter and resentful toward Michael, who does not yet understand the cost of her sacrifice. Finally speaking through the silence, Maria breaks the code of *omertà* when she explains why she continued to hide Italian culture from her grandchildren: "'Your grandfather never let me speak Italian in the house. . . . He never let me cook my own food. I missed that so much,' she said in the loneliest voice I had ever heard. 'He never let me sing you to sleep with the sweet songs from Italy I loved so much.'" When Michael recognizes the extent of his mother's sacrifice, he weeps uncontrollably, "an anthem" rising in him as his own cultural identity is finally affirmed (223). Whirling away from them in a death dance, the grandmother's final sensation is one of taste, just like her husband's. Recalling memories of the Italian foods prepared at Christmas, Maria's final words during her dance are, "'[I]t tastes so sweet, . . . just like I remember'" (224).

Maso reinforces the importance of stories from the past in part 5 of *Ghost Dance* when sister and brother reunite to mourn their losses and to create a space for themselves that is no longer life-denying. In *Writing Beyond the Ending*, Rachel Blau DuPlessis includes brother-sister ties in the list of narrative strategies that replace traditional narrative and cultural orders of fiction, such as romance, marriage, and motherhood. The brother-sister bond not only deemphasizes traditional narrative sequences but also embraces other narrative strategies germane to *Ghost Dance*, including lesbian ties and reparenting.[13]

Profoundly depressed, Vanessa expresses her need to reconnect with her mother through her relationships with two lesbian women: Marta, her college friend at Vassar, whose severe depression over the loss of her lover causes her to attempt suicide; and Sabine, her mother's lover of twenty-five years, with whom Vanessa makes love when they meet nearly a year after Christine's death. In both episodes, Sabine and Marta offer Vanessa another "angle," another way of seeing her situation, one that ultimately rejects death and self-abrogation as a means to end her suffering. Sabine tells Vanessa that "'we must learn to love her [Christine] from here now,'" suggesting the necessity of re-creation to aid in Vanessa's recovery (258). Marta's situation parallels Vanessa's: spending "so many months" dying for Natalie, she had forgotten her homeland in Venezuela. For the first time since she has fallen into a coma, Marta begins to remember the Vassar campus and the long-ago story of two women dancing on the lawn (Sabine and Christine?), rekindling her desire to live. Separating from Natalie's seductions, Marta experiences a pain that feels as if she "were giving birth" (262). In a similar way, Vanessa must pull herself up, "out of my mother's body," in order to recombine the pieces of her past (267). Before locating Fletcher, who is now living again in New York, Vanessa recalls the cast of characters of her past, many of whom are lost to her now: Michael, who has left the country, and her paternal grandparents, who have died (268).

Plowing through fields of snow on a particularly treacherous New York winter, Vanessa reaches Fletcher. Together, they perform the ghost dance ritual. As painful and difficult as it is to accept that their mother was killed in the prime of her life because of Ford Motor Company's gross negligence, brother and sister recall her presence during their ceremony. Nearly blinded by its "brilliant, jewel-like light," Fletcher and Vanessa see the "Topaz Bird," out of which steps their beautiful mother, dressed in white. Repeating to them the line "'I have loved you my whole life,'" Christine allows her children to say goodbye to her—as they must (272, 275).

Maso's final pages of *Ghost Dance* are history-laden. Vanessa accepts that she must live to tell the stories of loss about her family in America *and* about the American family. Like David of *A Bridge of Leaves*, Vanessa learns to contextualize her mother's loss, placing her in American history alongside other tragic occurrences: the death of a Vietnam veteran, the mutilation of a factory worker, the assassinations of President Lincoln and Martin Luther King, the death by starvation of a child in the Bronx. Unacceptable and inexplicably sad, these events in American history are the artist's canvas as she seeks to make meaning of the tragic. Throughout *Ghost Dance*, Maso suggests that when ancestral ties are broken, denied, or suppressed, characters inevitably suffer and eventually move toward the homeland in order to be healed. For Maso, like other Italian American writers, the call toward home becomes a journey of memory and imagination. By the novel's conclusion, Vanessa Turin becomes the brilliant Topaz Bird of her childhood stories, the voice of lyrical fiction.

*The Quick: A Novella and Stories* is Agnes Rossi's exploration of the power of loss to unite otherwise disparate characters.[14] Like Maso, Rossi submerges Italian American ethnicity and examines the consequences of doing so for a working-class Italian family in Paterson, New Jersey. That Rossi begins and ends her novel with the first-person narrator, Marie Russo, grieving her father's death reinforces the elegiac tone of the work. Despite her Italian surname, Marie Russo never once participates in *italianità*: culinary and musical traditions, holidays and saints' days, language and religion. In his review of Rossi's first novella, Stuart Dybek explains that she

> draws an unsentimental and convincing portrait of the working-class Russo family, whose Italian-American background has been largely erased. What's left is a narrowness without the compensation of ethnic identity, vitality or even much humor, and the father's brutal disappointment over what he perceives as the failure of his children to live up to his American dream of betterment through education. (15)

Despite Dybek's suggestion that the family's ethnicity has been erased, Rossi continues to inscribe features of the Italian American narrative in her allegiance to the family as a continuing presence in the first-person narrator's life. That Rossi offers a sustained response to loss in both the novella and the stories that follow relates well to Italian American literary traditions. Like Hendin's *The Right Thing to Do*, Rossi incorporates an illness narrative in her work; in doing so, she suggests the physical reality of the father's hard-won sacrifices: he dies of bone cancer. This cruel fact connects itself for Marie to the image of a "blackened bone," a memory of her neighbor dying without hope for survival when his house burns down. One of the stories that follows the novella, "What You Leave Out," offers a gloss on *The Quick* in the characters' ultimate revelation that family violence tore asunder their relationships. While Rossi is not thoughtlessly indebted to the code of *omertà*, her silence about the effects of the Italian father's anger not only on the children of the family but also on the mother—who remains a "woman of the shadows"—remains a provocative commentary on the costs of ethnic denial. Like Azpadu, Rossi suggests throughout *The Quick* that silences accumulate meanings inside the family. Marie Russo must discover a way to locate and articulate those silences.

What remains a positive force in Rossi's narrative is one of the staple features of Italian American culture and to several of its literary texts: sibling solidarity. Despite the fact that neither romance narrative nor heterosexual union is successful in Marie Russo's life, the brother-sister bond remains essential to Marie's understanding of her position in the family and of her ability to heal from the family's lack of nurturance. Rossi's inclusion of Marie's ride with her brother in his red Corvette remains for Marie her only soothing family memory. Driving the convertible herself, Marie's anxieties dissolve: "All I could do was perfectly matched with all I had to do. The car on the road. My hands on the wheel. Chris, his profile handsome and serious, beside me" (40). While her friend Phyllis gives Marie the courage and unflinching honesty with which to confront loss and death, Chris gives his sister the permanency of his friendship, which remains strong throughout their lives.

Rather than focus solely on the painful suffering and death of Marie's father, Rossi broadens her scope in order to include Marie's memory of the death of Phyllis's husband. Grieving the loss of her father, Marie spends most of the narrative remembering the past. In doing so, she is able to put some closure on the painful scenarios comprising her development into an adult. At the beginning of the narrative, Marie recalls the sudden death of Phyllis Macdonald's husband, an event that occurred twenty-five years before. This death is intimately connected with Marie's father's death, which also begins the narrative and is juxtaposed to the other losses in the narrator's life, exemplifying the major theme in this novella: that loss is ubiquitous but, at the same time, like grief, impermanent and cannot sustain us forever. The ordinary world presses in, muddying any thoughts we may have about the purity of our experience when death occurs:

> I thought death happened cleanly, thought you entered a separate realm where the death and its aftermath took place, where it was all by itself. I found out that death occurs in a perfectly ordinary context. All the regular stuff continues stubbornly around it. (59)

Marie Russo arrives at this understanding as a result of her friendship with Phyllis Macdonald, who becomes the lens by which Marie perceives her own losses.

With exacting honesty, Phyllis tells the story of her husband's death at his funeral service. She says to the congregation: "'Nothing I say here will tell you anything more about him. Jim died on June eighth at ten-twenty A.M. Today we bear witness to that. James Allen Macdonald is dead'" (49). Marie Russo recalls that she

> fell in love with Phyllis at that moment. No matter what else ever happened between us I knew I would love her for standing so straight and talking about her death in words that offered no comfort. I wanted to be with her, sit beside her, feel her ruthlessness and her courage. (49–50)

Throughout *The Quick*, Marie Russo symbolically sits beside Phyllis as she remembers with candor the events of loss in her life, beginning with the frustrations and tensions within the Russo household.

Marie Russo's father delivered milk for thirty-five years, working "for a tyrant." Forced to quit school at fifteen, Louis Russo never overcomes his extraordinary disappointment in his potential, displacing his anger and his expectations onto his children, for whom he wants college educations and middle-class status. Both children disappoint him: Marie graduates from college but fails as an elementary school teacher, taking a clerical job in her hometown, Paterson. Chris becomes a skilled mechanic, a working-class status that infuriates his father. Quickly dismissing the "romantic notion of home as a safe place," Marie Russo recalls "the volatile nature of things in my house" in an effort to probe the underlying reasons for the family's profound dissatisfaction (29, 70). Those reasons may very well lie in the family's attenuated relationship to their ethnic identity, symbolized by the destruction of a six-inch bust of Verdi, broken during a hostile fight between Marie's father and brother.

During this scene, Rossi examines the behavior of each family member, revealing the loss of the father's status as *capofamiglia*, a concern that Waldo and Hendin earlier thematized in their novels. Marie does not overtly describe her father's behavior as a reaction to his inability to maintain *l'ordine della famiglia*, but his violent response reveals his own impotence. When Chris disappears for five days, Louis Russo's searches prove ineffectual. When his son returns home in his red Corvette with a girlfriend, his father pushes and shoves Chris back into his house and beats him furiously until Chris sends his father reeling into the china closet. Rossi explains that this scene of violence ushers both children outside the parental home. Chris will never return: "I knew I'd never live with Chris again. That part of our lives was suddenly over" (84).

Rossi concludes the chapter by describing the objects broken when the china cabinet falls over:

> My mother's wedding dishes . . . and the flowered vase my father's relatives sent from Italy—Chris and I never considered ourselves related to my parents' relatives, especially the ones we never saw, the ones who were just blue airmail letters that lay around the house for a while and then were gone. My father's six-inch bust of Verdi had been on one of those shelves. (85)

That the children of Italian parents have so little communication with Italian relatives—*comari, compari*—in Italy and America suggests their status as orphans: without support from nuclear or extended families, with no evidence of godparent figures, with no reinforcement of their culture of heritage, it's no wonder Rossi describes the six-inch bust of Verdi as diminished and broken. For the father in Hendin's *The Right Thing to Do*, Verdi's opera, *Nabucco*, offers him solace in a world in which he feels alien; for the father in Rossi's *The Quick*, the sculpture of Verdi is stowed away and functions more as a decoration than a viable ethnic symbol.

Nonetheless, Marie Russo does not overlook the fact that her parents' culture has tumbled down around them: their loss is her loss.

Perhaps the character whose behavior is given the least attention in *The Quick* is Marie Russo's mother, whose identity is solely defined by her husband's anger. As much as her husband was domineering and cruel, the mother in *The Right Thing to Do* gained pleasure in life from the ordinary details of her Italian culture—stories, aphorisms, recipes—and the women in family and community with whom she shared her voice. In marked contrast, Marie Russo's mother, starved for any sign of devotion from her husband, sanctions his tirades and surrenders to his wishes. The mother neither sustains interests with relatives nor establishes close ties with her children. Rossi seems to be forcefully suggesting that the denial of ethnic identity has its most damaging effects on those who submit to its most chauvinistic, narrow definitions, in this case, Marie Russo's mother.

For Marie Russo, the violent family household that she leaves is unfortunately reproduced in her college liaison with a "skinny and frenetic" boy who humiliates her sexually and emotionally. Calling her "parochial," Marie's boyfriend, like Alex of *The Right Thing to Do*, uses sexual violence as a means of controlling her body and spirit (55). In order to cope with the fact that she was raped, Marie splits herself in two, refusing to confront questions about her gendered and working-class status. To escape from the limitations of her family and job, Marie retreats into a safe but ultimately dissatisfying marriage with Ralph, whom she eventually divorces. When the narrative begins, Marie's college-aged daughter, Rita, is distant from her mother. Unable to provide her daughter with sustaining features of Italian American culture, Marie Russo reproduces the unhappy relationship she had with her own mother.

Louis Russo's death not only symbolizes the end of a narrow and destructive rendition of *l'ordine della famiglia* but also represents the death of a generation of Italian Americans whose ethnicity was vitiated by several interrelated factors, one being economic struggle, immediately revealed in the first line of the novella: "[T]his is a neighborhood of people who aren't quite making it" (17). Other factors include a lack of visible means for maintaining and renewing one's relationship to ethnic ancestry, for example, a common language or dialect, a set of religious beliefs, and kinship patterns; and an absence of what Raymond A. Belliotti describes as "felt solidarity with other Italian Americans, and some measurable degree of continuity with earlier generations" (173). Certainly, sharing a consciousness of *italianità* is not dependent on one factor alone but is, rather, a realization that one's sense of self is strengthened and enhanced by shared feelings about ancestry. Rossi's *The Quick* exposes the costs of losing continuity between children and parents, Italy and America, old-world beliefs and new-world re-creation of those beliefs. Only Phyllis Macdonald and Chris Russo offer Marie solace, perhaps because they view their world in the context of relationships, something that Marie Russo may learn better how to do as a result of her ongoing friendship with them.

## Italian Signs in Ciresi, Calcagno, and Manfredi

Recent collections of stories—Rita Ciresi's *Mother Rocket*, Anne Calcagno's *Pray for Yourself and Other Stories*, and Renée Manfredi's *Where Love Leaves Us*—continue in the tradition of works by writers such as Carole Maso and Tina De Rosa in the belief that ethnicity is a governing identity and as such must be reinterpreted by every generation. Italian American ethnicity is inscribed in the stories through Italian signs, that is, specific references to Italian culture without necessarily the impetus of the Italian American family narrative. Moreover, each collection incorporates two topics that Italian American narratives often include: the fascination with duality and the loss of family members. In the first, characters possess a "double-consciousness" (Sollors's term) and are thus often attracted to mirrors, an activity of negotiation presented as early as Marion Benasutti's *No SteadyJob for Papa*. Second, the writers present characters in search of redemption, having lost parents, siblings, entire families, and the older generation. Reconstructing a viable relationship to the past is the goal of several protagonists as they seek to connect themselves to an ancestral heritage that gives meaning to their present lives. As Ciresi writes in one of her stories in *Mother Rocket*, "[T]he older you get, the easier it is to resurrect yourself" (34). In each of the collections, some reinvented version of the self as ethnic is presented.

Italian signs are peppered throughout *Mother Rocket*, Ciresi's first collection of stories.[15] Words, phrases, and sentences from Italian American cultural life are placed in stories about relationships—between siblings, spouses, children and parents, and mentors and protégées. Although the stories are not overtly about the Italian American culture or family, Ciresi's signaling of *italianità* reveals a sustained interest in the importance of cultural identity to enrich (and at times, proscribe) the characters' lives.

Perhaps the story that best epitomizes Ciresi's interest in the strength of cultural identity is the title story, "Mother Rocket." That this story is placed in the middle of the collection reinforces its centrality to one of Ciresi's abiding concerns: the tension between identity and ethnicity, a tension that motivates the movement of "Mother Rocket." One of the ways characters resolve this conflict is by changing the present course of their lives. Such an activity might be described as "getting off the road," a designation that I borrow from William Boelhower, who describes ethnicity as the "practice of digging up cultural origins . . . of staying behind, of getting off the road, of rediscovering place" (*Through a Glass Darkly* 64). For Jude Silverman, the protagonist of "Mother Rocket," getting off the road eases the pressure she regularly feels about being Jewish American.

At the beginning of the story, Jude Silverman makes her living as a dancer in the modern troupe called "Future/Dance/Theater," a name that has ironic significance for Jude because she is devoted to the past. At the beginning and the end of the story, Ciresi refers to Jude's reaction to a caged polar bear in Central Park, a structural doubling that reinforces Jude Silverman's feeling of duality. By the conclusion, however, Jude has come to terms with the single-most captivating event in her life: the death by explosion of her foster parents, Uncle Chaim and Aunt Mina, in Jerusalem in 1967. The then seventeen-year-old Jude Schitzman was photographed in a national magazine cradling the amputated arm of her uncle, a photograph that enjoyed considerable fame, winning for the photographer the Pulitzer Prize.

To reinforce Jude's obsessive connection to the past, Ciresi graphically refers to the tragic event twice in the story; the photograph is another framing device that captures the idea that Jude is harnessed by the past. Jude's relationship to the past is further exacerbated in the present by her choosing to marry a photographer, who remembers the 1967 award-winning photograph with envy. Jude's perversely humorous description of taking pictures and making love theatricalizes her ongoing relation to the past. To her future husband, she exclaims: "'Load your guns. . . . Fire away. . . . Mmm, then, photographer. Give me an F-stop I'll never forget. Fire away'" (59, 61). Of course, Jude has never forgotten. Her one memory emotionally enslaves her and has the potential to deprive her of developing a cultural identity that she accepts without hatred or arrogance.

Understanding her past as loathsome does not prevent Jude from feeling irresistibly tied to it. However entrapping her cultural identity feels, Jude wonders aloud what those Americans think about all day who are not ethnic. When her photographer husband replies with the words "'sex and death, . . . same as you, without the East Side accent,'" Jude realizes that her understanding of sex and death are indeed modified by the very fact of her ethnicity: "But it was the accent that made her." Jude interprets her identity *only* through the lens of ethnicity, believing that "she wasn't anything, she wasn't anybody, without all that behind her" (69). By the end of the story, however, Jude Silverman—like Anna Giardino of Bryant's text—is able to move beyond the past without losing it, a mental and spiritual shift accompanied by her having become pregnant.[16]

Jude eventually achieves a sense of continuity with the past without the self-dramatizing suicidal despair so apparent at the story's beginning. In choosing to "get off the road" by retiring from the dance troupe, Jude Silverman invests herself in a more affirming connection to her cultural heritage than that of the grotesque memory of her foster parents' death. Ciresi seems to suggest in this story that one's relationship to ethnicity is eminently subject to shifts in the angle of one's perceptions of it. On the brink of motherhood, Jude Silverman reinvents herself as a "Hebrew warrioress," no longer fighting off feelings of despair but fighting to survive for the future of her child (75).

Fighting for his life is precisely what Piero is doing in Anne Calcagno's "A River Fat with Life," a story from her collection *Pray for Yourself and Other Stories.*[17] Of the nine tales in the collection, two are set in Italy, revealing Calcagno's bicultural interest in both countries. Like Ciresi's collection, Calcagno's stories are insistently concerned with relationships—destructive and loving. Maintaining a commitment and conscious awareness of cultural identity is explored in depth in "A River Fat with Life," a story set in Italy that examines the extent to which a character will go to reaffirm cultural roots.

Italian-born Piero, whose birthplace is Tuscania, returns to his hometown with his Italian wife, Emilia, and two visiting Americans: a philosophy professor, Frank, and his former student, Sarah. Witnessing the ritual skinning and butchering of a sheep, eating a succulent lunch of fish, cheese, olives, and red wine, and visiting an abandoned monastery comprise the day's events. However, throughout the visit, Piero's excessive need to reinforce the importance of his provenance results in a perilous late-night drive home. Mocking death and terrorizing his passengers, Piero drunkenly speeds down the dark, narrow roads.

"A River Fat with Life" can be read persuasively as a modern story about alienation, each character failing the other in valuing intimacy as a means to overcome atomistic individualism. Calcagno's interest in ethnic identity, moreover, enriches the story's modernist emphasis on alienation. The impetus for Piero's trip home is his dire need to reaffirm his identity, without which he feels he will die. Calcagno's first paragraph functions like a thematic précis of the entire story. Like a much earlier American writer, Nathaniel Hawthorne, Calcagno tells the story twice, once in the first paragraph and again throughout the remainder of the story. Such a structural doubling, as we saw in Rossi and Ciresi, reveals the author's interest in ethnicity. Of Piero, the narrator writes:

> He had been counting on this day particularly because he had been feeling *pale*, slipping from himself, and in a recurring nightmare he fell into a river. . . . But he never sank. The river was a chemical and proceeded *to strip the color from his skin*, then usurped his weight. . . . There was no struggle, just disappearance. He was afraid he would die in his sleep. (italics mine, 44)

Calcagno employs color symbology to reflect the character's fear of annihilation through the loss of cultural identity. Such a strategy parallels the concerns of several Italian American writers, especially Dodici Azpadu in her recognition that the category of whiteness often vitiates the ethnic identity of her Sicilian characters, who do not identify as white. Because he is physically close enough to drive to his place of origin, Piero feels that he can reconstitute his relationship to cultural identity by returning home. This convenience was often denied the immigrants who left their hometown villages altogether and were compelled to create other ways to sustain and rejuvenate their sense of themselves as Italian.

Piero fears becoming the quintessential invisible man: no one will see that he has disappeared. To reassert his identity, Piero returns to his birthplace because he believes that there he will find a sense of continuity. As scholars of ethnic identity have written, in knowing one's origins "one finds to some degree the personal and social meaning of human existence. . . . To be without a sense of continuity is to be faced with one's own death" (De Vos and Romanucci-Ross, "Ethnicity: Vessel of Meaning" 364). Piero's fears result in excessive behavior, however, and Calcagno employs violent diction to enforce this: "Piero had this day by the throat and it was singing to him" (54).

Unable to respond to Tuscania in the same way as Piero, the other characters incur his scorn and become victims of Piero's insistent clinging to his cultural roots. If the stressing of one's ethnic identity becomes obsessive, it reveals "a flaw in one's self-conception as a unique multidimensional entity" (Devereux 67).[18] In this way, Piero is comparable to Jude Silverman of Ciresi's story, both characters verging on the grotesque because of their obsession about cultural background. Piero stubbornly insists on an identity that is rooted to his place of heritage; as a result, he diminishes what may be other equally decisive elements that spring from his age, his occupation, his marital status, and the like. When Piero leaps onto a thin rim of an orchard balcony at the monastery, he wants the earth to claim him, his body feeding his place of birth. Sarah, the American student, reveals her acuity in her private thought about her visit to Tuscania: "*[I]t's our illness that we eat ourselves*," she thinks, aware of Piero's overidentification with place, his excess of self (56). Ironically, Piero cannot be filled completely by his return home. In fact, in his desperate actions, Piero concomitantly becomes an excessive self *and* less of himself, a perverse caricature. Devouring the experience of self, Piero becomes like Kafka's hunger artist, never satiated yet always seeking the ideal meal.

While Ciresi locates her interest in ethnicity in Jewish American identity and Calcagno in native Italian identity, Renée Manfredi depicts the Little Italy section of Pittsburgh in "The Projectionist," the first story in her collection *Where Love Leaves Us.*[19] Of the three collections under consideration, Manfredi most directly characterizes Italian American family life, though her stories, like Ciresi's and Calcagno's, engage other plots and themes as well. "The Projectionist" functions much like a miniature narrative of the many ideas portrayed in the novels of Italian America: maintaining close family ties and relations between Italy and America; continuing invocations to the Madonna; challenging *l'ordine della famiglia*; losing the Italian language; dismantling the ethnic enclave; employing folk rituals; grieving the loss of the Italian homeland; and suffering from displacement in a new world.

Manfredi incorporates each of these ideas in her portrayal of an Italian American father, Nicolo, who sinks deeper into depression as he remembers how his first family was slaughtered in war-torn Italy. Serafina, the fifteen-year-old narrator of his second family in America, ultimately functions as a mediator between her father's old-world mentality and his new-world reality. Living in the rapidly changing Little Italy section in Pittsburgh, Nicolo has worked for fifteen years as the projectionist at the local theater.

Nicolo finds the changes he sees in his neighborhood and in his daughter, an *American* teenager, profoundly disturbing. Unable to adjust, the father descends into a depression that lasts much longer than his annual "crazy April," when he grieves for the death of his first wife and baby, who were killed in April 1945.

Serafina takes part in her father's recovery, although she refuses to submit to his definition of *rispetto* (respect), which would mean traveling to Italy and agreeing to an arranged marriage. Nonetheless, she guides her mother in the recipe to cure *mal'occhio*, revealing her ability to remember and engage family rituals. Mother and daughter use the *mal'occhio* ritual because they recognize the extent to which Nicolo is suffering from cultural malaise: Nicolo just learned that the Italian owners of his local grocery store committed suicide so as not to burden their children in old age. Serafina also observes her father's somnambulism. As he murmurs in Italian, she feels her own loss in recognizing that her father refused to teach the children the native language, considering American English a badge of status. Toward the conclusion of the narrative, Nicolo awakens Serafina and both go to the theater at three in the morning to watch *The Wizard of Oz*. Offering his brand of exegesis on the star of the movie, Judy Garland, Nicolo could be issuing a warning to his daughter about her future in America: "'I want to reach in and shake her. Warn her of the wolves like Minelli who turned her into a boozer and a doper, the bum. He gives Italians a bad name'" (17).

Wanting to save her from the inevitable pain of adulthood, Nicolo dramatizes his own painful history in Italy. Despite the fact that Nicolo is consumed by the memory of the death of his family in Sicily during the Second World War, he regularly envisions Italy as the place of milk and honey. In this way, he joins other characters in Italian American narratives who remember the homeland in unchanging terms, often a childhood memory of pleasure and satisfaction. When Nicolo tries to dissuade his fifteen-year-old daughter from dating an Italian American boy, he dreamily imagines the lives of fifteen-year-old girls in his homeland: "'In the old country girls still play with dolls at fifteen'" (5). Immediately correcting his misperception, the mother reminds her husband of actual history: "'The old country in your dreams, Sir. My mother was married at fifteen, my grandmother at thirteen'" (6).

During another conversation, Nicolo argues with Carlo Benedetti, Serafina's boyfriend, who has dropped out of college and plans to hitchhike across the country. Responding angrily to Carlo's decision to leave his family, Nicolo reminds him of how proud Carlo made his parents by receiving a scholarship to college. Uninterested in nostalgic stories of the past, Carlo responds, in typical teenage fashion, "'I have to live my life. There's more to life than earning money'" (10). Instead of responding directly to what he perceives as a betrayal of *l'ordine della famiglia*, Nicolo recalls southern Italy, a place that Robert Orsi explains is used by immigrant parents "as a reproach to the younger generation's emerging sense of the world." In his study of intergenerational conflict in Italian Harlem, Orsi contends that immigrant parents created the geographic idiom of "southern Italy" in order to discipline their children "with the other place": "As they imagined 'Southern Italy' for their children, it became a place of perfectly ordered and secure family relations . . . a land of mighty mothers and fathers whom no child would dare disobey. . . . It was a geographical fantasy of entropy" ("The Fault of Memory" 136–38).

Nicolo counters Carlo's adolescent comment with a series of questions that are impossible for Carlo and Nicolo's family to answer: "'What do you know of the value of money? What do you know of poverty? What do you know of not having enough money to get the hell out of a country where you forbid your wife to go to church for fear that it, also, will be under siege?'" (10). In seeking to discipline Carlo with "the other place," Nicolo uses the image of southern Italy against him. Realizing this, Carlo explains, "'But it isn't my fault that I don't [know about southern Italy, the war, famine, and so on]'" (10). Like many southern Italians, Nicolo is rooted to a memory of southern Italy that both pleases ("'I say you can see God in the people there'") and torments him ("'My wife and baby died. . . . I delivered the child from her dead body'") (9, 10). In either case, the memories are not necessarily intended to be "passed on."[20] Yet, in keeping with his profound belief in the strength of cultural heritage, Nicolo insists that it is the duty of

American-born children of immigrants to learn about the homeland, the sacrifices made in order for children to live better lives in the new world.

Manfredi's short story reiterates themes of importance to Italian American writers. That she has the daughter of the story function as a mediator between the culture about which she learns (southern Italy) and the one in which she is a part (Italian America) suggests the resiliency and creative possibilities of the topic of ethnicity. Increasingly, writers from the third and fourth generation explore the tensions between cultures and the sustaining nature of *italianità* by using multiple and interacting layers of plot, character, and theme. The influence of modernist narrative strategies on stories such as "Mother Rocket," "A River Fat with Life," and "The Projectionist" help emancipate ethnicity from traditionalism, to which it is too often narrowly aligned.[21] Writers of Italian American background in the 1980s and 1990s show little concern with "transcending" ethnic identity. For them, going home is a way of experimenting with *italianità*.[22] In this way, recent writers are similar to their Italian American sisters of the early period who defined home as creative ethnicists, building a bridge between Italy and America. As early as Mari Tomasi, negotiating the memories of Italy meant a conscious effort to sustain cultural traditions, from learning the Italian language to teaching a non-Italian the recipe for dandelion salad, as the capable ambassador of both cultures, Michelle Tiffone/Mister Tiff, did for Minna Douglas, the Scotch quarry owner, in *Like Lesser Gods.*

Claiming an identity that is neither all Italian nor American, the writers remember and imagine a homeland that nourishes their creative talents. While a devotion to their small villages remained preeminent in the minds of immigrant parents, Italian American women writers push those boundaries by exploring northern and southern Italy and by traversing both countries, Italy and America. Cavallo, for example, pays homage to the Florentine poet Dante *and* the Sicilian playwright Pirandello. Barolini writes about northern and southern Italy with a facility that comes with having lived in her grandparents' homeland and having learned the language skillfully enough to become, herself, a translator. Invoking the artistic magnificence of da Vinci, De Rosa claims a connection to the northern Italian artist's erudition as much as she embraces the oral traditions of her Neapolitan grandparents.

Communities where Italians settled in America become the imaginative topography for writers such as Benasutti and Waldo. Values of orientation antithetical to *la via vecchia* are often mediated by godparent figures, whose importance increases as children's memories of the homeland decrease. The writers reimagine the transatlantic crossing of their parents and grandparents, producing a saga of immigration that is woven into the fabric of American literary history. In this way, Italian American writers are also claiming a tradition that emerges from their relationship to American ideals of freedom and independence. Because of these ideals, Italian women experienced a loosening of strict Italian family codes. Many chose to write about the family in an effort to honor and challenge those traditions of *italianità* integral to their identities as women and as writers.

For the writers examined in these pages, going home is a radical act: an act of faith and defiance. To discover a female maternal ancestry, Italian American women writers return—in memory and actuality—to the homeland, to the homes of their grandmothers and mothers, and to their own writing desks where they take up pen and imagine convincingly. Writers of the 1990s and beyond, writers of the fourth and fifth generations, may look back to the works of Tomasi and Bryant and discover the maternal *literary* ancestry that is theirs to claim. To reiterate the belief of Adrienne Rich, whose words began this study, to claim an education rather than to receive one passively can literally mean the difference between life and death. In much the same way, claiming traditions of Italian American women writers is an act of vitality. Those of us dedicated to the study of Italian American literature participate in shaping the images germane to this cultural group.

Of Emily Dickinson, who lived and wrote her entire adult life under her father's roof, Rich (in the poem "'I Am in Danger—Sir—'") writes

> you chose
> silence for entertainment,
> chose to have it out at last
> on your own premises (*Adrienne Rich's Poetry* 31)

Italian American women are "having it out" in the kitchens, the front rooms, and the back streets of their imagination. Without claiming their efforts, we risk losing the complex beauty of ethnicity itself.

*Notes*
*Bibliography*
*Index*

# Notes

## Introduction

1. In "Where Are the Italian-American Novelists?," Talese refers to one Italian American woman writer: the academician Camille Paglia, who believes that Italian Americans are more *naturally* inclined toward film than books. Slipping into stereotyping, Talese reinforces the notion regarding Italians' need for display in his conclusion that Italians are essentially village-dwelling people and "crowd-pleasing performers" (29).

2. In *The Italian-American Novel: A Document of the Interaction of Two Cultures*, Green explores what she sees revealed in the fiction as the dominant pattern underlying each phase of the integration experience: "conflict, isolation, and assimilation." The end product of the novels is the subscription to this belief: "[T]he individual has the moral power to triumph in the struggle against a hostile environment" (19). Green's analysis of Italian American literature assumes that assimilation should be the thematic goal of the novels. Green cites Mario Puzo's *The Godfather* as *the* ultimate proof that the Italian American novel has come of age, joining the "general family," because it is evaluated "on equal terms with that of other writers" (368). Puzo's emphasis on criminality and organized violence appeals to a wider-ranging reading public than immigrant themes and should, according to Green, be applauded for doing so.

3. Washington writes, "[M]ore than anything else, . . . three literary events made it possible for serious Hurston scholarship to emerge": Robert Hemenway's biography, *Zora Neale Hurston: A Literary Biography* (1977); The University of Illinois Press edition of *Their Eyes*, which "made the novel available on a steady and dependable basis"; and Walker's *I Love Myself When I Am Laughing . . . And Then Again When I Am Looking Mean and Impressive: A Zora Neale Hurston Reader* (1979) (xi).

4. On the back cover of *The Dream Book*, Alice Walker writes this commendation:

> For years I have wanted to hear the voice(s) of the Italian American woman. Who is she? I have wondered. What is her view of life? Does she still exist? *The Dream*

*Book* answers these questions and more. Barolini's powerful introduction, exploding the silence of Italian American women writers, is an impassioned and magnificent contribution to our knowledge of what it has meant and what it means still, to be Ethnic American *and* Woman, in a society that validates authenticity in neither. It is a book of heroic recovery and affirmation.

5. Out of print for over a decade, *Paper Fish* nonetheless continued to inspire a coterie of scholars who taught and wrote about the novel, despite the scarcity of books. In 1995, Fred L. Gardaphé, author of *Italian Signs, American Streets: The Evolution of Italian American Narrative*, introduced De Rosa's novel to Florence Howe, publisher at The Feminist Press. She read it and republished it in 1996, making *Paper Fish* the first twentieth-century Italian American novel written by a woman to be republished by that press.

6. *From the Margin* is edited by three academics, two who work in departments of Italian, Anthony J. Tamburri and Paolo Giordano, and one who works in a department of English, Fred L. Gardaphé. I refer to their academic affiliations to reinforce the fact that literary analyses written about Italian American literature have captured the interest of scholars teaching in both Italian and English departments in the United States and Italy. The conversation about Italian American writers crosses cultures, continents, and academic disciplines. The American Italian Historical Association, founded in 1966, has annually brought together scholars from both America and Italy.

7. My edition, *The Voices We Carry*, includes selections of works-in-progress of fourteen Italian American women, five of whose published works were previously anthologized in Barolini's *The Dream Book*.

8. In the introduction to *The Invention of Ethnicity*, Werner Sollors defines ethnicity as an invention "of the general cultural constructedness of the modern world. . . . [B]y calling ethnicity—that is, belonging and being perceived by others as belonging to an ethnic group—an 'invention,' one signals an interpretation in a modern and postmodern context" (x, xiii). In his earlier work *Beyond Ethnicity* (1986), Sollors takes "the conflict between contractual and hereditary, self-made and ancestral, definitions of American identity—between *consent* and *descent*—as the central drama in American culture" (5–6). Sollors's paradigm is useful in understanding the underlying tension between old-world southern Italian culture and American mores in nearly all of the texts under consideration.

9. Chametzky argues that "we *need* these experiences of the particular; it is too early, socially and historically[,] to dismiss or minimize their importance" (248).

10. In 1861, Italy became a nation and Victor Emmanuel II was proclaimed king of Italy. To complete the *Risorgimento* (the years between 1815 and 1870 in which Italy achieved nationhood and became modern-

ized), the papal states were annexed by Italy in 1870. Northern and southern Italians highly identified with their regions and with the cultural mores and dialects specific to them. As one Italian immigrant says, "I say Italy; but for me, as for the others, Italy is the little village where I was raised" (qtd. in Williams 17). In response to the actual unification of Italy's provinces, the southern *contadini* (peasants) "unwittingly began [uniting] in a rebellion against the despised Bourbon oppressors." They had little desire to unite Italy, "an empty abstraction to them" (Gambino, *Blood of My Blood* 43).

11. The *Mezzogiorno* includes these regions: Abruzzi-Molise, Apulia, Basilicata, Calabria, Campania, Lazio, Sardinia, and Sicily. The word *Mezzogiorno* literally means "midday," but it also connotes the idea of "the land that time forgot."

12. According to Maddalena Tirabassi, however, the great Italian migration to the United States that began in the 1890s

> was from the outset characterized by a conspicuous number of women. From constituting just under 30 percent of the immigrants in the 1890s they reached 60 percent of the total in the 1980s and today slightly outnumber the men in the Italian American population. (135)

13. Census figures indicate that perhaps as many as 80 percent of Italian immigrants came from southern Italy. However, that figure is taken

> from statistics of American immigration authorities, who began to keep separate counts of "northern" and "southern" Italians starting in 1899. These counts are not fully trustworthy because the intent of their distinction was racial, and accordingly, a peculiar definition of a *southerner* was employed, which included anyone from central and even some from northern Italy. According to the Bureau of Immigration's definition, "southern" Italians included anyone from the "peninsula proper" . . . so that "even Genoa [the northern port city] is South Italian." (Alba 41 n. 4)

14. For discussions of anti-Italian bigotry, see Richard Gambino's *Vendetta*, which details the 1891 lynching of Italian Americans in New Orleans; Andrew Rolle's chapter "The Roots of Discrimination" in *The Italian Americans: Troubled Roots*; Leonard Covello's "The Southern Question in Italy in Its Bearing on Italo-American Problems" in *The Social Background of the Italo-American School Child*; and Jerre Mangione and Ben Morreale's chapter "New Orleans—Wops, Crime, and Lynchings" in *La Storia: Five Centuries of the Italian American Experience.* As early as 1806, a distinction was being made between the more industrialized culture of northern Italy and the agricultural *Mezzogiorno*: "Europe ends at Naples, and it ends there badly enough. Calabria, Sicily, all the rest is African" (Creuzé de Lesser, *Voyage en Italie et en Sicile*, qtd. in Williams 1).

15. See Micaela di Leonardo's chapter "'The Family is *Soprattutto*':

Mobility Models, Kinship Realities, and Ethnic Ideology" in *The Varieties of Ethnic Experience.*

16. The word *campanilismo* is derived from the word *il campanile,* defined as the bell tower or belfry of a church (Covello, Appendix A). Gambino explains that the attitude of village-mindedness is "limited to those who live within hearing range of their village's church bell [*campana*]" (*Blood of My Blood* 65).

17. Williams is quoting from an article by Emily F. Meade, "Italian Immigration into the South," *South Atlantic Quarterly* 14 (July 1905): 218.

18. In her essay "The Italian Immigrant Women Who Arrived in the United States Before World War I," Valentine Rossilli Winsey describes the Italian woman's "heritage of fatalism" as nurtured by

> her religion, her extreme poverty combined with a continuous succession of such violent natural forces as volcanic eruptions, hot winds from the African Sirocco, etc. . . . Her heritage of fatalism was inescapable—one's life was predetermined by one's "destino," a belief which, unbeknownst to her, was tacitly encouraged by the nobles and clergy whose welfare depended on submission of the peasant class. (200)

19. I am indebted to M. Giulia Fabi for providing me with fuller information about the distinction between masculine and feminine use of words (personal correspondence with the author, August 1990).

20. King-Kok Cheung's "'Don't Tell': Imposed Silences in *The Color Purple* and *The Woman Warrior*" focuses on how the daughters overcome their culture's predisposition to secrecy by channeling their anger into creativity. The same attitude toward silence and creativity can be seen in the Italian American novels under consideration.

21. For many Italian American writers, Gillan's poem "Public School No. 18: Paterson, New Jersey" has become a theme song for reclaiming the voices of their ethnic heritage. Gillan's poem has been reprinted in several books, including her own *Where I Come From: Selected and New Poems.*

22. Sister Blandina Segale's *At the End of the Santa Fe Trail* (1948) is the memoir of a Sister of Charity in the Southwest during the frontier days—1872–93. Frances Vinciguerra, encouraged by an editor to anglicize her surname to Winwar, wrote historical novels and biographical studies, the most famous of which is *Poor Splendid Wings* (1933), a biographical study of the Rossetti family and the pre-Raphaelite circle. Rosa Cassettari's oral memoirs told to Marie Hall Ets relate stories that she heard as a child in her northern village and that she experienced during her migration to America (*Rosa: The Life of an Italian Immigrant*). Each of these authors, writing in different genres and for different purposes, was intimately connected to her culture of heritage. After her work in the Southwest, Sister Blandina labored for thirty-five years on behalf of

the Italian immigrants of Cincinnati, opening up an institute and three schools. Among her score of historical biographies, Winwar also published *Pagan Interval* (1929), a novel that uses the Mediterranean island of Ennios as its setting. A storyteller at the Chicago Commons (a settlement house) and Northwestern University, Rosa Cassettari regularly recited stories from her native village in northern Italy.

## 1. *Family Novels of Development: Mari Tomasi's* Like Lesser Gods *and Marion Benasutti's* No SteadyJob for Papa

1. This is paraphrased from M. H. Abrams's definition of the bildungsroman in *A Glossary of Literary Terms* (132).

2. For an analysis of the problems inherent in the generic use of the bildungsroman as a form for women's novels and the problem of the concept of identity itself, see Lazzaro-Weis.

3. I am distinguishing between women writing in the English and Anglo-American traditions from more recent ethnic women writers, whose allegiance to two cultures highly informs their writing. Several texts by Anglo-descended and Anglo-American women writers focus on the issue of gender as it proscribes the female protagonist's freedom: Kate Chopin's *The Awakening*, Edith Wharton's *The House of Mirth*, George Eliot's *The Mill on the Floss* and *Middlemarch*, and Doris Lessing's volumes of *Children of Violence* are just a few examples.

4. Sollors explains in his essay "Ethnicity" that "it makes little sense to define 'ethnicity-as-such,' since it refers not to a thing-in-itself but to a relationship: ethnicity is typically based on a *contrast*" (288).

5. In *The Varieties of Ethnic Experience*, di Leonardo challenges several sociological surveys and mobility studies from the 1960s and 1970s that characterize the Italian American "family culture" as creating an "ambitionless, self-reproducing, urban working class" (95). In particular, the sociological study by Herbert J. Gans, *Urban Villagers: Group and Class in the Life of Italian Americans* (1962), and the mobility study by Stephan Thernstrom, *The Other Bostonians: Poverty and Progress in an American Metropolis, 1880–1970* (1973), fail to consider shifting economies and changing social mobility. These works and several like them characterize immigrants as immutable peasants who disparage change and are unaffected by economic and social influences. Tomasi and Benasutti tell a different story.

6. In *Blood of My Blood*, Gambino explains that the creative ethnicist "uses his ethnic background as a point of departure for growth rather than as proof of his worth" (329).

7. Tomasi's own family followed the first wave of granite sculptors

and artisans to Barre. She writes, "[T]hese immigrants were not granite workers; they came to establish small businesses in this booming Vermont town" ("The Italian Story" 77–78).

8. In this way, Tomasi can be compared with Eudora Welty, who explains that "long before I wrote stories, I listened for stories" (14).

9. Added to the paucity of material on strikes and tension between ethnic groups, Barolini notes Tomasi's silences on other pressing topics:

> Mari Tomasi did not address any of the sensitive areas in the stoneworkers' stories . . . the radical political and anti-church leanings of many of the *Northern Italians*; the sense of discrimination experienced by Italian immigrants in this country, the reasons for their *shame* and *guilt* during the second World War when Italy was an enemy. ("The Case of Mari Tomasi" 181)

Rudolph J. Vecoli attributes the silence of old-time residents of Barre, Vermont, on the subject of anarchism (Barre was a world center of anarchism in the first decades of the twentieth century) to what he calls "historical amnesia": with respect to the radical antecedents of immigrant families,

> the second generation, the children of the immigrants [of which Tomasi is a member], had the difficult task of reconciling its Old World traditions with the new ways of America. That task was made more difficult if one's parents were identified as "reds," as well as foreigners. ("Finding, and Losing" 7)

10. An earlier version of Rosa's article is called "The Novels of Mari Tomasi." For an interpretation on the quarry town as a frontier environment, see Garroni.

11. Perhaps Di Donato's *Christ in Concrete* best captures how Italian workers in New York City were abused by their bosses and the state bureaucracy that supported big business over and above the concerns of workers. In their jobs as construction workers at dangerous work sites, the immigrants are literally buried alive in concrete.

12. Dust-removing equipment was not installed in closed sheds until it was required by law in 1937. By then, as Vecoli explains, Barre experienced "the dominant and terrible fact in that history": "the premature death of an entire generation of immigrant stoneworkers (including other nationalities, as well) who fell victims to the insidious dust in the sheds" ("Finding, and Losing" 7).

13. The phrase "female realism" is taken from Mike Gold's memoir, *Jews Without Money*: "With female realism she tried to beat the foolish male dreams out of his head" (qtd. in Ewen 191).

14. Rolle explains that "[t]he Madonna had been a mother but scarcely a wife. Accordingly, the Italian woman has historically reduced the power and importance of sexuality by accepting a *mater dolorosa* role" (111).

15. In *The Dream Book*, Barolini appropriately reprints the conclusion

of book 1 of *Like Lesser Gods*, for it dramatizes in breathtaking detail the lengths to which Maria will go in order to prevent her husband from illness.

16. In "The Case of Mari Tomasi," Barolini contends that, because he is a man, Pietro Dalli was given the freedom to love his art more than his family:

> He is allowed that. Maria, the wife and mother, the family pinion, must embody the traditional womanly traits—she must be stolid, enduring, silent, sacrificial. It is a powerful contrast that Tomasi implicitly makes in the difference of choices available to men and women of the Dalli's background. Could Tomasi have felt in her own life that, as a woman, she could not, as Pietro did, give everything to her art? (180)

17. Da Vinci's painting is historically known as *Virgin of the Rocks*. Tomasi substitutes the word "Madonna" to emphasize the relationship between motherhood and strength and between Maria Dalli and the Mother Mary.

18. Characterizations of fathers who are weak-minded or physically ill in Italian American novels are not limited to the writers discussed in this book. Antonia Pola's *Who Can Buy the Stars?*, Julia Savarese's *The Weak and the Strong*, and Mario Puzo's *The Fortunate Pilgrim* depict immensely strong immigrant mothers who help the family survive the early years in America. For the most part, the mothers in these novels remain in the more familiar province of home; the men, in contrast, are separated from the home world and often feel out of place in the work force. The writers often characterize their fictional males as divided selves, suffering eventual illness and even death.

19. Green underemphasizes Tomasi's focus on family and community by interpreting Pietro Dalli as the protagonist and the patriarchal father figure who exercises "his born right as head of the family" (137).

20. Tomasi was baptized with the name "Marie" at St. Augustine's Church in Montpelier. She changed her name to "Mari" (pronounced like "Mary") at school because her "real name was 'too foreign'" (Barolini, "The Case of Mari Tomasi" 182). Tomasi's decision sounds more like a defensive measure than a celebration of embracing two cultures, as she has Michele Tiffone do. By endowing Michele Tiffone/Mister Tiff with two names, Tomasi may very well have been considering the importance of both her baptismal name and her self-chosen name.

21. Tiffone achieves the status of community adviser because he is unafraid of danger, of taking chances, or of using benevolent bribery to effect change for the good of the people. In book 2, for example, Tiffone successfully resolves the political chief's illicit love affair, and he encourages Gabbi Dalli (the youngest daughter) to accept her fiance's decision to work the stone, even though she wants her future husband to have white-collar status.

22. Likewise, Mari Tomasi's only sister, Marguerite, became a regis-

tered nurse in Montpelier. One of her three brothers, Ernest, became a practicing physician also in Montpelier (Tomasi, "The Italian Story" 79).

23. Tomasi's first novel, *Deep Grow the Roots*, is set in the Piedmont region of northern Italy during the beginnings of the Fascist regime and centers around the tragic love story of two peasants, Luigi and Nina. The novel was well reviewed by contemporary novelists such as Dorothy Canfield Fisher, Mary Ellen Chase, and Faith Baldwin. Overlooked by the reviewers but compelling are the images of strong, unconventional, independent female characters, including the midwife La Tonietta and the Bottani sisters, who live in seclusion in the mountains.

24. See Benasutti's essay "The Making of an Italian American Writer."

25. Green offers a more balanced interpretation of the father's situation of employment:

> Papa's unsteady odyssey with employment, however, is not a matter of indolence. Following an injury in a soft-coal mine, he goes to work in the Navy Yard in Philadelphia. A frail man, temperamentally unsuited to hard labor, he is only the residue of his vanquished hope of becoming a scholar or an artist. (195)

26. In her study of Ascoli Piceno, a city in the region of Le Marche, 130 miles northeast of Rome, Lola Romanucci-Ross found evidence that controverted the Banfield notion of

> "amoral familism," that is, the emphasizing of family loyalty above all other considerations. . . . Seduction of the woman is feared not from the stranger, but from the *compare*, *cugino*, and *cognato* ("godfather," "cousin," and "brother-in-law"). . . . Very often one hears, *La vita è una fregature. Chi non sa fregare rimane fregato* ("Life is a rape scene. He who is not the aggressor in the act will be the victim") [Romanucci-Ross's translation]. (202–3)

For information on marital arrangements in Italian culture, see Winsey.

27. I am using the terms "consent" and "descent" as Sollors does in *Beyond Ethnicity* (5–6).

28. Nathalia Wright explains that Italy provided American artists and writers with an intellectual and moral experience not available to them in a young country like America. I am distinguishing Italian American writers' perception of Italy as Edenic from American writers in the nineteenth century, who used the myth of the garden of Eden in their Italianate fiction. According to Wright, American writers examined moral issues often by depicting Italian civilization as corrupt; the Italian past, however, promised good. One of the most commonly employed images to expand on this theme was the garden of Eden (29, 33, 256).

29. Five fairly recent works portray a narrator or character who returns to Italy in order to negotiate issues of identity: Robert Ferro's novel of Italian American and gay identity, *The Family of Max Desir*; Susan Caperna Lloyd's autobiographical narrative, *No Pictures in My Grave: A*

*Spiritual Journey in Sicily*; Anna Monardo's female bildungsroman, *The Courtyard of Dreams*; Anne Calcagno's collection of short stories, *Pray for Yourself and Other Stories*; and Fred L. Gardaphé's autobiographical essay, *The Italian-American Writer: An Essay and an Annotated Checklist.*

30. The narrator of John Fante's short story collection, *The Wine of Youth*, describes the mother's anger in "A Wife for Dino Rossi" as she unsuccessfully represses her rage at her abusive husband: "She worked in a fury, the sweat clinging like mist across the lines of her forehead. . . . [The father] was whistling *'La Donna è mobile'* when he left. . . . It made Mamma so furious that she took the large fish platter and sent it crashing over the floor" (92, 94).

31. In *The Italian-American Novel*, Green also makes the connection between Alcott's Jo and Benasutti's Rosemary, both girls growing "from childhood to the brink of womanhood" (195).

32. In *The Dream Book*, Barolini contrasts the Italian writer Grazia Deledda (Nobel Prize Laureate for Literature in 1926), who was married with children, to the childless great women writers of the Anglo and Anglo-American tradition: Jane Austen, George Eliot, Emily Dickinson, and Edith Wharton. Deledda perceived her family as integral to her art, not as a threat to literary expression. Deledda's writings included thirty-three novels and eighteen collections of stories (28–29).

33. Fante's short story "The Odyssey of a Wop" also details the response of the boy narrator when he is the victim of an ethnic slur:

> I don't like the grocer. My mother sends me to his store every day, and instantly he chokes up my breathing with the greeting: "Hello, you little Dago! What'll you have?" So I detest him, and never enter his store if other customers are to be seen, for to be called a Dago before others is a ghastly, almost a physical humiliation. My stomach expands and contracts, and I feel naked. (135–36)

34. According to historian Donna Gabaccia:

> [M]others of neither immigrant group [Italian or Jewish] prepared daughters for menstruation, adult sexuality or maternity, but Jewish daughters nevertheless used birth control and chose hospital birth more often than Italian daughters. (Italians' daughters' fertility did decline, relative to their mothers, however). ("Italian American Women" 45)

35. In the 1860s, Sister Blandina Segale chose her vocation as a Sister of Charity and spent twenty-one years doing missionary work in the Southwest. Though her father commanded her not to leave on such a far-away mission, Sister Blandina listened to an authority higher than her father's and left the Midwest. As a nun in the Southwest, Sister Blandina's pioneering work was not beset by the hardships of pregnancy and motherhood. Her position as a nun liberated her from the expectations exacted of women in nineteenth-century society.

## 2. *"Growing Down": Arrested Development in the Family Narratives of Octavia Waldo's* A Cup of the Sun *and Josephine Gattuso Hendin's* The Right Thing to Do

1. For an ethnographic analysis of the interdependent concepts of honor and shame, the related practices that govern family identity, and the virginity of young girls in Mediterranean societies, see Jane Schneider's "Of Vigilance and Virgins: Honor, Shame and Access to Resources in Mediterranean Societies." Schneider focuses primarily on pastoral communities that developed codes of honor and shame as their own means of social control. Her analysis of the code of honor as it resides in the women is useful to understanding the Italian American father's desire to control the daughter's sexuality:

> [I]f the family or lineage is inherently unstable, or at least has no long-term, indivisible economic interests in common, what besides family name provides a focus for honor? The repository of family and lineage honor, the focus of common interest among the men of the family or lineage, is its women. A woman's status defines the status of all the men who are related to her in determinate ways. The men share the consequences of what happens to her, and share therefore the commitment to protect her virtue. She is part of their patrimony. (17–18)

2. Rolle explains that

> the repression imposed on the family by fathers who needed to remain outwardly dominant endangered the very structure of family life. In a permissive American setting, the school, the police, and the courts assumed the functions of the father as a mediator between the outside world and the family. These institutionalized forces made his regimentation seem outmoded and eroded his power. (114)

3. By examining models of leadership in Italian American culture, I attempted to gauge the effectiveness of godparent figures to aid in the emotional and spiritual development of young Italian Americans in two novels, Tomasi's *Like Lesser Gods* and Waldo's *A Cup of the Sun*. See my "Italian/American Women Writers: Family Shapes Community."

4. According to Pratt, novels such as Fanny Fern's *Rose Clark* (1856) and Hannah More's *Coelebs in Search of a Wife* (1808) provide young women models of behavior appropriate for success in the marriage market. As a result, young women are expected to be content with their submission and service to others (14).

5. Perhaps Rudolph Bell best describes the conditions of *miseria* in *Fate and Honor, Family and Village: Demographic and Cultural Change in Rural Italy since 1800*:

> Of course *la miseria* means being underemployed, having no suit or dress to wear for your child's wedding, suffering hunger most of the time, and welcoming death.

. . . *La miseria* is a disease, a vapor arising from the earth, enveloping and destroying the soul of all that it touches. Its symptoms are wrinkles, distended bellies, anomic individualism, hatred of the soil, and the cursing of God. (113)

6. In his chapter "L'Uomo di Pazienza—The Ideal of Manliness," Gambino controverts the belief in destino or fatalism in the males of southern Italy and Sicily, describing instead a fiercely held belief in *pazienza*—patience:

A fatalist is resigned to whatever fortune will bring. . . . The stoic learns to love and actively embrace what destiny brings. . . . In contradistinction to fatalists and stoics, the contadino of the Mezzogiorno was determined *not* to be resigned to a life that presented itself without pity and with only little hope. (*Blood of My Blood* 119)

The novels under consideration suggest that a character may believe in her *destino* without being resigned to her fate.

7. Two other novels that incorporate practices of and attitudes towards *il mal'occhio* include Nino Ricci's *The Book of Saints* and Louisa Ermelino's *Joey Dee Gets Wise: A Novel of Little Italy.*

8. Lawrence Di Stasi dedicates his book-length study to analyzing the origins and meanings of the evil eye. His idea that the *mal'occhio* situation is striking in its normalcy accounts for the fact that no particular person is immune to its effects:

[S]omeone could not help admiring the beauty of a child. That is really the idea that soaked through to the bone, that beauty and excellence attract the eye, and that the admiring eye thus attracted, no matter how benign it may appear, is *mal*, is evil, and capable of causing harm. (23–24)

9. In *Mal Occhio*, Di Stasi explains that the *jettatore* is significantly a person of some status: nobleman, priest, king, or even the pope (33). Thus I use the pronoun "he" in describing this personification of the evil eye as opposed to other involuntary casters.

10. Appel and Di Stasi both attribute the impotence of *il jettatore* to the conflict of ideas during the period of Illuminism (as the Enlightenment was called in Italy) that was introduced to the kingdom of Naples in the second half of the 1600s. Appel explains in "The Myth of the *Jettatura*":

Without a strong bourgeoisie the ideas of Illuminism, which had been predicated on the rationalization of society, were unable to take a real hold in Neapolitan life. . . . In all sectors of society, both in the capital and in the countryside, the sense of impotence to act, to rationally determine the events of the future, was predominant. (23)

Di Stasi writes, "[T]hus the *jettatore*, a rational human being who involuntarily brings destruction onto others, symbolizes the frustration and ambivalence of Neapolitan intellectuals" (34–35).

11. The standard cures for the evil eye read like a recipe:

Take a bowl of water, drop three drops of oil into it, cross yourself and say:

> *Two eyes have looked at you,*
> *Two saints have enjoyed you,*
> *Father, Son, Holy Ghost;*
> *Enemies, run away!*

This is repeated three times, three drops of oil being allowed to drip into the water each time. If the oil coagulates, it means the patient is afflicted with the evil eye; if the oil "disappears," his sickness is not due to the evil eye.

These cures were not transcribed but were passed down by word of mouth, usually by grandmothers and mothers to daughters and nieces (Appel 18).

12. See especially Covello 149–91.

13. In her analysis of western Sicilian agrotowns, Donna Gabaccia offers a historical reading of the Sicilians' desire to accrue respect:

> The end of feudalism, the emergence of new landowning classes and the extension of new forms of cultivation led to a century of intense competition for land, for material goods and for social status in Sicily. . . . Respect was a form of social judgment, and largely a product of gossip, so competition for respect itself then encouraged families to try to build social ties based on the exchange of information about the moral and social behavior of others. (*From Sicily to Elizabeth Street* 8–9)

14. Waldo has published other works under the names Capuzzi and Locke. On a resume located in the Immigration History Research Center, she writes her full name as Octavia Capuzzi Waldo Locke. In this chapter, I will refer to her as Waldo as her name appears on *A Cup of the Sun.* Waldo was awarded a Fulbright grant to Italy to study fine arts. In 1965, Waldo was the recipient of a Bread Loaf fellowship, and in 1970, she was a Yaddo guest (from Locke, Papers).

15. Written under the surname of Capuzzi, the short stories "Portrait of a Family" and "The Collection" recall Waldo's abiding interest in the psychological effects of the family on its members. "Portrait of a Family" revolves around Miguel Almaden's fight to keep his house after the death of his wife. "The Collection," more complicated because of its modernist structure, explores the narrator's conflicted relation to her past with her family. Both stories reflect Waldo's skill in interweaving the internal voices of characters in pain.

16. Plots of exhaustion or decline describe novels in the American literary tradition that hold to the philosophy of determinism: human beings are controlled by their instincts and passions or by their social and economic environment. As a result, the character moves steadily downward in his or her quest to achieve materially and emotionally in a world that is governed by forces over which he or she has no control. Though Octavia Waldo does not subscribe to the philosophy of naturalism, her

interest in the power of the family to control the will of another results in a narrative of decline for one of the characters.

17. Gabaccia explains that

> migration left untouched the important Sicilian distinction between artisanal and dirty-dependent work, but that life in the United States eliminated many of the social and economic differences that in Sicily separated the two occupational categories of artisan and peasant. (*From Sicily to Elizabeth Street* 109)

18. The school and the factory took sons and daughters away from home in America. This removal from parental guidance was considered "a significant and undesirable change for the artisan minority, a significant but familiar form of failure for the former peasant majority" (Gabaccia, *From Sicily to Elizabeth Street* 101).

19. Gambino's description of the children of Italian immigrants who fought in World War II parallels Waldo's fictional depiction of the conflicts between *Mezzogiorno* and American ideals:

> World War II came during the young adulthood of this generation. Whether they actually attacked the homeland of their parents, as many did, or merely read of the fighting in Italy, for them it was a special kind of war. It was a civil war. They had struggled throughout their childhoods with the conflicting demands of Mezzogiorno and American cultures. The outbreak of war represented a cruel peak in this generation's extreme culture conflict. (*Blood of My Blood* 287)

20. In his review of Tom Lutz's *American Nervousness*, Michael Vincent Miller explains that throughout history, certain illnesses have been elaborated into an "explanation, a kind of allegory, for the additional burdens that social life inevitably heaps upon the human condition" (1). In a similar vein, Waldo portrays characters suffering from illnesses that provide an explanation for their lives as second-generation Italian Americans who have failed to maintain their idealized vision of the family.

21. In *Writing Beyond the Ending: Narrative Strategies of Twentieth-Century Women Writers*, DuPlessis defines writing beyond the ending to mean the

> transgressive invention of narrative strategies, strategies that express critical dissent from dominant narrative. These tactics, among them reparenting, woman-to-woman and brother-to-sister bonds, and forms of the communal protagonist, take issue with the mainstays of the social and ideological organization of gender, as these appear in fiction. Writing beyond the ending . . . produces a narrative that denies or reconstructs seductive patterns of feeling that are culturally mandated, internally policed, hegemonically poised. (5)

22. It will be recalled that the term *campanilismo* describes the unity of those who live within the sound of the church bell, *il campanile*. In

the *Mezzogiorno*, the sound of the bell "was a physical fact defining the perceptible social boundary of a southern Italian's world" (Alba 23).

23. Note the similarity in the Italian poet Mariella Bettarini's enraged expression toward her father in *Paternale* (from *The Defiant Muse: Italian Feminist Poems from the Middle Ages to the Present*):

> but then what do you know about the rights of suffocated
> genitals
> . . . years in the family prison? of geraniums not to be
> touched
> because "you're menstruating"? of big grown up things
> about sex (paternal) the prick perpetually pricked
> (pricking) our bodies all wrapped up instead
> in chastity . . . (107)

24. Perhaps Waldo could not conceive of a "double" bildungsroman for the brother-sister pair without irreparably damaging Niobe's chances for freedom. In this sense, *A Cup of the Sun* compares with George Eliot's *The Mill on the Floss*, which similarly deprives the brother, Tom, of achieving a successful adulthood. For an article that examines Eliot's novel in the context of the bildungsroman, see Susan Fraiman's "*The Mill on the Floss*, the Critics, and the *Bildungsroman*."

25. In 1970, Hendin published her first academic study, *The World of Flannery O'Connor* (1970). During her tenure at the New School of Social Research, Hendin wrote articles for *Harper's*, the *New York Times Book Review*, and *Psychology Today*. After she returned to full-time teaching at New York University, Hendin published her second critical study, *Vulnerable People: A View of American Fiction Since 1945* (1978), an ALA Notable Book. Hendin's novel *The Right Thing to Do* is slated for republication by The Feminist Press.

26. Jane Smiley's review of Hendin's novel for the most part criticizes Hendin for passing up the opportunity to create "intriguing dramatic scene[s] . . . in favor of pages of discussion about what Gina and other members of the younger generation should be doing" (20).

27. In his analysis of Italian Catholicism, Vecoli explains that

> the peasants were intensely parochial and traditional. While nominally Roman Catholics, theirs was a folk religion, a fusion of Christian and pre-Christian elements, of animism, polytheism, and sorcery with the sacraments of the Church. . . . Their brand of Christianity . . . had little in common with American Catholicism. ("Prelates and Peasants" 228, 230)

See also Richard Juliani's "The Interaction of Irish and Italians: From Conflict to Integration."

28. In their essay "Depression and the American Dream: The Struggle with Home," Robert D. Romanyshyn and Brian J. Whalen maintain that depression is the soul's response to a loss of home, abetted by the myth

of the American dream, which encourages the "self-made" man to forget his past: "As the other face of the American dream, as a reminder to the self-made man of what he would forget, depression is the call of home" (217). That Nino in his final days dreams of the "homecoming place," his village in Ventimiglia, and speaks only in dialect suggests that his home is in Sicily, not America.

29. *Nabucco* (1842) was one of Verdi's early operas. As John Louis DiGaetani explains:

> Verdi's own commitment to the *Risorgimento*, Italy's political movement for unification and freedom from foreign domination, colored many of his early operas. *Nabucco* includes the famous chorus "Va, pensiero," which represents the yearning and homesickness of Israelites lamenting that they must live under Babylonian rule. (36)

30. For a starkly comical depiction of a Jewish man and Italian American woman's relationships to in-laws and relatives, see Rita Ciresi's *Blue Italian*.

31. In "Religion and Ethnicity in America," Timothy L. Smith observes that the "acts of uprooting, migration, resettlement, and community-building became for the participants a theologizing experience, not the secularizing process that some historians have pictured." After the migration experience, the folk theology and religious piety that flourished in immigrant churches "were not merely traditional but progressive. Belief and devotion were powerful impulses to accommodation and innovation; and both helped legitimate the behavior, the perceptions, and the structures of association that sustained the processes of change" (1181).

32. The conclusion of Di Prima's poem "To My Father—2" parallels Nino's deathbed vision of "the homecoming place" in Ventimiglia, his Sicilian village:

> If only you'd lie down
> to die in an orchard. . . .
> You are dying of grief
> on the rooftops / of yr mind, but things
> grow in the ground. (149)

## 3. *Remembering Their Names: The Developmental Journeys in Diana Cavallo's* A Bridge of Leaves *and Dorothy Bryant's* Miss Giardino

1. For book-length studies of the traditional bildungsroman, see Beebe; Buckley; Swales; and Moretti. An article that challenges the actual origin of the generic term "bildungsroman" is Jeffrey L. Sammons's "The Mystery of the Missing *Bildungsroman*, or: What Happened to Wilhelm

Meister's Legacy?" Laura Sue Fuderer provides a useful introduction and a thorough listing of women's novels of development in *The Female Bildungsroman in English: An Annotated Bibliography of Criticism.* For book-length studies of the female bildungsroman, see Christ; Pratt; Abel, Hirsch, and Langland; and Dalsimer. Useful articles on the female bildungsroman include Rita Felski's "The Novel of Self-Discovery: A Necessary Fiction?"; Carol Lazzaro-Weis's "The Female *Bildungsroman*: Calling It into Question"; and Fraiman's "*The Mill on the Floss*, The Critics, and the *Bildungsroman.*"

2. In "The Female *Bildungsroman*: Calling It into Question," Lazzaro-Weis articulates the challenge made by feminist deconstructionists:

> [N]otions of a coherent self, the possibility of representation, and finally, one of the most basic tenets of feminism, the belief that "women's truth-in-experience-and-reality is and always has been different from men," have, however, all been attacked by male and female supporters of deconstructive criticism. Feminist deconstructionists dismiss experientially based politics as being inherently reactionary and incapable of recognizing one's constant complicity with existing patriarchal structures. (19)

3. See Buckley's introductory chapter in *Season of Youth* for an overview of the traditional male youth on his journey toward understanding his role in the world (1–27).

4. Articles focusing on the ethnic text as a bildungsroman include Bonnie Hoover Braendlin's "*Bildung* in Ethnic Women Writers" and Sondra O'Neale's "Race, Sex and Self: Aspects of *Bildung* in Select Novels by Black American Women Novelists."

5. Through the metaphor of the psychic voyage, Susan Sontag makes a connection between the nineteenth-century tubercular, who is exiled to a sanatorium, and the person suffering from insanity:

> [T]he psychic voyage is an extension of the romantic idea of travel that was associated with tuberculosis. To be cured, the patient has to be taken out of his or her daily routine. It is not an accident that the most common metaphor for an extreme psychological experience viewed positively—whether produced by drugs or by becoming psychotic—is a trip. (36)

6. Cavallo's publications include her first novel, *A Bridge of Leaves*, republished by Guernica in 1997, and the nonfiction work *The Lower East Side: A Portrait in Time.* Her work has also appeared in three anthologies of Italian American writers: *The Dream Book* (ed. Barolini); *From the Margin* (ed. Tamburri, Giordano, and Gardaphé); and *The Voices We Carry* (ed. Bona). She is currently completing a fictional work entitled *Juniper Street Sketches.* All citations from *A Bridge of Leaves* are taken from Cavallo's 1961 edition.

7. Included in Katharine Newman's list of "eccentric" ethnic novels

is Di Donato's *Christ in Concrete*. According to Newman, all ethnic novels contain

> extraneous material, or disproportions of plot, or distortions of character, or variations of tone or style. Even a book which seems "perfectly constructed" can deviate in some way, revealing some ambiguity in the attitude of the author to his subject, or within the subject itself. (9)

8. My definition of ethnic symbols differs from Gans's theory of symbolic ethnicity, based on a belief in "straight-line" acculturation and assimilation and eventual absorption of the ethnic group into the general population. Gans defines ethnic symbols as "frequently individual cultural practices that are taken from the older ethnic culture; they are 'abstracted' from that culture and pulled out of its original moorings, so to speak, to become stand-ins for it" (194, 204).

9. Italian American works spanning several generations and incorporating a grandparent figure include the previously cited Fante story "The Odyssey of a Wop," Pola's *Who Can Buy the Stars?*, Carole Maso's *Ghost Dance*, and Lisa Ruffolo's story "My Grandfather's Suit" (in *From the Margin*, ed. Tamburri, Giordano, and Gardaphé). For an analysis of grandparent imagery in various ethnic texts, see Sollors's chapter "First Generation, Second Generation, Third Generation . . . : The Cultural Construction of Descent" in *Beyond Ethnicity* (208–36).

10. According to Birnbaum, the black Madonna "may be considered a metaphor for a memory of the time when the earth was believed to be the body of a woman and all creatures were equal." Having traveled to many of the significant sanctuaries of black Madonnas in Italy, Birnbaum hypothesizes that each was located on or near archaeological evidence of the pre-Christian woman divinity (*Black Madonnas* 3).

11. In *Liberazione della Donna*, Birnbaum cites the Italian feminist Carlamaria Del Miglio who believes that for women to be liberated, a knowledge of mother-daughter relationships is necessary: "Every woman is a daughter and many women are mothers. When they are oppressed by a role imposed by others, women themselves become oppressors in their relationships with their daughters" (190). In Cavallo's novel, the mother's debilitating depression oppressed the daughter, accounting for Laura's inability to develop a coherent sense of self.

12. In *Women's Madness: Misogyny or Mental Illness?*, Jane Ussher discusses the reality of her own mother's "madness," severely exacerbated by the "positioning of madness as a deadly secret, a fear, a means of dismissing and controlling women, and a means of pathologizing distress." Laura's mother's "madness" likewise positioned her as other and as "invariably feminine," especially because the mother's illness is associated with her daughter's birth (13, 12).

13. As Marina Warner writes, "[B]lue is the colour of the Virgin, 'the sapphire,' as Dante wrote, who turns all of heaven blue . . . [and] signified that the wearer was a child of Mary. . . . [Mary] was the culmination of womanhood" (xx). Warner's agnostic father thought it a good religion for a girl. Cavallo implicitly challenges this idea by equating the catatonic Laura to a life-sized statue of the Virgin; passivity will not give Laura the tools to fashion her own identity.

14. I am indebted to George De Vos and Lola Romanucci-Ross's explanation of the vital meaning of ethnicity. They write:

> To know one's origin is to have not only a sense of provenience, but perhaps more importantly, a sense of continuity in which one finds to some degree the personal and social meaning of human existence. . . . To be without a sense of continuity is to be faced with one's own death. ("Ethnicity: Vessel of Meaning" 364)

15. Dorothy Bryant has published ten novels, three plays, and the nonfiction work *Writing a Novel.* Her most recent novel, *Anita, Anita,* details the life of Anita Garibaldi, wife of the Italian liberator. The Feminist Press has republished three of Bryant's novels: *Miss Giardino, Ella Price's Journal,* and *Confessions of Madame Psyche.* All citations from *Miss Giardino* are taken from the Ata Books edition.

16. For information about Bryant's northern Italian relatives and her parents' migration to America, see her autobiographical essay, "Dorothy Bryant," in *Contemporary Authors Autobiography Series* 26.

17. Although I do not discuss Savarese's *The Weak and the Strong,* her novel offers a disturbing account of suffering and illness in urban America during the depression of the 1930s, the national catastrophe acutely affecting immigrants in New York City tenements. One of the characters, Mr. Black, willfully loses his memory, the pain of his past too unbearable. Unlike Anna Giardino, Mr. Black experiences no process of recuperation; he remains a tabula rasa, without memory or a past.

18. Robert Orsi explains in "The Fault of Memory" that

> parents and children lived in different linguistic universes, and the way they talked to each other expressed their mutual refusal to acknowledge the reality of their respective worlds: in a common pattern in immigrant communities, parents in East Harlem spoke only in Italian to their children, who would respond only in English. (134)

Although Anna Giardino's family emigrated from northern Italy and lived in the West, the same linguistic behavior occurred as a result of generational conflict.

19. This is Frances Beale's term to describe being not only black but also female in American society (qtd. in O'Neale 34).

20. Marianne Hirsch analyzes how the Oedipus story has been used by women writers to explore the relationship between plot and gender. She insists that feminist rethinking must reject the biased distinction

made between maternal and nonmaternal women, a distinction challenged and explored in Bryant's text. See *The Mother/Daughter Plot* (1–8).

21. In "Progressive Pedagogy and Political Struggle," Valerie Walkerdine explains that women teachers historically have been trapped "inside a concept of nurturance which held them responsible for the freeing of each little individual, and therefore for the management of an idealist dream, an impossible fiction" (16). However authoritative and uncompromising a teacher she is, Anna Giardino is trapped within this concept of nurturance.

22. Lazzaro-Weis explains in "The Female *Bildungsroman*" that traditionally epiphanic moments in the genre do not translate into obvious material gains. She also notes that Swales's *The German Bildungsroman* and Sammons's "The Mystery of the Missing *Bildungsroman*" offer examples of how protagonists claim "to have learned some essential truth. Usually, however, this knowledge neither applies to nor produces any drastic change in the lived world of the protagonist" (30 n. 46). Anna Giardino's many changes at the end of her memory journey affect both her interior life and the lives of those surrounding her. Thus, her change is indeed momentous.

23. Even though she conceives of the future as keeping the past at bay, Sethe in Toni Morrison's *Beloved* describes the processes of memory in terms similar to Anna's:

> Some things just stay. I used to think it was my rememory. You know. Some things you forget. Other things you never do. But it's not. Places, places are still there. If a house burns down, it's gone, but the place—the picture of it—stays, and not just in my rememory, but out there, in the world. (35–36)

24. O'Neale quotes from Bernard Boelen's *Personal Maturity* in order to make an important distinction between the terms "adulthood" and "maturity," a distinction that illuminates Anna Giardino's development:

> [T]he terms "adulthood" and "maturity" are not synonymous. "Adulthood" denotes the end point of the process of growth and development, or a fixed, plateau-like state of being. "Maturity," on the other hand, denotes the achievement of one's full potentialities, ripeness, self-actualization. (36)

## 4. *A Process of Reconstruction: Recovering the Grandmother in Helen Barolini's* Umbertina *and Tina De Rosa's* Paper Fish

1. *Umbertina* was originally published by Seaview Books in 1979; the copy that I am using is the Bantam Edition. All page references hereafter will be taken from this text.

2. Barolini's subscription to realism in writing *Umbertina* is equally evident in her research prior to writing the novel: she interviewed other

women immigrants and researched immigration history (Interview, tape 1).

3. In *The Italian Americans: Troubled Roots*, Rolle records personal ruminations from each generation of Italian Americans. The second generational response offers a useful gloss on Barolini's depiction of Carla and Sam, both children of immigrant parents:

> *Second Generation*: "I'm a second generation Italian. My name is Jodi Desmond, but I was born Josephina Dessimone and oh how I hated that. For the first fourteen years of my life I was Josephina Dessimone and rebelling every moment. I was ashamed of my parents, they spoke with a broken accent and I am ashamed of being ashamed now, but I wasn't then. I just ignored them." (183–84)

4. In *Italian Signs, American Streets*, Gardaphé writes, "[I]mmigrant *figurae* represent historical mysteries that require explanation" (121). Gardaphé suggests that what is reinvented by third-generation writers such as Barolini and De Rosa is the concept of *italianità*.

5. See Gardaphé's "From Oral Tradition to Written Word" for a fuller appreciation of oral characteristics in the literary traditions of Italian American writers.

6. At a reading during the Italian American Heritage Month in Chicago in October 1988, Tina De Rosa described her epilogue as "snapshots of people who are leaving." William Boelhower defines snapshots as "irreducibly discontinuous moments lacking an implicit narrative thread" ("The Ethnic Trilogy" 17). That De Rosa concludes her novel in this narrative fashion reinforces her elegiac tone throughout *Paper Fish*. Nonetheless, Carmolina assures Grandma that "nothing goes away" in section 6 of the epilogue; De Rosa suggests here that the novel celebrates the uses of memory to recapture the past.

7. Barolini's *Umbertina* is actually the combined manuscripts of two separate novels, *The Last Abstraction* and *Umbertina*. Barolini's working title for *Umbertina* was *The Tin Heart*, a reference to the heart-shaped holder that belonged to Barolini's grandmother, who was said to have worn the heart around her waist when she was tending to the goats on the hills of Calabria (Barolini, Papers). Receiving an NEA grant in 1976 allowed Barolini to "take all these different pieces just like the bedspread [the fictional character Umbertina's matrimonial bedspread], put them together, make a pattern out of it" (Interview, tape 1).

8. For information regarding Barolini's use of Italy in *Umbertina*, see Tamburri's article "Looking Back: The Image of Italy in Helen Barolini's *Umbertina*."

9. The word "*terrone*" disparages peasant origins. Thus, Alberto's comment is more critical than descriptive. Helen Barolini's Italian husband once said to her, "[T]he only way I a Northerner could have married you, a Southerner, was by way of at least two generations of purgatory in America on your part" ("A Circular Journey" 116). For several more

autobiographical connections between *Umbertina* and Barolini's life, see "A Circular Journey."

10. The designation of "hyphenated" comes from Daniel Aaron's "The Hyphenate American Writer."

11. In *Gender, Fantasy, and Realism in American Literature,* Alfred Habegger explains that Isabel Archer

> does indeed share the tendency so common and so admired in contemporary [nineteenth-century] women's fiction of mistaking maternal protectiveness for love. . . . Yet she didn't fully realize she had substituted the maternal for the "wifely," that what she felt for Osmond had little in common with sexual love. (70)

In contrast, Marguerite marries Alberto to *receive* maternal protection from him. Feeling unmothered all her life, Marguerite seeks the maternal in her husband.

12. The connection between peasant women and elementary strength is examined in Birnbaum's *Black Madonnas*: "Peasant women, resembling the primordial goddess and formidable black madonnas, were fiercely nurturant, teaching their children the realities of life and death early on" (49). Marguerite is persuasive when she connects primitive strength to her grandmother.

13. For a thorough examination of American writers' relationship to Italy, see Wright.

14. Like her fictional creation Marguerite Morosoni, Helen Barolini learned Italian and began translating several Italian works into English, including her husband's (Antonio Barolini's) novel, *A Long Madness.* Besides her edited collection, *The Dream Book*, Barolini has written a second novel, *Love in the Middle Ages*; a combination memoir and recipe book, *Festa: Recipes and Recollections of Italian Holidays*; and a critical study of the pioneering scholar-publisher Aldus Manutius, *Aldus and His Dream Book.* Her collection of essays, *Chiaroscuro: Essays of Identity*, comprises both personal and critical writings. *Umbertina* has been republished by The Feminist Press.

15. For a delightful inside look at the literary prize business in Italy, see Barolini's "Neruda vs. Sartre at the Sea."

16. In *Women and Madness*, Phyllis Chesler explains that Demeter and Persephone "were the central figures of a mother-daughter religion—the Eleusinian mysteries—in ancient Greece. . . . Both women still symbolize the sacrifices of self that biology and culture demand of women" (n. pag.). See also Adrienne Rich's chapter "Motherhood and Daughterhood" for an explanation of the religious mystery of Eleusis and the mother-daughter myth of Demeter and Persephone in *Of Woman Born.* While Marguerite ultimately is defined by her maternal body, Tina is able to transcend the limitations of her sex without denying the possibility of motherhood and marriage in her future.

17. *Paper Fish* was originally published by the now defunct Wine Press

(Chicago, 1980); all citations from *Paper Fish* in the chapter are taken from this edition. De Rosa has also published a biography called *Bishop John Baptist Scalabrini: Father to the Migrants*, dedicated to her paternal grandmother, Della De Rosa.

18. Gans defines symbolic ethnicity as "an ethnicity of last resort," hardly promising language for writers interested in probing their cultural background for literary focus (193). Gardaphé offers a balanced assessment of Gans's construction of symbolic ethnicity: it seems

> to suggest a superficial expression that lacks sincerity and authenticity, yet the Italian American writers of the third-generation are anything but superficial in their constructions of *Italianità*. . . . Gans's notion of symbolic ethnicity . . . can help us read the symbols generated by writers who are the grandchildren of immigrants. (*Italian Signs, American Streets* 120)

19. Of her fictional treatment in *Paper Fish* of her great-grandparents, De Rosa explains: "There is a section in the novel that deals with my great-grandparents, about whom I know nothing. I imagined my great-grandparents and Italy. I have had people who have read the book ask me if I have been there" ("An Interview" 23).

20. In her analysis of the care of dependents, Williams writes, "[I]n America as in Italy, Italians are no more willing to commit feeble-minded dependents to institutions than they are the aged." In *Paper Fish*, during their family meeting about Doriana, Aunt Katerina suggests sending the child to the nuns, perhaps a residual reminder that monks and nuns in monasteries provided in Italy "the first institutional care of the sick" (193, 171).

21. In her afterword to *Paper Fish*, Edvige Giunta explains that the opening words of the first section, "This is my mother," which appear under the title "Prelude," "stand almost as a subtitle, suggesting that the writing that follows is itself the 'mother,' the locus of creativity that brings the past, through memory, back to life, incorporating it in a continuum in which past, present, and future are inseparable" (128).

22. Part 3, "The Family," is placed numerically in the middle of the book, but the chapter is actually "off-center," coming as it does before the middle of the text. This may suggest the eccentric quality of ethnic fiction itself as well as the BellaCasa's particular family struggle, where the uneven, the irregular, are the standards by which we evaluate the novel. For this quality of unevenness in ethnic literature, see Newman.

23. A patrolman for twenty-four years for the city of Chicago, De Rosa's father performed the "sad and hidden work of society" and "came home and hid his face in the little world of us. . . . [T]his man taught his daughter how to be an artist." De Rosa explains that we receive our "inheritances unexpectedly": "It is an amazing revelation to me, as I look at the silent children of my books, to see, finally, what the writing *is*, to me,

and to see, finally, that my father is the one who taught me how to do this" ("My Father's Lesson" 15).

24. Carmolina's destruction of the doll recalls an earlier fictional portrayal by Toni Morrison in her first novel, *The Bluest Eye.* In that novel, the child narrator, Claudia, dismembers white baby dolls, attempting to annihilate what is valued in American culture (whiteness) at the expense of black lives. Claudia recognizes to her horror her same violent impulse toward living white girls. Carmolina's own wish to destroy what she cannot fully understand or control is tempered by her love for Doriana. Claudia discovers a similar "hiding place" in love in *The Bluest Eye*, though this discovery is not seen as a necessarily positive improvement in Morrison's novel.

25. I take the phrase "specialist in survival" from Romanucci-Ross's anthropological investigation of her native Italian provenance, Ascoli Piceno, and the Italians who immigrated to America, Australia, and Canada. Romanucci-Ross refers to the immigrants as "specialists in survival," "winning and losing [being] irrelevant categories" to them (220).

26. When asked the meaning of the title *Paper Fish*, De Rosa responded, "[T]he people in the book were as beautiful and as fragile as a Japanese kite, so the title" ("An Interview" 23).

27. La Belle writes:

> [T]he daughter is in part a genetic replication of the mother, a biological mirroring that can be signified by the image in the glass as the girl becomes what her mother became—old. . . . In one's mother's mirror, there is a double image, the echo and re-echo, the reflection of the self and the ghostly unseen presence of the parent. (80)

In De Rosa's *Paper Fish*, the interrelationships between generations of mothers and daughters are depicted, for the most part, positively, as in the preparations before the wedding scene.

28. Gardaphé explains that the marriage ceremony in *Paper Fish*

> recreates the traditional procession of the Madonna, a staple of Italian culture, through which the people receive the blessing of God's mother. . . . Blue is the color traditionally associated with the Madonna, and it is fitting that the blue-eyed matriarch of the BellaCasa family wears it as she is carried up to see her granddaughter. (*Italian Signs, American Streets* 137)

29. De Rosa describes the feeling of being doubly alienated—first from her family and community and second from the educated world she entered as a third-generation Italian American. She learns to accept the "gift and burden" of a dual heritage through the act of writing:

> I know now that where I belong is with myself, knowing that I don't really belong anywhere. That is the inheritance, that is the curse, of being born into a world and into a family that wants you to enter another. You say partially goodbye to one,

partially hello to another, some of the time you are silent, and if you feel a little bit crazy—and sometimes you do—then you write about it. ("An Italian-American Woman Speaks Out" 39)

## 5. *Recent Developments in Italian American Women's Literary Traditions*

1. Perry observed in the course of her fieldwork in Toronto the role behaviors described to her by the community. Although the whore in the community may be considered unacceptable to the legitimate wife, she nonetheless provides a function in a system of "mutual exploitation of sex for economic gain and the physiological needs of sexual satisfaction" (224).

2. Sedgwick also explains how a gay person's revelation can result in closeted behavior by the heterosexual listener: "The pathogenic secret itself, even, can circulate contagiously *as* a secret: a mother says that her adult child's coming out of the closet with her has plunged her, in turn, into the closet in her conservative community" (53). Philip Gambone writes similarly about his mother's response to his gayness in "Learning and Unlearning and Learning Again the Language of *Signori*."

3. In *Goat Song*, Azpadu's second novel, one of the lesbians, olive-complected, was orphaned at birth and does not know her ethnic origins. Although Azpadu does not identify her as a Sicilian American, the fact that she is depicted as an orphan may very well be Azpadu's way of explaining the racial ambiguity and loss of homeland of Sicilian Americans. For a less ambiguous rendering of Sicilian identity, see Azpadu's "Desert Ruins."

4. Italian Americans have examined in creative and critical writings the "not-yet-white" perceptions of their cultural group. Rose Romano's essay "Coming Out Olive in the Lesbian Community" and two books of poetry, *Vendetta* and *The Wop Factor*, examine color symbology, explaining how southern Italians and Sicilians are neither white people nor persons of color. Orsi coins the term "racial in-betweenness" to describe Italian American history that began in "racially inflected circumstances everywhere in the United States" ("The Religious Boundaries" 314).

5. Donald Tricarico examines "not-yet-whiteness" in the urban youth subculture of New York City, which calls itself "Guido" or "Cugine." Appropriating black youth style elements, punk, and New Wave, Guido maintains antagonisms and boundaries between youth groups. Adopting the label "Guinea" (an anti-Italian epithet derived from the name given black slaves from West Africa), Guido youth culture "mock[s] this slur by celebrating Italian ethnicity" and by recalling a time

in Italian American history when Italians were not yet considered white ethnics (56). Vecoli also examines the relation between race and identity in "Are Italian Americans Just White Folks?"

6. Of *Saturday Night in the Prime of Life*, Bonnie Zimmerman writes that the categories of class and ethnicity separate Lindy and Neddie: "[T]he strong ties that bind Neddie to her Sicilian family are hard for the Nordic Lindy to comprehend" (*The Safe Sea of Women* 114). Lindy never learns to understand Neddie's familial life. Lindy often speaks for Neddie throughout the narrative, but when Neddie does speak, she reveals a thorough understanding of her parents' protective and overbearing behavior. Toward the end of the narrative, Neddie is still explaining to Lindy her mother's needy reasons for manipulation: "'I know I can't ignore my mother. Regardless of her tricks. Scheming is the only way for her to take care of herself'" (87). In contrast, Lindy, decades ago, cut off all communication with her parents, who were as repulsed by Neddie's lesbianism as they were her ethnic and class background. Lindy has no idea whether her parents are dead or alive; such a situation is utterly unthinkable for Neddie Zingaro.

7. Saint Lucy's Day is December 13. In *Festa*, Barolini explains that Santa Lucia was said to have "gouged out her eyes because their beauty attracted a heathen suitor; or, alternatively, her eyes were plucked out by her torturers. . . . Her name itself derives from *lux*, *lucis*, the Latin word for light" (24).

8. Maso has written five other novels: *The Art Lover*, *Ava*, *The American Woman in the Chinese Hat*, *Aureole*, and *Defiance*. While Italian American identity is not the focus of any of these novels, Maso continues to explore issues of identity as they intersect with illness and madness. In the highly experimental *Ava*, Maso departs completely from a conventional linear narrative, producing a postmodern text about Ava Klein's internal thoughts on the last day of her life. Before publishing *Ava*, Maso experienced "an end to narrative as I once understood it" ("An Essay" 27). In 1995, Maso became the director of the creative writing program at Brown University.

9. In defining the construction of traditions, Orsi explains in "The Fault of Memory" that immigrants depended on

> materials already available, consciously and unconsciously, to the people involved in the act of reimagining a tradition. . . . Traditions always exist as themes and variations, with the latter determined by and expressing historical circumstance, psychological need, political pressures, and so on. The immigrants did not invent a tradition *ex nihilo*; rather they improvised on the polysemous "tradition" (all that they understood or fantasized about themselves and where they had come from and where they were going) they had inherited, in some inchoate fashion, from their own elders. (n. 38, 145–46)

10. At the conclusion of *Christ in Concrete*, Di Donato depicts Paul, the protagonist, holding his dying mother, Annunziata, as she croons a final lullaby. Maso similarly complicates the traditional image of the *mater dolorosa* by having the son embrace his dying parents. After the World's Fair, Michael's father begins his journey back to a simpler time; his death ultimately allows his wife to attend to her own grieving over the loss of the Italian homeland.

11. The underlying principle of the Ghost Dance doctrine, James Mooney writes, "is that the time will come when the whole Indian race, living and dead, will be reunited upon a regenerated earth, to live a life of aboriginal happiness, forever free from death, disease, and misery" (19). See also Weston La Barre's *Ghost Dance: Origins of Religion.* Maso not only refers to the historical occasion of the Ghost Dance but also uses the term metaphorically throughout her novel to bear witness to several other dances: between Fletcher and Vanessa; between Sabine and Christine; between Vanessa and Sabine; and on the lawn of the nursing home, where the paternal grandmother dances her final tarantella.

12. The grandmother's imperatives to Vanessa stem from her belief in possessing useful knowledge of natural life. She literally offers her granddaughter recipes for living. The use of repetition and present tense in Maria's directives are two characteristics of oral cultures, a hearkening back to Italian storytelling traditions. Another story that uses oral traditions to teach lessons about the natural world is Ree Dragonette's "This Is the Way We Wash Our Hands."

13. I am using DuPlessis's definition of reparenting as it relates to the collaboration of mother and daughter as artists: "[T]he female artist is given a way of looping back and reenacting childhood ties, to achieve not the culturally approved ending in heterosexual romance, but rather the reparenting necessary to her second birth as an artist" (94). It is interesting to note that Maso herself claims that her mother, a nurse, was her first and only mentor: "She took me very seriously . . . demanded that I came home with all A's. I worked hard and took myself very seriously—it became very bound up in my love for her" ("Interview by Joyce Hackett" 68).

14. Agnes Rossi's second novel, *Split Skirt*, examines the relationship between two women who are jailed for a weekend. Rossi alternates chapters to examine the ways each woman responds emotionally and psychologically to her predicament. Different in age, temperament, and social status, the two women ultimately share poignant stories about how they ended up in jail. Rossi's use of a minor Italian American character who suffers physical abuse from her husband combines features of both women and remains both a disturbing and fascinating cameo appearance in the novel. For an analysis of Rossi's narrative technique, see Giunta's "Rein-

venting the Authorial/Ethnic Space: Communal Narratives in Agnes Rossi's *Split Skirt.*"

15. Ciresi's *Mother Rocket* won the Flannery O'Connor award for short fiction. Ciresi's debut novel, *Blue Italian*, depicts an Italian American protagonist whose familial life causes her much distress. *Pink Slip*, Ciresi's second novel, received the 1997 Pirate's Alley Faulkner Award. Ciresi recently completed a collection of linked stories, tentatively titled *Sometimes I Dream in Italian.* Ciresi teaches creative writing in the department of English at the University of South Florida.

16. Along the lines of a Flannery O'Connor story, Jude Silverman's change at the end of "Mother Rocket" might also be called a conversion experience, a narrative strategy with which Ciresi is obviously familiar.

17. For stories in *Pray for Yourself and Other Stories*, Calcagno received the James D. Phelan Award and was awarded fellowships from the NEA and the Illinois Arts Council. Born in San Diego, Calcagno was raised in Rome, returning to the United States to attend college. Calcagno maintains a dual citizenship in Italy and the United States; she presently teaches creative writing at DePaul University.

18. A particularly virulent example of obsessive emphasis on ethnic identity that George Devereux identifies is the Nazi SS member who pleads that in "performing atrocities he only obeyed commands implicitly affirmed[,] that his SS status took precedence over all his other group identities, including his membership in the human estate" (67).

19. In 1993, Manfredi became the first Italian American to win the Iowa Short Fiction Award, adding to her NEA fellowship and a Pushcart Prize. She teaches in the department of English at the University of Alaska-Fairbanks and is currently working on a manuscript tentatively entitled *Running Away with Frannie.*

20. I am reminded of the conclusion of Toni Morrison's *Beloved*, in which we read the cryptic line "this is not a story to pass on," suggesting both that the story (of slavery, the middle passage, infanticide) should not be continued but will not (and should not) easily be forgotten. Orsi wonders in "The Fault of Memory" if the immigrants created "a particular understanding of 'Southern Italy' which not only could not be 'passed on,' but was never intended to be" (136). For children of immigrants, "southern Italy," the land of *miseria*, cannot be passed on but continues in the imaginative recreation of the writers.

21. The relationship between cultural identity and innovative narrative strategies is highlighted in the works of Mary Caponegro and Laura Marello. Both write stories about how the female self crafts an identity within the family. See especially Caponegro's "Materia Prima" in her collection *The Star Cafe and Other Stories* and Marello's "Catch Me Go Looking."

22. Experimenting with *italianità* is also demonstrated in recent publications of memoirs by Italian American women. They include Marianna De Marco Torgovnick's *Crossing Ocean Parkway: Readings by an Italian American Daughter*, Louise De Salvo's *Vertigo: A Memoir*, and Mary Cappello's *Night Bloom*. For an interesting reflection on writing memoirs, see Torgovnick's new afterword to the 1996 reprint of *Crossing Ocean Parkway*: "So, What Did Your Mother Think?" (175–86).

# *Bibliography*


Aaron, Daniel. "The Hyphenate American Writer." *Rivista di studi anglo-americani* 3.4–5 (1984–85): 11–28.

Abel, Elizabeth, Marianne Hirsch, and Elizabeth Langland, eds. *The Voyage In: Fictions of Female Development.* Hanover: UP of New England, 1983.

Abrams, M. H. *A Glossary of Literary Terms.* 6th ed. Fort Worth: Harcourt Brace College P, 1993.

Ahearn, Carol Bonomo. "Interview: Helen Barolini." *Fra Noi* Sept. 1986: 47.

Alba, Richard D. *Italian Americans: Into the Twilight of Ethnicity.* Englewood Cliffs: Prentice, 1985.

Appel, Willa. "The Myth of the *Jettatura*." *The Evil Eye.* Ed. Clarence Maloney. New York: Columbia UP, 1976. 16–27.

Azpadu, Dodici. "Desert Ruins." *The Voices We Carry: Recent Italian/American Women's Fiction.* Ed. Mary Jo Bona. Montreal: Guernica, 1994. 187–99.

——. *Goat Song.* Iowa City: Aunt Lute, 1984.

——. *Saturday Night in the Prime of Life.* Iowa City: Aunt Lute, 1983.

Barolini, Helen. *Aldus and His Dream Book.* New York: Italica P, 1992.

——. "Becoming a Literary Person Out of Context." *Massachusetts Review* 27.2 (1986): 262–74.

——. "The Case of Mari Tomasi." *Italians and Irish in America.* Ed. Francis X. Femminella. Proc. of the Sixteenth Annual Conference of the American Italian Historical Association. Staten Island: American Italian Historical Association, 1985. 177–86.

——. *Chiaroscuro: Essays of Identity.* Lafayette, IN: Bordighera, 1997. Rev. ed. Madison: U of Wisconsin P, 1999.

——. "A Circular Journey." *Texas Quarterly* 21.2 (1978): 109–26.

——. *Festa: Recipes and Recollections of Italian Holidays.* New York: Harcourt, 1988.

——, ed. *The Dream Book: An Anthology of Writings by Italian American Women.* New York: Schocken, 1985.

———. "The Finer Things in Life." *Arizona Quarterly* 29.1 (1973): 26–36.

———. "Going to Sicily." *Paris Review* 22 (1980): 178–87.

———. Interview (unedited) with Helen Barolini. 2 tapes. American Audio Prose Library, 1982.

———. *Love in the Middle Ages.* New York: William Morrow, 1986.

———. "Neruda vs. Sartre at the Sea." *Paris Review* (Winter 1975): 206–15.

———. Papers. Immigration History Research Center. University of Minnesota.

———. *Umbertina.* New York: Bantam, 1979. New York: Feminist P, 1999.

Bartky, Sandra Lee. "Foucault, Femininity, and the Modernization of Patriarchal Power." *Femininity and Domination: Studies in the Phenomenology of Oppression.* New York: Routledge, 1990. 63–82.

Baym, Nina. *Women's Fiction: A Guide to Novels by and about Women in America, 1820–1870.* Ithaca: Cornell UP, 1978.

Beebe, Maurice. *Ivory Towers and Sacred Founts: The Artist Hero in Fiction from Goethe to Joyce.* New York: New York State UP, 1964.

Bees, Julian. "Stonecutters of Carrara." *Attenzione* May 1980: 60–66.

Bell, Rudolph. *Fate and Honor, Family and Village: Demographic and Cultural Change in Rural Italy since 1800.* Chicago: U of Chicago P, 1979.

Belliotti, Raymond A. *Seeking Identity: Individualism Versus Community in an Ethnic Context.* Lawrence: UP of Kansas, 1995.

Benasutti, Marion. "The Making of an Italian American Writer." *Fra Noi* Feb. 1988: 31.

———. *No SteadyJob for Papa.* New York: Vanguard, 1966.

Bettarini, Mariella. *The Defiant Muse: Italian Feminist Poems from the Middle Ages to the Present.* Ed. Beverly Allen et al. New York: Feminist P, 1986. 107–8.

Birnbaum, Lucia Chiavola. *Black Madonnas: Feminism, Religion and Politics in Italy.* Boston: Northeastern UP, 1993.

———. *Liberazione della Donna: Feminism in Italy.* Middletown, CT: Wesleyan UP, 1986.

Boelhower, William. "The Ethnic Trilogy: A Poetics of Cultural Passage." *MELUS* 12.4 (1985): 7–23. Rpt. as "Ethnic Trilogies: A Genealogical and Generational Poetics." *The Invention of Ethnicity.* Ed. Werner Sollors. New York: Oxford UP, 1989. 158–75.

———. "The Immigrant Novel as Genre." *MELUS* 8.1 (1981): 3–13.

———. *Through a Glass Darkly: Ethnic Semiosis in American Literature.* New York: Oxford UP, 1987.

Bona, Mary Jo. Afterword. *A Bridge of Leaves.* By Diana Cavallo. Toronto: Guernica, 1997.

———. Afterword. "Escaping the Ancestral Threat?" *The Right Thing to Do.* By Josephine Gattuso Hendin. New York: Feminist P, 1999. 213–37.

———. "Broken Images, Broken Lives: Carmolina's Journey in Tina De Rosa's *Paper Fish.*" *MELUS* 14.3–4 (1987): 87–106.

———. "Italian/American Women Writers: Family Shapes Community." *Taking Parts: Ingredients for Leadership, Participation, and Empowerment.* Ed. Eloise Buker et al. Lanham, MD: UP of America, 1994. 135–49.
———. "Mari Tomasi's *Like Lesser Gods* and the Making of an Ethnic *Bildungsroman.*" *Voices in Italian Americana* 1.1 (1990): 15–34.
———. "*Mater Dolorosa* No More? Mothers and Writers in the Italian/American Literary Tradition." *Voices in Italian Americana* 7.2 (1996): 1–19.
———, ed. *The Voices We Carry: Recent Italian/American Women's Fiction.* Montreal: Guernica, 1994.
Braendlin, Bonnie Hoover. "*Bildung* in Ethnic Women Writers." *Denver Quarterly* 17 (Winter 1983): 75–87.
Bryant, Dorothy. *Anita, Anita.* Berkeley: Ata, 1993.
———. "Blood Relations." *The New Family.* Ed. Scott Walker. St. Paul: Graywolf P, 1991. 75–80.
———. *Confessions of Madame Psyche.* Berkeley: Ata, 1986. New York: Feminist P, 1998.
———. *A Day in San Francisco.* Berkeley: Ata, 1983.
———. "Dorothy Bryant." *Contemporary Authors Autobiography Series* 26. Detroit: Gale Research, 1997. 47–63.
———. *Ella Price's Journal.* Berkeley: Ata, 1972. New York: Feminist P, 1997.
———. *The Garden of Eros.* Berkeley: Ata, 1979.
———. *Killing Wonder.* Berkeley: Ata, 1981.
———. *The Kin of Ata Are Waiting for You.* New York: Random, 1971.
———. *Miss Giardino.* Berkeley: Ata, 1978. New York: Feminist P, 1997.
———. *Myths to Lie By.* Berkeley: Ata, 1984.
———. *Prisoners.* Berkeley: Ata, 1980.
———. *The Test.* Berkeley: Ata, 1991.
———. *Writing a Novel.* Berkeley: Ata, 1978.
Buckley, Jerome H. *Season of Youth: The Bildungsroman from Dickens to Golding.* Cambridge: Harvard UP, 1974.
Calcagno, Anne. *Pray for Yourself and Other Stories.* Evanston, IL: Northwestern UP, 1993.
Caponegro, Mary. *The Star Cafe and Other Stories.* New York: Macmillan, 1990.
Cappello, Mary. *Night Bloom.* Boston: Beacon P, 1998.
Capuzzi [Waldo Locke], Octavia. "The Collection." *Triquarterly* 40 (1977): 213–36.
———. "Portrait of a Family." *New Orleans Review* 4.4 (1975): 355–61.
———. "The Rocks." *New Orleans Review* 3.3 (1973): 380–83.
Caroli, Betty Boyd, Robert F. Harney, and Lydio F. Tomasi, eds. *The Italian Immigrant Woman in North America.* Proc. of the Tenth Annual

Conference of the American Italian Historical Association. Toronto: Multicultural History Society, 1978.

Cateura, Linda Brandi. *Growing Up Italian.* New York: William Morrow, 1987.

Cavallo, Diana. *A Bridge of Leaves.* New York: Atheneum, 1961. Toronto: Guernica, 1997.

——. "The Dark Watcher." *Confrontation* 50 (1992): 110–20.

——. *The Lower East Side: A Portrait in Time.* New York: Macmillan, 1971.

Chametzky, Jules. "Ethnicity and Beyond: An Introduction." *Massachusetts Review* 27.2 (1986): 242–51.

Chesler, Phyllis. *Women and Madness.* 1972. New York: Harcourt, 1989.

Cheung, King-Kok. "'Don't Tell': Imposed Silences in *The Color Purple* and *The Woman Warrior.*" *PMLA* 103 (1988): 162–74.

Chodorow, Nancy. *The Reproduction of Mothering: Psychoanalysis and the Sociology of Gender.* Berkeley: U of California P, 1978.

Christ, Carol P. *Diving Deep and Surfacing: Women Writers on Spiritual Quest.* Boston: Beacon P, 1980.

Ciongoli, Kenneth A., and Jay Parini, eds. *Beyond the Godfather: Italian American Writers on the Real Italian American Experience.* Hanover: UP of New England, 1997.

Ciresi, Rita. *Blue Italian.* Hopewell, NJ: Ecco, 1996.

——. *Mother Rocket.* Athens: U of Georgia P, 1993.

——. "Paradise Below the Stairs." *Italian Americana* 12.1 (1993): 17–22.

——. *Pink Slip.* New York: Delacorte P, 1999.

Clément, Catherine. *Opera, Or the Undoing of Women.* Minneapolis: U of Minnesota P, 1988.

Cornelisen, Ann. *Women of the Shadows.* Boston: Little, 1976.

Covello, Leonard. *The Social Background of the Italo-American School Child.* Diss. New York U, 1944. Leiden: Brill, 1967.

Dalsimer, Katherine. *Female Adolescence: Psychoanalytic Reflections on Works of Literature.* New Haven: Yale UP, 1986.

De Rosa, Tina. *Bishop John Baptist Scalabrini: Father to the Migrants.* Darien, CT: Insider P, 1987.

——. "An Interview with Tina De Rosa." By Fred Gardaphé. *Fra Noi* May 1985: 23.

——. "An Italian-American Woman Speaks Out." *Attenzione* May 1980: 38–39.

——. "Lady in Waiting." Interview by Connie Lauerman. *Chicago Tribune* 2 Sept. 1996, sec. 5: 1+.

——. "My Father's Lesson." *Fra Noi* Sept. 1986: 15.

——. *Paper Fish.* Chicago: Wine P, 1980. New York: Feminist P, 1996.

De Salvo, Louise. *Vertigo: A Memoir.* New York: Dutton, 1996.

Devereux, George. "Ethnic Identity: Its Logical Foundations and Its

Dysfunctions." *Ethnic Identity: Cultural Continuities and Change.* Ed. George De Vos and Lola Romanucci-Ross. 1975. Chicago: U of Chicago P, 1982. 42–70.

De Vos, George. "Ethnic Pluralism: Conflict and Accommodation." *Ethnic Identity: Cultural Continuities and Change.* Ed. George De Vos and Lola Romanucci-Ross. 1975. Chicago: U of Chicago P, 1982. 5–41.

De Vos, George, and Lola Romanucci-Ross, eds. *Ethnic Identity: Cultural Continuities and Change.* 1975. Chicago: U of Chicago P, 1982.

———. "Ethnicity: Vessel of Meaning and Emblem of Contrast." *Ethnic Identity: Cultural Continuities and Change.* 1975. Chicago: U of Chicago P, 1982. 363–90.

deVries, Rachel Guido. *How to Sing to a Dago.* Toronto: Guernica, 1996.

———. *Tender Warriors.* Ithaca: Firebrand, 1986.

Di Donato, Pietro. *Christ in Concrete.* 1939. New York: Signet, 1993.

DiGaetani, John Louis. *An Invitation to the Opera.* New York: Anchor, 1986.

di Leonardo, Micaela. *The Varieties of Ethnic Experience: Kinship, Class, and Gender among California Italian-Americans.* Ithaca: Cornell UP, 1984.

Di Prima, Diane. *Pieces of a Song: Selected Poems.* San Francisco: City Lights, 1990.

Di Stasi, Lawrence. *Mal Occhio: The Underside of Vision.* San Francisco: North Point, 1981.

Dragonette, Ree. "This Is the Way We Wash Our Hands." *The Dream Book: An Anthology of Writings by Italian American Women.* Ed. Helen Barolini. New York: Schocken, 1985. 374–79.

Du Bois, W. E. B. *The Souls of Black Folk.* 1903. Millwood, NY: Kraus-Thomson, 1973.

DuPlessis, Rachel Blau. *Writing Beyond the Ending: Narrative Strategies of Twentieth-Century Women Writers.* Bloomington: Indiana UP, 1985.

Dybek, Stuart. Rev. of *The Quick: A Novella and Stories*, by Agnes Rossi. *New York Times Book Review* 14 June 1992: 14–15.

Ermelino, Louisa. *Joey Dee Gets Wise: A Novel of Little Italy.* New York: St. Martin's, 1991.

Ets, Marie Hall. *Rosa: The Life of an Italian Immigrant.* Minneapolis: U of Minnesota P, 1970. 2nd ed. Madison: U of Wisconsin P, 1999.

Ewen, Elizabeth. *Immigrant Women in the Land of Dollars: Life and Culture on the Lower East Side, 1890–1925.* New York: Monthly Review P, 1985.

Fante, John. *The Wine of Youth: Selected Stories.* 1940. Santa Rosa, CA: Black Sparrow, 1985.

Feder, Lilian. *Madness in Literature.* Princeton: Princeton UP, 1980.

Felski, Rita. "The Novel of Self-Discovery: A Necessary Fiction?" *Southern Review* 19 (1986): 131–48.

Ferro, Robert. *The Family of Max Desir*. New York: Plume, 1983.
Fischer, Michael M. J. "Ethnicity and the Post-Modern Arts of Memory." *Writing Culture: The Poetics and Politics of Ethnography*. Ed. James Clifford and George E. Marcus. Berkeley: U of California P, 1986. 194–233.
Foucault, Michel. *The History of Sexuality. Volume I: An Introduction*. New York: Vintage, 1980.
Fraiman, Susan. "*The Mill on the Floss*, the Critics, and the *Bildungsroman*." *PMLA* 108 (1993): 136–50.
Fuderer, Laura Sue. *The Female Bildungsroman in English: An Annotated Bibliography of Criticism*. New York: MLA, 1990.
Fuss, Diana. "Inside/Out." *Inside/Out: Lesbian Theories, Gay Theories*. New York: Routledge, 1991. 1–10.
Gabaccia, Donna. *From Sicily to Elizabeth Street: Housing and Social Change among Italian Immigrants, 1880–1930*. Albany: State U of New York P, 1984.
——. "Italian American Women: A Review Essay." *Italian Americana* 12.1 (1993): 38–61.
Gambino, Richard. *Blood of My Blood: The Dilemma of Italian-Americans*. New York: Doubleday, 1974. Toronto: Guernica, 1996.
——. *Vendetta*. New York: Doubleday, 1977.
Gambone, Philip. "Learning and Unlearning and Learning Again the Language of *Signori*." *Fuori: Essays by Italian/American Lesbians and Gays*. Ed. Anthony J. Tamburri. West Lafayette, IN: Bordighera, 1996. 60–80.
Gans, Herbert J. "Symbolic Ethnicity: The Future of Ethnic Groups and Cultures in America." *On the Making of Americans: Essays in Honor of David Reisman*. Ed. Herbert J. Gans et al. Philadelphia: U of Pennsylvania P, 1979. 193–220.
Gardaphé, Fred L. *Dagoes Read: Tradition and the Italian/American Writer*. Toronto: Guernica, 1996.
——. "From Oral Tradition to Written Word: Toward an Ethnographically Based Literary Criticism." *From the Margin: Writings in Italian Americana*. Ed. Anthony J. Tamburri, Paolo Giordano, and Fred L. Gardaphé. West Lafayette, IN: Purdue UP, 1991. 294–306.
——. Introduction. *Christ in Concrete*. By Pietro Di Donato. New York: Signet, 1993. ix–xviii.
——. *The Italian-American Writer: An Essay and an Annotated Checklist*. Spencertown, NY: Forkroads P, 1995.
——. *Italian Signs, American Streets: The Evolution of Italian American Narrative*. Durham: Duke UP, 1996.
Garroni, Maria Susanna. "Coal Mine, Farm and Quarry Frontiers: The Different Americas of Italian Immigrant Women." *Storia Nordamericana* 5.2 (1988): 115–36.

Gates, Henry Louis. Afterword. "Zora Neale Hurston: 'A Negro Way of Saying.'" *Their Eyes Were Watching God.* By Zora Neale Hurston. New York: Harper, 1990. 185–95.

Gever, Martha. "The Names We Give Ourselves." *Out There: Marginalization and Contemporary Cultures.* Ed. Russell Ferguson et al. New York: New Museum of Contemporary Art, 1990. 191–202.

Gillan, Maria Mazziotti. *Where I Come From: Selected and New Poems.* Toronto: Guernica, 1995.

Gilligan, Carol. *In a Different Voice: Psychological Theory and Women's Development.* Cambridge: Harvard UP, 1982.

Gilman, Sander L. *Disease and Representation: Images of Illness from Madness to AIDS.* Ithaca: Cornell UP, 1988.

Giovannini, Maureen J. "A Structural Analysis of Proverbs in a Sicilian Village." *American Ethnologist* 5 (1978): 322–33.

Giunta, Edvige. Afterword. "'A Song from the Ghetto.'" *Paper Fish.* By Tina De Rosa. New York: Feminist P, 1996. 123–42.

——. "Blending 'Literary' Discourses: Helen Barolini's Italian/American Narratives." *Romance Languages Annual* 6 (1995): 261–66.

——. "Reinventing the Authorial/Ethnic Space: Communal Narratives in Agnes Rossi's *Split Skirt.*" *Constructions and Confrontations: Changing Representations of Women and Feminisms, East and West.* Ed. Cristina Bacchilega and Cornelia N. Moore. Vol. 12 of *Literary Studies East and West.* Honolulu: University of Hawaii, 1996. 90–102.

——, guest ed. *Voices in Italian Americana.* Special Issue: Italian/American Women Authors 7.2 (1996).

Green, Rose Basile. *The Italian-American Novel: A Document of the Interaction of Two Cultures.* Rutherford, NJ: Fairleigh Dickinson UP, 1974.

Habegger, Alfred. *Gender, Fantasy, and Realism in American Literature.* New York: Columbia UP, 1982.

Hansen, Marcus Lee. "The Third Generation in America." *Commentary* 14 (1952): 492–500.

Hendin, Josephine Gattuso. Interview. *Voices in Italian Americana* 1.1 (1990): 53–62.

——. *The Right Thing to Do.* New York: Feminist P, 1999.

Hirsch, Marianne. *The Mother/Daughter Plot: Narrative, Psychoanalysis, Feminism.* Bloomington: Indiana UP, 1989.

——. "The Novel of Formation as Genre: Between Great Expectations and Lost Illusions." *Genre* 3.3 (1979): 293–311.

Hurston, Zora Neale. *Their Eyes Were Watching God.* 1937. New York: Harper, 1990.

Johnson, Barbara. "Apostrophe, Animation, and Abortion." *Diacritics* 16.1 (1986): 29–45.

Johnson, Colleen Leahy. *Growing Up and Growing Old in Italian-American Families.* New Brunswick, NJ: Rutgers UP, 1985.

——. "The Maternal Role in the Contemporary Italian-American Family." *The Italian Immigrant Woman in North America.* Ed. Betty Boyd Caroli, Robert F. Harney, and Lydio F. Tomasi. Proc. of the Tenth Annual Conference of the American Italian Historical Association. Toronto: Multicultural History Society, 1978. 234–44.

Juliani, Richard. "The Interaction of Irish and Italians: From Conflict to Integration." *Italians and Irish in America.* Ed. Francis X. Femminella. Proc. of the Sixteenth Annual Conference of the American Italian Historical Association. Staten Island, NY: American Italian Historical Association, 1985. 27–34.

Kazin, Alfred. Introduction. *Call It Sleep.* By Henry Roth. New York: Farrar, 1991. ix–xx.

La Barre, Weston. *Ghost Dance: Origins of Religion.* New York: Dell, 1970.

La Belle, Jenijoy. *Herself Beheld: The Literature of the Looking Glass.* Ithaca: Cornell UP, 1988.

Lazzaro-Weis, Carol. "The Female *Bildungsroman*: Calling It into Question." *NWSA Journal* 2.1 (1990): 16–34.

Lloyd, Susan Caperna. *No Pictures in My Grave: A Spiritual Journey in Sicily.* San Francisco: Mercury, 1992.

Locke, Octavia Waldo. Papers. Immigration History Research Center. University of Minnesota.

Maglione, Connie, and Carmen Anthony Fiore. *Voices of the Daughters.* Princeton: Townhouse P, 1989.

Manfredi, Renée. *Where Loves Leaves Us.* Iowa City: U of Iowa P, 1994.

Mangione, Jerre, and Ben Morreale. *La Storia: Five Centuries of the Italian American Experience.* New York: HarperCollins, 1992.

Marello, Laura. "Catch Me Go Looking." *New Directions in Prose and Poetry* 53 (1989): 88–121.

Masini, Donna. *About Yvonne.* New York: Norton, 1997.

Maso, Carole. *The American Woman in the Chinese Hat.* Normal, IL: Dalkey Archive, 1994.

——. *The Art Lover.* Hopewell, NJ: Ecco, 1990.

——. *Aureole.* Hopewell, NJ: Ecco, 1996.

——. *Ava.* Normal, IL: Dalkey Archive, 1993.

——. *Defiance.* New York: Dutton, 1998.

——. "An Essay." *American Poetry Review* 24.2 (1995): 26–31.

——. *Ghost Dance.* Hopewell, NJ: Ecco, 1986.

——. "Interview by Joyce Hackett." *Poets and Writers* 24.3 (1996): 64–73.

——. "Interview by Nicole Cooley." *American Poetry Review* 24.2 (1995): 32–35.

Mathias, Elizabeth, and Richard Raspa. *Italian Folktales in America: The Verbal Art of an Immigrant Woman.* Detroit: Wayne State UP, 1985.

Miller, Michael Vincent. Rev. of *American Nervousness*, by Tom Lutz. *New York Times Book Review* 7 July 1991: 1+.

Minh-ha, Trinh T. *Woman Native Other: Writing Postcoloniality and Feminism*. Bloomington: Indiana UP, 1989.

Monardo, Anna. *The Courtyard of Dreams*. New York: Doubleday, 1993.

Mooney, James. *The Ghost-Dance Religion and the Sioux Outbreak of 1890*. 1896. Chicago: U of Chicago P, 1965.

Moretti, Franco. *The Way of the World: The Bildungsroman in European Culture*. London: Verso, 1987.

Morrison, Toni. *Beloved*. New York: Knopf, 1987.

——. *The Bluest Eye*. New York: Pocket, 1970.

——. *Song of Solomon*. New York: Penguin, 1977.

Newman, Katharine. "An Ethnic Literary Scholar Views American Literature." *MELUS* 7.1 (1980): 3–19.

O'Neale, Sondra. "Race, Sex and Self: Aspects of *Bildung* in Select Novels by Black American Women Novelists." *MELUS* 9.4 (1982): 25–37.

Orsi, Robert. "The Fault of Memory: 'Southern Italy' in the Imagination of Immigrants and the Lives of Their Children in Italian Harlem, 1920–1945." *Journal of Family History* 15.2 (1990): 133–47.

——. "The Religious Boundaries of an Inbetween People: Street *Feste* and the Problem of the Dark-Skinned Other in Italian Harlem, 1920–1990." *American Quarterly* 44.3 (1992): 313–47.

Ostendorf, Berndt. "Literary Acculturation: What Makes Ethnic Literature 'Ethnic.'" *Le Facteur Ethnique aux Etats-Unis et au Canada*. Ed. Monique Lecomte and Claudine Thomas. Trauvaux: Université de Lille III, 1983. 149–61.

Papajohn, John, and John Spiegel. *Transactions in Families: A Modern Approach for Resolving Cultural and Generation Conflicts*. San Francisco: Jossey-Bass, 1975.

Peragallo, Olga. *Italian-American Authors and Their Contribution to American Literature*. New York: Vanni, 1949.

Perry, Harriet. "The Metonymic Definition of the Female and the Concept of Honour Among Italian Immigrant Families in Toronto." *The Italian Immigrant Woman in North America*. Ed. Betty Boyd Caroli, Robert F. Harney, and Lydio F. Tomasi. Proc. of the Tenth Annual Conference of the American Italian Historical Association. Toronto: Multicultural History Society, 1978. 222–32.

Pipino, Mimi. "*Ella Price's Journal*: The Subv/mersion of Ethnic and Sexual Identity." *Voices in Italian Americana* 7.2 (1996): 35–54.

Pola, Antonia. *Who Can Buy the Stars?* New York: Vantage, 1957.

Pratt, Annis. *Archetypal Patterns in Women's Fiction*. Bloomington: Indiana UP, 1981.

Puzo, Mario. *The Fortunate Pilgrim*. New York: Lancer, 1964.

Ricci, Nino. *The Book of Saints.* New York: Picador, 1990.
Rich, Adrienne. *Adrienne Rich's Poetry.* Ed. Barbara Charlesworth Gelpi and Albert Gelpi. New York: Norton, 1975.
——. *Of Woman Born: Motherhood as Experience and Institution.* 1976. New York: Norton, 1986.
——. *On Lies, Secrets, and Silence: Selected Prose 1966–1978.* New York: Norton, 1979.
Roediger, David R. *Towards the Abolition of Whiteness: Essays on Race, Politics, and Working Class History.* London: Verso, 1994.
Rolle, Andrew. *The Italian Americans: Troubled Roots.* New York: Free P, 1980.
Romano, Rose. *la bella figura: a choice.* San Francisco: malafemmina p, 1993.
——. "Coming Out Olive in the Lesbian Community." *Social Pluralism and Literary History: The Literature of the Italian Emigration.* Ed. Francesco Loriggio. Toronto: Guernica, 1996. 161–75.
——. *Vendetta.* San Francisco: malafemmina p, 1990.
——. *The Wop Factor.* Brooklyn: malafemmina p, 1994.
Romanucci-Ross, Lola. "Italian Ethnic Identity and Its Transformations." *Ethnic Identity: Cultural Continuities and Change.* Ed. George De Vos and Lola Romanucci-Ross. 1975. Chicago: U of Chicago P, 1982. 198–226.
Romanyshyn, Robert D., and Brian J. Whalen. "Depression and the American Dream: The Struggle with Home." *Pathologies of the Modern Self: Postmodern Studies on Narcissism, Schizophrenia, and Depression.* Ed. David Michael Levin. New York: New York UP, 1987. 198–220.
Rosa, Alfred. Afterword. *Like Lesser Gods.* By Mari Tomasi. Shelburne, VT: New England P, 1988. 291–98.
——. "The Novels of Mari Tomasi." *Italian Americana* 2.1 (1975): 66–78.
Rossi, Agnes. *The Quick: A Novella and Stories.* New York: Norton, 1992.
——. *Split Skirt.* New York: Random, 1994.
Rotunno, Marie, and Monica McGoldrick. "Italian Families." *Ethnicity and Family Therapy.* Ed. Monica McGoldrick et al. New York: Guilford P, 1982. 340–63.
Ruffolo, Lisa. "My Grandfather's Suit." *From the Margin: Writings in Italian Americana.* Ed. Anthony J. Tamburri, Paolo Giordano, and Fred L. Gardaphé. West Lafayette, IN: Purdue UP, 1991. 75–81.
Sammons, Jeffrey L. "The Mystery of the Missing *Bildungsroman*, or: What Happened to Wilhelm Meister's Legacy?" *Genre* 14 (1981): 229–46.
Savarese, Julia. *The Weak and the Strong.* New York: Putnam's, 1952.
Scapp, Ron, and Anthony J. Tamburri, eds. *Differentia: Review of Italian Thought.* Special Issue: Italian American Culture 6–7 (1994).

Schneider, Jane. "Of Vigilance and Virgins: Honor, Shame and Access to Resources in Mediterranean Societies." *Ethnology* 10.1 (1971): 1–24.

Scholes, Robert. *Protocols of Reading*. New Haven: Yale UP, 1989.

Sedgwick, Eve Kosofsky. "Epistemology of the Closet." *The Lesbian and Gay Studies Reader*. Ed. Henry Abelove et al. New York: Routledge, 1993. 45–61.

Segale, Sister Blandina. *At the End of the Santa Fe Trail*. Milwaukee: Bruce, 1948.

Silko, Leslie Marmon. *Ceremony*. New York: Penguin, 1977.

Smiley, Jane. "Getting Away from Daddy." Rev. of *The Right Thing to Do*, by Josephine Gattuso Hendin. *New York Times Book Review* 13 Mar. 1988: 20.

Smith, Timothy L. "Religion and Ethnicity in America." *American Historical Review* 83.4 (1978): 1155–85.

Sollors, Werner. *Beyond Ethnicity: Consent and Descent in American Culture*. New York: Oxford UP, 1986.

——. "Ethnicity." *Critical Terms for Literary Study*. Ed. Frank Lentricchia and Thomas McLaughlin. Chicago: U of Chicago P, 1990. 288–305.

——. "Introduction: The Invention of Ethnicity." *The Invention of Ethnicity*. Ed. Werner Sollors. New York: Oxford UP, 1989. ix–xx.

Sontag, Susan. *Illness as Metaphor*. New York: Farrar, 1977.

Swales, Martin. *The German Bildungsroman from Wieland to Hesse*. Princeton: Princeton UP, 1978.

Talese, Gay. "Where Are the Italian-American Novelists?" *New York Times Book Review* 14 Mar. 1993: 1+.

Tamburri, Anthony J., ed. *Fuori: Essays by Italian/American Lesbian and Gays*. West Lafayette, IN: Bordighera, 1996.

——. "Looking Back: The Image of Italy in Helen Barolini's *Umbertina*." *MELUS* 22.3 (Fall 1997): 83–101.

——. *A Semiotic of Ethnicity: In (Re)cognition of the Italian/American Writer*. New York: State U of New York P, 1998.

Tamburri, Anthony J., Fred Gardaphé, Edvige Giunta, and Mary Jo Bona, eds. *Italian/American Literature and Film: A Select Critical Bibliography*. West Lafayette, IN: Bordighera, 1997.

Tamburri, Anthony J., Paolo Giordano, and Fred L. Gardaphé, eds. *From the Margin: Writings in Italian Americana*. West Lafayette, IN: Purdue UP, 1991.

Tirabassi, Maddalena. "Bringing Life to History: Italian Ethnic Women in the United States." *The Italian Diaspora: Migration Across the Globe*. Ed. George E. Pozzetta and Bruno Ramirez. Ontario: Multicultural History Society, 1992. 135–54.

Tomasi, Mari. *Deep Grow the Roots*. Philadelphia: Lippincott, 1940.

——. "The Italian Story in Vermont." *Vermont History* 28 (1960): 73–87.

———. *Like Lesser Gods.* Milwaukee: Bruce, 1949. Shelburne, VT: New England P, 1988.

———. "Stone." *The Literature of Vermont: A Sampler.* Ed. Arthur W. Biddle and Paul A. Eschholz. Hanover, NH: UP of New England, 1973. 312–20.

Torgovnick, Marianna De Marco. *Crossing Ocean Parkway: Readings by an Italian American Daughter.* Chicago: U of Chicago P, 1994.

Tricarico, Donald. "Guido: Fashioning an Italian-American Youth Style." *Journal of Ethnic Studies* 19 (1991): 41–66.

Ussher, Jane. *Women's Madness: Misogyny or Mental Illness?* Amherst: U of Massachusetts P, 1991.

Vecoli, Rudolph J. "Are Italian Americans Just White Folks?" *Italian and Italian/American Images in the Media.* Ed. Mary Jo Bona and Anthony J. Tamburri. Proc. of the 27th Annual Conference of the American Italian Historical Association. Staten Island: American Italian Historical Association, 1996. 3–17.

———. "Finding, and Losing, the Gems of Barre's Italian Immigrant Past: Anarchism, Silicosis, and a Slip of the Community Mind." *Times Argus* 26 Oct. 1989: 7+.

———. Foreword. *Rosa: The Life of an Italian Immigrant.* By Marie Hall Ets. Minneapolis: U of Minnesota P, 1970. v–xi.

———. "Prelates and Peasants: Italian Immigrants and the Catholic Church." *Journal of Social History* 2 (1969): 217–68.

Waldo, Octavia. *A Cup of the Sun.* New York: Harcourt, 1961.

Walkerdine, Valerie. "Progressive Pedagogy and Political Struggle." *Feminisms and Critical Pedagogy.* Ed. Carmen Luke and Jennifer Gore. New York: Routledge, 1992. 15–24.

Warner, Marina. *Alone of All Her Sex: The Myth and the Cult of the Virgin Mary.* New York: Vintage, 1976.

Washington, Mary Helen. Foreword. *Their Eyes Were Watching God.* By Zora Neale Hurston. New York: Harper, 1990. vii–xiv.

Welty, Eudora. *One Writer's Beginnings.* Cambridge: Harvard UP, 1983.

Williams, Phyllis H. *South Italian Folkways in Europe and America: A Handbook for Social Workers, Visiting Nurses, School Teachers, and Physicians.* New York: Russell and Russell, 1938.

Winsey, Valentine Rossilli. "The Italian Immigrant Woman Who Arrived in the United States Before World War I." *Studies in Italian American Social History: Essays in Honor of Leonard Covello.* Ed. Francesco Cordasco. Totowa, NJ: Rowman and Littlefield, 1975. 199–210.

Winwar, Frances. *Poor Splendid Wings: The Rossettis and Their Circle.* Boston: Little, 1933.

Wright, Nathalia. *American Novelists in Italy: The Discoverers Allston to James.* Philadelphia: U of Pennsylvania P, 1965.

Young, Robyn. "Barre's Anarchists." *Times Argus* 22 Sept. 1989: 3A+.

Zimmerman, Bonnie. "Exiting from Patriarchy: The Lesbian Novel of Development." *The Voyage In: Fictions of Female Development.* Ed. Elizabeth Abel, Marianne Hirsch, and Elizabeth Langland. Hanover: UP of New England, 1983. 244–57.

——. *The Safe Sea of Women: Lesbian Fiction 1969–1989.* Boston: Beacon, 1990.

# Index

Mary Jo Bona is presently teaching in the Italian American Studies Program at the State University of New York at Stony Brook and is an associate professor of English and chair of Women's Studies at Gonzaga University. She has coedited, with Anthony J. Tamburri, *Through the Looking Glass: Italian and Italian/American Images in the Media* and edited *The Voices We Carry: Recent Italian/American Women's Fiction.*